# *Culture and Customs of the United States*

# Culture and Customs of the United States

*Volume 1*
*Customs and Society*

## EDITED BY BENJAMIN F. SHEARER

Culture and Customs of North America

GREENWOOD PRESS
Westport, Connecticut • London

**Library of Congress Cataloging-in-Publication Data**

Culture and customs of the United States / edited by Benjamin F. Shearer.
    p. cm.—(Culture and customs of North America, ISSN 1940–1132)
   Includes bibliographical references and index.
   ISBN 978–0–313–33875–5 (set : alk. paper)—ISBN 978–0–313–33876–2
(vol. 1 : alk. paper)—ISBN 978–0–313–33877–9 (vol. 2 : alk. paper)
  1. United States—Civilization.   2. United States—Social life and
customs.   3. United States—Social conditions.   I. Shearer, Benjamin F.
   E169.1.C843   2008
   973—dc22       2007039174

British Library Cataloguing in Publication Data is available.

Library of Congress Catalog Card Number: 2007039174
ISBN-13: 978–0–313–33875–5 (set)
       978–0–313–33876–2 (vol 1)
       978–0–313–33877–9 (vol 2)
ISSN: 1940–1132

First published in 2008

Greenwood Press, 88 Post Road West, Westport, CT 06881
An imprint of Greenwood Publishing Group, Inc.
www.greenwood.com

Printed in the United States of America

The paper used in this book complies with the
Permanent Paper Standard issued by the National
Information Standards Organization (Z39.48–1984).

10  9  8  7  6  5  4  3  2  1

# Contents

# Preface

*CULTURE AND CUSTOMS of the United States* is part of the Greenwood Culture and Customs of North America series. As such, this work provides a glimpse into contemporary U.S. culture and a context through which to understand it. A chronology is provided as well as a detailed index to the complete work. Bibliographies may be found at the end of each chapter, and a selected general bibliography is also provided.

The first chapter is a general overview of the land, climate, people, language, and history of the United States. The vastness and abundance of the land is one key to understanding the American character—how Americans think of themselves. Likewise, regional variations also help to define Americans' understanding of themselves and introduce a certain diversity into what it means to be an American. Indeed, diversity is the hallmark of this nation of immigrants. The ethnic mix of the country has always been and remains ever in flux, and Americans have never been shy to borrow what they like from any ethnic group to the effect of redefining their culture and customs.

The following chapters delve into particular aspects of the American cultural experience. Chapter 2 explores American religions, overwhelmingly Christian, and how religious thought affects the political and social arenas. Gender, marriage, family, and educational issues are considered in chapter 3. In chapter 4, American holiday customs and leisure time activities, including sports, are the subjects. Chapter 5 takes a look at the eclectic world of American food and fashion. U.S. literature is covered in the sixth chapter, media and cinema in the next. Chapter 8 covers the performing arts, and finally, the last chapter discusses American art and architecture as well as housing.

# Chronology

| | |
|---|---|
| 30,000 B.C.E. | Migrating groups from Asia and South America begin populating North America. |
| 1492 | Christopher Columbus lands in the New World. |
| 1565 | Spanish found St. Augustine, Florida. |
| 1607 | Jamestown, Virginia, colony founded by the British. |
| 1619 | First African slaves arrive in Virginia. |
| 1620 | Pilgrims land at Plymouth and sign the Mayflower Compact. |
| 1621 | First Thanksgiving at Plymouth. |
| 1626 | Dutch found New Amsterdam on Manhattan. |
| 1636 | Harvard College founded. |
| 1638 | Sweden founds a colony in Delaware. |
| | First Baptist church in America is founded. |
| 1692 | Witchcraft trials in Salem, Massachusetts. |
| 1718 | French found New Orleans. |
| 1729 | Benjamin Franklin buys the *Pennsylvania Gazette* and is its publisher. |
| 1741 | Jonathan Edwards gives sermon "Sinners in the Hands of an Angry God," epitomizing America's religious Great Awakening. |

1769        Fr. Junipero Serra founds mission at San Diego, California.

1775        American Revolution breaks out with the battle of Lexington and Concord.

1776        Newly named United States of America declares independence from Great Britain.

1781        American victory in the battle of Yorktown ends the American Revolution; Articles of Confederation become the law of the land.

1783        Treaty of Paris officially ends the Revolution and expands American territory to the Mississippi River.

            The *Pennsylvania Evening Post* is the first daily newspaper in America.

1789        Constitution replaces Articles of Confederation as America's governing document; George Washington becomes first president.

1790        The first U.S. census counts 3,893,874 people, of whom 694,207 are slaves.

1793        Eli Whitney invents the cotton gin, which proves a boon for the use of slave labor.

1796        Amelia Simmons publishes *American Cookery,* the first cookbook in America.

1800        Congress convenes in the new U.S. capital, Washington, D.C.

1803        America purchases Louisiana from France, doubling the size of the nation.

1808        Importation of slaves ends by federal law.

1812        War of 1812, ended with the Treaty of Ghent in 1814, settles no American issues.

1817        The New York Stock and Exchange Board is established.

1818        United States and Great Britain agree on U.S.-Canadian border.

1819        Writer Washington Irving's *Sketchbook* first appears.

1821        The Adams-Onís Treaty with Spain, negotiated in 1819, is ratified, ending Spanish claims on Oregon and U.S. claims on Texas and giving the United States a southwestern border and Florida.

1826        James Fenimore Cooper publishes *The Last of the Mohicans.*

| 1830 | President Andrew Jackson signs the Indian Removal Act into law. |
| | Joseph Smith founds a church in New York that takes the name Church of Jesus Christ of Latter-day Saints (Mormons) in 1838. |
| 1838 | The Trail of Tears begins as the Cherokee are forced to migrate to Indian Territory. |
| 1844 | With the aid of government funding, Samuel F. B. Morse proves the commercial efficacy of the telegraph. |
| 1846 | First officially recorded baseball game takes place at Elysian Fields in Hoboken, New Jersey, between the New York Base Ball Club and the New York Knickerbockers. |
| 1847 | Frederick Douglas starts the abolitionist newspaper the *North Star.* |
| 1850 | Nathaniel Hawthorne publishes *The Scarlet Letter.* |
| 1851 | Herman Melville publishes *Moby Dick.* |
| 1852 | Roman Catholicism becomes America's largest single religious denomination. Harriet Beecher Stowe publishes *Uncle Tom's Cabin.* |
| 1857 | In the Dred Scott case, the U.S. Supreme Court decides that African Americans have no rights. |
| 1861 | The Civil War begins and ends in 1865 with defeat of the Confederate States. Henry Wadsworth Longfellow publishes "Paul Revere's Ride." |
| 1867 | The United States purchases Alaska from Russia. |
| 1868 | Louisa May Alcott publishes *Little Women.* |
| 1870 | New York City's Metropolitan Museum of Art is founded. |
| 1873 | Levi Strauss and Jacob Davis patent blue jeans. |
| 1874 | Alexander Graham Bell invents the telephone. |
| | The Women's Christian Temperance Union is founded in Cleveland, Ohio. |
| 1875 | Mary Baker Eddy publishes *Science and Health,* the basis for Christian Science. |
| 1876 | Walter Camp, the father of American football, writes the first rules for American football at the Massasoit Convention. |
| | Samuel Clemens (Mark Twain) publishes *The Adventures of Tom Sawyer.* |

1877        Henry James publishes *The American.*

1879        Thomas Edison invents the lightbulb.

1889        The *Wall Street Journal* begins publication.

1890        Massacre at Wounded Knee becomes the last battle of the Indian
            wars that began in the seventeenth century.

1891        James Naismith invents basketball at Springfield College (Massa-
            chusetts) for the YMCA and writes the first rules the next year.

1896        U.S. Supreme Court decision in *Plessy v. Ferguson* establishes
            "separate but equal" practice in race relations, thus reinforcing
            segregation.

1898        The United States annexes Hawaii.

            The Spanish-American War leaves the United States with the
            Philippines, Guam, Puerto Rico, and Cuba.

1903        Orville and Wilbur Wright successfully fly their airplane in North
            Carolina.

            America's first narrative film, the 10-minute "The Great Train
            Robbery," is shown in theaters.

1908        Henry Ford produces the first Model-T automobile.

            Ashcan School (artists William Glackens, Robert Henri, George
            Luks, and John Sloan) exhibit their works in New York City.

1909        The National Association for the Advancement of Colored
            People is founded in Springfield, Illinois.

1911        Radical magazine the *Masses* starts publication.

1913        Cecil B. DeMille makes Hollywood's first full-length feature
            film, *The Squaw Man,* a smash hit that helped to establish
            Hollywood films.

1915        T. S. Eliot publishes "The Love Song of J. Alfred Prufrock."

1916        Margaret Sanger opens America's first birth control clinic in
            Brooklyn, New York.

1917        United States enters World War I.

1920        Nineteenth Amendment to the Constitution gives women the
            right to vote.

            KDKA in Pittsburgh, Pennsylvania, becomes the first radio
            broadcasting station in the United States.

Edith Wharton publishes *The Age of Innocence.*

Census reveals that most Americans now live in urban areas.

1924    All native-born Indians are given U.S. citizenship.

George Gershwin's *Rhapsody in Blue* is first performed in New York City.

1925    F. Scott Fitzgerald publishes *The Great Gatsby.*

John Scopes is convicted in court for teaching evolution at a Tennessee public school.

1926    Ernest Hemingway publishes *The Sun Also Rises.*

1929    The Museum of Modern Art in New York City opens to the public.

William Faulkner publishes *The Sound and the Fury.*

Stock market crash precipitates the Great Depression.

1930    Wallace Fard Muhammad founds a mosque in Detroit that is the origin of the Nation of Islam.

1931    Boris Karloff stars in the film *Frankenstein.*

Construction of the Empire State Building is completed.

1932    Americans are introduced to European architecture as the International Style exhibition opens at the Museum of Modern Art.

1934    George Balanchine and Lincoln Kerstein found the School of American Ballet.

1935    Federal homesteading ends, except for Alaska.

1936    Charlie Chaplin's film *Modern Times* appears in theaters.

1937    Walt Disney's *Snow White and the Seven Dwarfs* is the first animated full-length feature film.

1939    WRGB makes the first network television broadcast from New York City to Schenectady, New York.

Professional baseball and football games are televised for the first time.

John Steinbeck publishes *Grapes of Wrath.*

*Gone with the Wind* is a Hollywood smash hit.

1941    The National Gallery of Art opens on the mall in Washington, D.C.

Orson Welles's *Citizen Kane* revolutionizes filmmaking.

United States enters World War II after Japanese attack on Pearl Harbor, Hawaii.

1943     Artist Jackson Pollock has his first one-man show.

1948     Architect Philip Johnson builds his glass house.

1949     Arthur Miller's *Death of a Salesman* premiers.

1950     United States enters Korean War, which ends with armistice in 1953.

1951     J. D. Salinger publishes *The Catcher in the Rye.*

1954     In the case of *Oliver L. Brown et al. v. the Board of Education of Topeka (KS) et al.,* the U.S. Supreme Court overturns the separate but equal provision of *Plessy v. Ferguson,* allowing for the racial integration of schools.

1955     Rosa Parks refuses to give her seat to a white man, thus starting a bus boycott in Montgomery, Alabama, as a civil rights protest.

         First McDonald's restaurant opens in Des Plaines, Illinois.

         Disneyland opens in Anaheim, California.

1956     Elvis Presley makes his first number one hit, "Heartbreak Hotel."

1957     Jack Kerouac publishes *On the Road.*

1958     New York City's Solomon R. Guggenheim Museum, designed by Frank Lloyd Wright, opens.

1960     Televangelist Pat Robertson purchases a small Virginia station and calls his operation the Christian Broadcasting Network, thus beginning conservative Christian network television.

1961     President John F. Kennedy sends 100 special forces troops to Vietnam.

1962     Pop artist Andy Warhol executes oil on canvas, painting "200 Campbell's Soup Cans."

1963     Civil rights march on Washington, D.C.

         Bob Dylan records "Blowin' in the Wind."

1964     Civil Rights Act signed into law, prohibiting discrimination based on race, color, religion, or national origin.

1965     National Endowment for the Arts and National Endowment for the Humanities founded.

Antiwar marches in Washington, D.C., and race riots in Los Angeles.

1967        Film *The Graduate* is in theaters.

1968        Dr. Martin Luther King Jr. and Robert F. Kennedy are assassinated.

1969        Group exhibit of conceptual art is mounted in New York City.

            Woodstock music festival takes place.

            Stonewall riot in New York begins the gay liberation movement.

            Neil Armstrong becomes first man on the moon on July 20.

1970        *Jesus Christ Superstar* is performed on Broadway.

            The movie *M*A*S*H* is in theaters.

1971        *All in the Family* initiates socially conscious comedy on television.

1972        The Equal Rights Amendment, which prohibits the denial or abridgement of equality of rights on account of sex, passes Congress and is sent to the states for ratification.

            *Ms.* magazine appears on newsstands.

            Movie *The Godfather* sets opening day records.

            Burglars break into Watergate headquarters of the Democratic Party National Committee Offices.

1973        President Richard M. Nixon declares "peace with honor" in Vietnam.

            Evangelists Paul and Jan Crouch found the Trinity Broadcasting Network, which claims to be the largest Christian broadcasting network in the United States.

            U.S. Supreme Court overturns state abortion restrictions in *Roe v. Wade*.

            *People* magazine begins publication.

1975        *Jaws* is a megahit in theaters.

1976        Alex Haley publishes *Roots*.

            Barbara Walters becomes first woman to anchor a U.S. network news broadcast.

1977        First installment of *Star Wars* hits theaters.

1978        Woody Allen's film *Annie Hall* starts a new fashion trend.

            Herman Wouk publishes *War and Remembrance.*

1979        Cable sports network ESPN is launched.

1980        CNN begins 24-hour televised news reporting.

1981        The IBM PC enters the market.

            MTV comes to cable TV.

1982        The Equal Rights Amendment fails to be ratified by the states.

            Gannett launches the nationwide newspaper *USA Today.*

            Michael Jackson's "Thriller" is a best-selling album.

1985        Quantum Computer Services, which became America Online, is founded.

1986        Fox becomes America's fourth national TV network, along with ABC, CBS, and NBC.

1987        Toni Morrison publishes *Beloved.*

1990        United States sends troops to liberate Iraqi-occupied Kuwait in the Persian Gulf War.

1991        Condoms advertised on American television for the first time.

1992        Race riot breaks out in Los Angeles when police are acquitted of beating Rodney King, an African American man.

1993        Terrorists set off a car bomb in the garage of the World Trade Center in New York City.

            The military adopts a "don't ask, don't tell" policy in regard to homosexuals in the service.

1995        *Toy Story* is the first digitally animated full-length feature film.

1996        The Defense of Marriage Act, which does not recognize same-sex marriage, becomes federal law.

1997        Blogs first appear on the Internet.

1999        President Bill Clinton is acquitted in his impeachment trial.

2001        Terrorists attack the World Trade Center in New York City and the Pentagon.

            United States invades Afghanistan in Operation Enduring Freedom.

2002    Playwright Suzan Lori-Parks wins the Pulitzer Prize for Drama for *Topdog/Underdog.*

2003    United States invades Iraq in Operation Iraqi Freedom, and President George W. Bush soon declares the mission accomplished.

2006    The population of the United States hits 300 million.

        Broad Republican defeat in the November elections viewed as repudiation of Bush administration's handling of the Iraqi War.

# Introduction

THE HOPE FOR new lives with new opportunities that brought millions of immigrants to the United States in the past continues today. The United States has always been a nation of immigrants and therefore constantly in flux as new waves of migration from without and within redefined the American experience.

The United States is not the world's biggest country, but most Americans like to think it is and act as if it were. The richness and enormity of American resources make the nation virtually self-sufficient in many areas, most notably in agriculture. With such abundance, Americans are big consumers with generally high incomes, at least by world standards.

"America the Beautiful," a patriotic poem and song by Katharine Lee Bates, sums up Americans' emotion about their homeland: from sea to shining sea, beautiful, spacious skies overlook majestic purple mountains, amber waves of grain, and fruited plains. God shed his light on the United States, where freedom spreads across the wilderness and alabaster cities gleam. When this song is sung at public functions, it is not unusual for the audience to sing along, many with tears in their eyes.

For many Americans, the land itself is proof of a good God and a God-given destiny. Space—unknown and often unowned—gave early Americans in real terms a sense of individual freedom. This is an old tradition. When the Reverend Roger Williams of the Church of England arrived in Boston in 1631, he refused to serve the church there because he no longer believed in an established church. In fact, he had become, like the Puritans he later served for a while, a separatist, but too radical even for them. He criticized the Massachusetts Bay Company—even questioning the legality of its charter—and the churches. He befriended the natives and supported their ownership of the land. Williams refused to quiet himself or retract his positions and was given six weeks to remove himself from Massachusetts. He found his own space, Providence, where he could practice his own ideas the way he wanted. Eight years later, he had a royal patent for a united Rhode Island. For colonists and the immigrants who followed them, the New World was freedom from the constraints of the Old World and freedom to pursue individual wants and desires in a bountiful land.

It has been said that if something—anything—exists, it can probably be found in the United States. The United States seems to have it all, from all the extremes and everything in between. Americans take pride in this. They are an industrious and inventive people on the go, who value risk taking and its rewards. They like to think that any person born in the United States can grow up to be president, a belief attributable to their sense of independence, self-reliance, fair play, and hard work.

Yet the culture of the United States seems to be filled with contradiction. America fashions itself to be a peace-loving nation, but its armed forces have been involved in some 250 international military actions since the end of the eighteenth century, from Peru to Turkey, the Fiji Islands to Tripoli, Sumatra to Uruguay, and nearly everywhere in between. The U.S. Constitution gives citizens the right to bear arms but does not recognize equal rights for women. Hollywood films have defined American culture internationally, however erroneously, but have never been beyond censorship at home, rights to freedom of artistic expression and free speech aside. In the so-called Land of Equality, African Americans and Latinos earn less than whites, and women earn less than men. White educational attainment far surpasses that of most minority groups. In a society that values scientific advancement, debates about the teaching of evolution in public schools stubbornly persist in school boards across the country. Even presidential candidates have to declare themselves for or against evolution.

These often deep ethnic, economic, political, social, educational, and religious divisions are, however, sources of vitality in American culture. In the end, the culture of the United States is based on a series of compromises, which, taken together, are a source of self-identity and pride for most Americans. Indeed, the Founding Fathers understood this quite well, creating a nation that, from its beginning, declared freedom and liberty for its citizens and let slavery stand. Americans believe they can work out their problems in time.

Americans believe that their country is the best place to live on earth. In spite of the fact that the United States of America occupies a space in the

Americas, specifically North America, only its citizens refer to themselves as Americans. In the U.S. lexicon, Americans do not include Canadians, Venezuelans, Argentineans, Hondurans, or any other citizens of nations in the Americas. Throughout this work, the predilection for U.S. linguistic hegemony is maintained by using the terms *America* and *Americans* to refer only to the United States and its residents.

# 1

# Context: The Land, the People, the Past, the Present

## Benjamin F. Shearer

The United States themselves are essentially the greatest poem.

—Walt Whitman

THE UNITED STATES is a vast land that features most of the geological elements known to humankind: mountains, deserts, swamps, plateaus, glaciers, lakes, rivers, caves, volcanoes, canyons, mesas, seashores, plains, and even geysers and tar pits. The country was patched together over time, not always peaceably, out of Native American territories that had been settled and or claimed by England, France, Holland, Sweden, Spain, Mexico, and Russia. American culture was from the first, therefore, a conglomeration of all these early influences. Africans, brought to America in slavery, and the immigrants who eventually poured into the country from other nations also affected American culture and life from early times.

American culture, always in a state of redefinition, can be understood in terms of the nation's increasingly diverse ethnic groups and the regional variations that engender differences in dialects, food, clothing, the arts, and even religion. Yet beyond ethnic and regional differences, there is something that is distinctly American. The citizens of the United States, clustered largely around the major cities, value the freedom to say what they want, dress as they like, eat what they want, and live where they want. They believe religiously that their hard work will be rewarded with a piece of the American pie.

## THE LAND

Some basic information may help to illustrate the vastness of the United States. The United States occupies 3,794,083 square miles of the earth. About 79,000 square miles of that area are inland water areas made up mostly by the five Great Lakes—Lake Michigan (22,342 square miles), Lake Superior (20,557 square miles), Lake Huron (8,800 square miles), Lake Erie (5,033 square miles), and Lake Ontario (3,446 square miles). Of all the freshwater lakes in the country, and Minnesota alone claims to have 10,000 of them, only two others—Green Bay in Wisconsin and the Great Salt Lake in Utah—have areas of more than 1,000 square miles.[1]

The United States has 58,618 miles of ocean shoreline and 3,962,830 miles of rivers and streams, all feasts for outdoor and sport enthusiasts. Twenty-six of the rivers are over 500 miles long, and 13 are over 1,000 miles long. The Missouri River is the longest at 2,540 miles. It flows from Red Rock Creek in Montana to Missouri, where it dumps into the Mississippi River above St. Louis. It has a drainage area of 529,000 square miles. The Mississippi River, although second in length to the Missouri at 2,340 miles, drains an area of 1,150,000 square miles as it flows from Minnesota to Louisiana. The nation's most obvious topographical feature, it divides and unites the country. Alaska's Yukon River is the third longest at 1,980 miles, and the St. Lawrence and Rio Grande are tied at 1,900 miles.

If these kinds of data are dizzying, it is not much help to break it all down by state. Texas (268,581 square miles), California (163,696 square miles), Montana (147,042 square miles), Florida (65,255 square miles), New Hampshire (9,350 square miles), and New Jersey (8,721 square miles) would all fit handily into the nation's largest state, Alaska, with 663,267 square miles. Imagine the liberating change in mind-set that the western European immigrants who largely populated America underwent. The United Kingdom and Ireland together are the size of New Mexico. France, western Europe's largest nation in area, Denmark, Belgium, Liechtenstein, Luxembourg, Vatican City, Monaco, and the Netherlands all would fit into Texas. Germany and Switzerland together are smaller than California. Spain, Portugal, and Italy would fit nicely into Montana, Nevada, and Arizona, with room to spare. Less than half of Alaska would be needed to contain Norway and Sweden.

Another perspective might be more useful. From Boston on the Atlantic coast to Los Angeles on the Pacific coast is a 3,406-mile drive—when you get to Kansas City, Missouri, you are about halfway there. (A commercial airline flight is only six and a half hours.) A north–south jaunt from Duluth, Minnesota, to San Antonio, Texas, is 1,415 miles. If you decided to take a drive from Seattle, Washington, to Prudhoe Bay up on the Arctic Ocean in Alaska, you could do it, but it might be more an adventure than a little drive in the country. Once you get to Anchorage, Alaska's largest city, located in the south on the Gulf of Alaska, after 2,435 miles, you would still have another 847 miles up to your intended destination.[2]

It is astounding that the United States remains a rural country into the twenty-first century, at least in terms of land use. Of America's total land surface of 1,937,700,000 acres (this excludes Alaska and Washington, D.C.), 71.1 percent is rural land that consists of cropland (21.7%), pasture-land (6.1%), rangeland (20.9%), and forests (20.9%). The federal government owns 20.7 percent of the nation's land, which includes 91.9 percent of Nevada, 66.5 percent of Utah, 66.4 percent of Idaho, 50.6 percent of Wyoming, and 50.2 percent of Arizona. Water areas occupy 2.6 percent of the land. The remaining 5.5 percent is developed land. America's large urban and built-up areas occupy only 4 percent of that developed land, and if Alaska were included, that figure would, of course, shrink even further.

The geography and climate of the United States provide for an almost easy abundance of bountiful harvests and views of unbridled natural beauty. The coastal plains along the Atlantic Ocean and the Gulf of Mexico have natural ports and inland access through river systems. While the mean elevation of the United States is 2,500 feet above sea level, the Atlantic and Gulf coastal states have very low mean elevations: Delaware, with 60 feet; Georgia, with 100 feet; Florida, with 150 feet; and Louisiana, with 100 feet. The old Appalachian Mountains divide the coastal plains from the broad interior plains, drained by the Mississippi River, that stretch to the Rocky Mountains. The flat to rolling plains are home to America's tremendously productive agricultural industry. Above the central plains, the Canadian Shield, cut up by ancient glaciers, descends, leaving one of the world's largest deposits of iron. The Rockies rise dramatically above the plains. Colorado's mean elevation is 6,800 feet; Wyoming's is 6,700 feet. The Rockies give way westward to interior plateaus that grow wider northward all the way to the Yukon Basin in Alaska. These plateaus, some carved into canyons, are rugged, subject to extreme elevation changes, and have little population. The national parks in this area—Grand Canyon, Yellowstone, Glacier—preserve these scenic wonders and make them accessible. There are significant oil shale deposits where Utah, Colorado, and Wyoming meet. Gold, silver, zinc, lead, and uranium have long been mined there.

The Sierra Nevadas and the Cascades form the western borders of the plateaus. California has the highest point of elevation among the 48 contiguous states (Mt. Whitney at 14,495 feet) and the lowest (Death Valley at 280 feet below sea level), both making for spectacular sights. California's giant redwood and sequoia forests also nicely contrast with its Mojave Desert. Between California's Coast Ranges and the Sierras and Cascades lies the Central Valley, which, with the Puget Sound area and the Willamette Valley, produces a variety of crops more diverse than those grown on America's interior plains. The Cascades have a number of volcanoes, some of which, like those in Alaska and Hawaii, are still active.

The United States is said to have a moderate climate. Generally, this is true, unless standing on a mountaintop, but there are noticeable regional variations. The average daily mean temperature of Boston in New England is 51.6 degrees (Fahrenheit; *Celsius* is another term foreign to Americans). The South's premier city of Atlanta's is 62.2 degrees. The midwestern hub of Chicago's is 49.1 degrees. The mile-high city of Denver's is 50.1 degrees, while Phoenix's is 72.9 degrees. Honolulu's 77.5 degrees is fairly constant. Averages can, however, be somewhat misleading. Summer temperatures in Phoenix frequently rise above 100 degrees, but because the air contains little humidity, the deleterious effect on the human body is somewhat mitigated. The opposite is the case in many southern cities. Miami, with an average daily mean temperature of 76.6 degrees, is quite pleasant in the winter, but in the summer, when humidity levels rise to 90 percent and the temperature to 90 degrees and more, the climate becomes nearly unbearable.

The temperatures in the Midwest are subject to tremendous seasonal variation. Chicago, for example, has a daily mean temperature of 22 degrees in January, but 73.3 degrees in July, whereas Los Angeles has mean temperatures of 57.1 degrees in January and 69.3 degrees in July. The climatic conditions that make the Midwest an agricultural capital—hard freezes in winter that help to break up the soil in spring thaws and hot, humid summers—make life difficult in the extremes of summer and winter. Claims, perhaps spurious, have been made that it is so hot along the Mississippi River in St. Louis during mid-August that car tires will melt. At least eggs can be fried on the street. In Chicago, summer buildups of heat and humidity often lead to the deaths of those who have no air-conditioning or fans. On the other hand, an early February walk down Lakeshore Drive, with the tall buildings on each side tunneling the cold, stiff breeze off Lake Michigan, can only be described as an Arctic version of hell.

Precipitation is generally abundant across the nation. The midwestern agricultural breadbasket averages from 30 to 40 inches of rain per year. Boston averages a bit over 40 inches per year; the southern cities of Mobile, New Orleans, and Miami vie for the title of rainiest city, with Mobile on top at 66.29 inches per year, beating Miami and New Orleans by 8 inches. In the arid southwest, however, Phoenix averages only about 8 inches of precipitation and Los Angeles a little over 13 inches. Dams and water diversions provide these two major cities with water. Many believe Seattle to be on top of the list of America's rainiest cities, confusing fog, clouds, and drizzle for actual rainfall, which averages only about 37 inches per year.

The United States has made significant progress in improving air quality since 1970, even though it has refused to become a signatory to the international Kyoto Accords, which establish acceptable levels of pollution in an effort to prevent global warming. In the last 30 years of the twentieth century, the United States significantly reduced particulate matter and carbon monoxide emissions. Lead emissions were eliminated. Sulfur dioxide and volatile organic compound emissions were cut in half. Only nitrogen dioxide emissions rose slightly. Particulate matter comes from miscellaneous sources, but the single largest sources of carbon monoxide, volatile organic compounds, and nitrogen dioxides are the millions of gasoline and diesel cars, trucks, and off-highway vehicles. Sulfur dioxide is produced in fuel combustion by industries and electrical utilities. In all of these emission categories, however, the ambient air concentrations meet or exceed the government's air quality standards.

Water quality is a different matter. A sampling of American water quality conditions in 2000 revealed that 39 percent of the rivers and streams were polluted, agriculture being the largest contributor of the pollution, and another 8 percent were threatened. Forty-seven percent of the sampled lakes, reservoirs, and ponds were found to be polluted and another 8 percent threatened, mostly by urban runoff and storm sewers, with agriculture as a distant second culprit. Contaminated sediments polluted 78 percent of the shoreline sampled along the Great Lakes.

The quality of life in the United States, like any country, is affected by environmental policy as well as nature's whims, which can sometimes turn violent. Americans, however, tend to view major natural disasters as things that happen only in other countries, mainly third world countries. They believe that nature is something that, with ingenuity, can either be harnessed or avoided. The 29 locks and dams on the Mississippi River between Minneapolis and St. Louis are a prime example. Built during the 1930s, the locks and dams were constructed to maintain a nine-foot ship channel for navigation and to prevent the flooding that had characterized the river's history. Much of the nation's grain harvest is floated to distribution points on barges up and down the river when the waterway is not frozen.

Americans' willingness to tame nature one way or the other has minimized the effects of potentially catastrophic events. In 2002, for example, only 49 Americans lost their lives in floods and flash floods. Lightning killed

51 people. Tornadoes, which occur largely in the South and Midwest in what is called *Tornado Alley,* killed only 55. One hurricane hit the mainland and resulted in 51 deaths. What cannot be controlled can be known. The United States has developed excellent sources of instant information through media—radio, television, Internet, telephone, and cell phone—that can alert people to imminent natural dangers so that they can seek immediate safety or prepare to evacuate.

The horrendous floods, earthquakes, and tsunamis that have taken place around the world, ending tens of thousands of lives, are mediated experiences for Americans, who believe such things could not happen in the United States. Americans typically pour out their hearts and open their wallets for the victims left behind in these tragedies. When Hurricane Katrina struck the Gulf Coast in August 2005, Americans saw what looked to all the world like any other natural disaster, with people clinging on to loved ones and whatever belongings they could carry as they tried to escape the ravages of total devastation. Hundreds died along the Gulf Coast from Alabama and Mississippi to Louisiana, and hundreds of thousands were homeless. Most of New Orleans, the place where the good times rolled, was under water.

The American people were no less stunned by this event than they were by the 9/11 terrorist bombings in New York and Washington, D.C. The notion that America, so long isolated geographically from the world's troubles, could be attacked and thousands could lose their lives was unimaginable. The blow to the American psyche was bewildering—Americans had never viewed themselves as powerless victims. Likewise, the natural devastation of New Orleans again made America look and feel powerless, victimized, and unprepared for something that its technology was designed to prevent. It was reported that some people from New Orleans radio stations managed to get back on the air in the midst of the flooding. When one of the broadcasters referred to the wandering homeless as refugees, a fellow broadcaster corrected him with these words: "They are not refugees; they are Americans."

## Regions

Suppose you wanted to do a road trip to see the country, got in your car, and began traveling America's nearly 4,000,000 miles of highways. No matter where you set out, what direction you took, or where you stopped, you would experience a kind of American megaculture created by corporate America. It is connected by interstate highways and defined by a common media universe, where English is spoken, dollars are traded, and peaceful commerce is maintained by an overarching belief in American values. From sea to shining sea, you could overnight at Holiday Inns, Ramadas, Marriotts, Hampton Inns, Days Inns, Hiltons, Econo-Lodges, and Sheratons. You could shop at Wal-Marts (America's biggest employer), J.C. Penneys, Sears, and Targets. You could satisfy your hunger with all-American hamburgers at McDonald's, Wendy's, or Burger King; with chicken at Chick-fil-A, Church's, or Kentucky Fried Chicken; with pizza at Pizza Inn or Pizza Hut; with sandwiches at Subway or Arby's; with fish at Long John Silver's; with steak at Western-Sizzlin or Ponderosa; with Mexican food at Taco Bell; with Italian food at Fazoli's or Olive Garden; with coffee at Starbucks; and with dessert at Baskin & Robbins or Dairy Queen. If you were in the mood for a delightfully tacky yet unrefined dining experience, Hooters would happily fill that need.

There is a certain comfort after traveling hundreds or thousands of miles that the currency has not changed, the language remains understandable, and the Big Mac at McDonald's tastes the same as the Big Mac back home. Indeed, Americans take it for granted and would even expect to converse about the same major news stories with anyone they might meet along the way. This layer of megaculture is a kind of affirmation of America's greatness, values, and way of life. Yet at the same time, it is also a monument to mass production and mass marketing designed to appeal to everyone and offend no one. Beyond the highways and the shopping mall parking lots, the many other layers of racial, ethnic, religious, linguistic, and cultural diversity may be discovered that exist in all the regions of America.

Regions are difficult to define exactly, but there is no doubt that there are regional differences within U.S. culture that are based on early migration patterns, historical and current immigration patterns, topography, climate, and religion. These differences are expressed in language, custom, food, fashion, architecture, leisure activities, and the arts. On a wide scale, most Americans would agree that the nation divides culturally into East, West, North, and South, although to real southerners, any fellow American not a southerner may be considered just another Yankee. There are indeed some variations in the cultural identity of the people in these four broad regions. Fifty-five percent of African Americans in the United States live in the South. Forty-nine percent of Asians and 55 percent of Mexicans live in the West. Forty percent of Americans who claim heritage of two or more races also live in the West.

Certainly, within and around these rather artificial boundaries are unique cultural areas. The East may be further divided between the Mid-Atlantic states and the states of New England, each area having evolved from different historical roots. The Midwest, in the center of the country, defies the easy boundary of the Mississippi River, straddling both its shores. Southern coastal culture differs from the culture of the Deep South. What might be called the *Northlands* near the Canadian border and in Alaska are sparsely populated lands that are unique and not easily classed into four regions. Some have spoken of the space between Boston and Washington, D.C., and Los Angeles and San Diego as being essentially densely populated megacities, gigantic cities of population centers of millions tied together by transportation lines and an urban culture. The mountain areas of Appalachia and the Ozarks have developed distinctive cultures during years of relative isolation. The Pacific Northwest, also geographically isolated during its early development, has developed special characteristics distinct from the general western culture. Certainly, the Southwest has likewise developed a regional culture that is neither entirely western nor southern.

One problem with trying to identify regions is that they have fuzzy boundaries. Another is that if you ask Americans how they identify themselves when asked where they are from, Texans will say Texas and Californians will say California. Alaskans do not identify themselves as westerners, and neither do Hawaiians. No one from a Mid-Atlantic state will identify himself or herself as a Mid-Atlantican. Yet New Englanders, southerners, midwesterners, and westerners do identify strongly with their regions. A buckeye from Ohio may just as well say "I'm from the Midwest" as "I'm from Ohio." Only circumstance would determine the answer. If the Ohioan is talking with a fellow midwesterner, Ohio would be the obvious choice for the answer. If, however, a New York City native asks where he is from, the buckeye will answer that he is from the Midwest, in deference to the known fact that that New Yorkers have a skewed geographical sense of anything west of the Hudson River.

### New England

New England is the prototypical picture of an idyllic America to many Americans. Including the states of Maine, Vermont, New Hampshire, Massachusetts, Connecticut, and Rhode Island, New England is home to small towns with steepled churches, small farms, town meetings, and craggy landscapes from its mountains to its shoreline. It is in many senses the birthplace of America—its democracy, its literature, its poetry, its spirit. Plymouth Rock in Massachusetts marks the landing of the first Pilgrims in America, and the Old North Bridge marks the beginning of the American Revolution. New Hampshire's motto, "Live Free, or Die," sums up the spirit of New England independence in stark choices. New England spawned Nathaniel Hawthorne, Ralph Waldo Emerson, and Herman Melville. Another son of New England, writer Henry David Thoreau, is a national symbol of American independence and Americans' love of its natural landscape.

With 6,130 miles of shoreline, life in New England has always been tied closely to the sea. Whaling at one time was big business; fishing has always been. Clam chowder and codfish remain culinary highlights of New England fare. No one has ever visited Maine without eating a lobster or visiting one of the lighthouses that line the rugged and rocky Maine coast. Cape Cod possesses miles of beautiful sandy beaches and its own architectural style. Shipbuilding, not surprisingly, has been a mainstay of New England industry, supported by forests that cover the interior.

The highest point in New England is Mt. Washington, 6,288 feet in elevation. It is situated in New Hampshire's White Mountains, which, like the Green Mountains of Vermont and the Berkshire Hills in Massachusetts, seem like tame little hillocks compared to the Rockies and the Sierra Nevadas out West. Yet these beautiful mountains and the streams that flow from them provide incredible outdoor recreational opportunities. Skiing is a major industry in winter, and there is usually plenty of snow. Nature walks, fishing, canoeing, kayaking, and rock climbing are popular leisure activities in the

Covered bridges and colorful fall foliage add to the idyllic image of New England. Getty Images/PhotoDisc.

less frozen months, but L.L. Bean will certainly have the right boots and clothing for any New England outdoors enthusiast.

Boston is New England's premier city. It is a financial, educational, and cultural center, with a history dating back to 1630. Boston's natural harbor has been the entry point for millions of new Americans and the export point for New England manufactured products. That harbor was the site of one of the colonists' first major protests against England, the Boston Tea Party. The Freedom Trail that winds through Boston for a couple miles passes some of the colonial landmarks in the birth of American democracy. Boston's nickname, "Beantown," commemorates its Puritan past—the Puritans were said to have served and eaten beans frequently.

### The Mid-Atlantic

The Mid-Atlantic states of Pennsylvania, Maryland, New Jersey, and New York share a colonial heritage with the New England states. Delaware declared its independence from Pennsylvania and Great Britain in 1776, thus becoming the thirteenth colony and, finally, the first state. Although all these states were part of the original British colonies, they were much more culturally diverse than New England. New York began as a Dutch colony, Delaware was full of Swedish settlements, Quakers controlled Pennsylvania, and Roman Catholics were in Maryland. The Mid-Atlantic states, therefore, never shared New England's Puritan heritage.

Four very different major cities dominate the Mid-Atlantic states, three of them—New York City, Philadelphia, and Baltimore—being major ports for commerce and immigration. Washington, D.C., or the District of Columbia, is the nation's capital city. New York City is America's truly international city. With 578 miles of waterfront, an excellent harbor, access to the Great Lakes from the Hudson and Mohawk river systems, and service from three airports, New York City is a major commercial and transportation hub. There are over 1,000,000 flights from New York's airports each year. It is the financial center of the country, if not the world, and home to the New York Stock Exchange and many major banks. The city gave birth to America's film industry, and it remains the cultural capital of American theater, fashion, art, architecture, advertising, and media.

New York City has long welcomed the "huddled masses yearning to be free" to American shores. The Statue of Liberty in New York harbor is an important American icon, an enduring symbol of freedom. New York City has never stopped accepting new people. Today, 36 percent the people who live within the city's 303 square miles were born outside of the United States, and 48 percent speak a language other than English at home. Twenty-seven percent of the people are Hispanic or Latino, and 10 percent are Asian. Like many international cities around the globe, New York City represents the world's diversity in microcosm. It is home to over 400 ethnic neighborhoods, where more than 100 languages are spoken.

It seems that everything in New York City is bigger and better than anywhere else, at least according to one noted Manhattan real estate developer. More than 40,000,000 people visit the city each year, staying in its 70,545 hotel rooms and spending more than $21,000,000,000. There are over 17,300 restaurants and 12,000 licensed taxis; 4,465 buses make 44,550 trips per day over 1,871 miles of bus routes carrying 2,200,000 people on the average workday; 6,247 subway cars make 7,400 trips a day over 685 miles of track carrying 4,800,000 people a day to work, picking them up and dropping them off at 490 stations. The Staten Island ferry makes 104 trips a day with 70,000 passengers.[3]

In a very real sense, New York City is bigger than its boundaries. New York's major art museums—the Museum of Modern Art, the Metropolitan Museum of Art, the Whitney—are national treasures. The Metropolitan Opera is America's premier opera house. Its ballet companies belong to the nation, not just to New York City. Broadway plays and musicals, which are attended by more than 11,000,000 theatergoers each year, define American theater.[4] They frequently find a wider audience in film and become the stuff of high school, college, and community theater performances throughout America. With the headquarters of traditional network television companies in New York City, news and entertainment programming as well as commercials spread across America, serving to unite the country in a certain universe of shared information. There are more than 100 soundstages in the city. Some 40,000 films, television shows, music videos, and commercials are filmed there every year.

Like New York City, Philadelphia had the advantage of a good port and an accessible hinterland that promoted its growth. Philadelphia lies between the Delaware and Schuylkill rivers. Independence Hall is an icon of American democracy—the place where independence was born. While there is still some evidence of William Penn's carefully laid out rectangles in his design of the city, Philadelphia now appears to be a sprawling, meandering metropolis, America's sixth largest city. The evidence, however, of Penn's Quaker roots and the early immigration of Germans to the Philadelphia area abounds. Quaker or Friends' meetinghouses can be found all over the countryside, and soft pretzel vendors seem to be on every city street corner. In Philadelphia, by the way, soft pretzels are to be eaten with mustard. North and west of the city is Pennsylvania Dutch country, which, of course, is not Dutch, but Deutsch, that is, German. German and Swiss pietistic sects were welcome in tolerant Pennsylvania. Today, Amish and Mennonite communities thrive there.

Pittsburgh is Pennsylvania's second largest city. Its skyline is dotted with skyscrapers and many bridges, as the Allegheny and Monongahela rivers merge to form the Ohio River within the city. Corbis.

Maryland shares with Pennsylvania a history of religious toleration. Quakers settled in Maryland as well as Pennsylvania, and Amish communities remain in both states. Baltimore, Maryland's largest city, has the distinction of being the first Roman Catholic archdiocese in the United States, organized in 1808. Now in the midst of revitalization, Baltimore's Inner Harbor has become a major tourist destination on the coast. While Baltimore, with a population of 629,000, is a major Atlantic port, it lacks the developed supporting hinterland that allowed cities like New York and Philadelphia to develop. Black urban migration from the South helped the city's population to swell at one time—African Americans number 64.3 percent of Baltimoreans— but the city actually lost 11.5 percent of its population in the last decade of the twentieth century. On the other hand, the Maryland suburbs around the nation's capital—Silver Spring, Bethesda, Chevy Chase—seem to have grown exponentially and are stark contrasts to Maryland's eastern shore, a bucolic area on the shore of Chesapeake Bay where Maryland crab cakes are served in abundance.

Washington, D.C., only 35 miles from Baltimore, is surrounded by Maryland, which donated the land for a federal capital. Washington, like Philadelphia, is a planned city, but not with the rectilinear clarity of old Philadelphia.

Washington is designed as a series of wheels (traffic circles) and connecting spokes (major arteries) that serve to confound most tourists driving in the district. Happily, tourists do not have to drive because the subway system is easy to use and gets tourists to the district's many attractions as well as people to work.

It is an American rite of passage to visit the nation's capital. A trip to Washington is often the first family vacation many children remember. It is a lesson in citizenship. The Constitution and the Declaration of Independence are on display at the National Archives in what feels like a temple's most sacred space. Visits to the neoclassical buildings that house the three branches of government—the U.S. Capitol, the Supreme Court, and the White House—recall the ancient world's democracies, which America consciously replaced. The museums chronicle the development of American technology and display America's artistic riches and cultural heritage. Memorials to past presidents—Jefferson, Lincoln, Franklin Roosevelt—and the heroes of American wars make patriotic hearts stir.

Regional definitions have blurred somewhat owing to the extensive urban and suburban growth along the East Coast from north of Boston all the way to the nation's capital. A trip south down multilane Interstate 95 from

Millions of visitors come to the Vietnam Memorial Wall in Washington, D.C. every year. Many make pencil rubbings of the names of family members or loved ones whose lives were lost during the Vietnam War. Getty Images/PhotoDisc.

Portsmouth, New Hampshire, around Boston and through Providence, Rhode Island, on further through Fairfield and Stamford, Connecticut, into New York and past New York City to Newark, New Jersey, then right through Philadelphia, past Wilmington, Delaware, under the Fort McHenry Tunnel at Baltimore, and finally to Washington, D.C. will prove exciting or harrowing, depending on one's psychic disposition. There is plenty of time for sightseeing from the car while under way, unless trucks block the view, because the multiple lanes of the highway are randomly closed every few miles to repair parts of the road that have crumbled under the weight of millions of tons of daily traffic, salt to melt ice in the winter, and the natural effects of winter freezing and spring thaws. Thus, during the frequent stops and starts of an I-95 adventure, the sightseer will find it nearly impossible, save for highway signs, to tell one city from the next or where one city begins and another ends as suburban sprawl blends together any sense of boundaries.

### The South

The South includes the states of Virginia, West Virginia, North Carolina, South Carolina, Georgia, Florida, Kentucky, Tennessee, Alabama, Mississippi, Arkansas, Louisiana, and the eastern part of Texas as well as parts of Missouri and Oklahoma. Most of the South is unique among America's regions because it once seceded from the Union to establish the Confederate States of America. The Civil War served to solidify from within and without the identity of southerners as regionally separate.

Today, the South refers to itself as the New South. The Old South of white-haired, white-suited colonels sitting in rocking chairs on the verandas of their plantation houses and sipping mint juleps with favored ladies in pastel hoop skirts exists only in tourist attractions. Indeed, this old stereotype never explained the complexity of the South that southern writers like William Faulkner, Eudora Welty, and Flannery O'Connor understood and portrayed so well. There was never one South. Within the southern region, there are cultural variations among the Gulf Coast, the southern highlands, the Georgia-Carolinas Piedmont, and the northern interior. Certainly the Creoles and Cajuns in French Catholic Louisiana never quite fit the old stereotype.

Some remnants of the Old South do persist. The New South is still filled with cotton fields, peanut fields, and farms with tobacco allotments. Southern hospitality remains a valued commodity that is only enhanced by a southern drawl. Grits, biscuits, and red-eye gravy can still be found on southern breakfast menus, pork is still more popular than beef, and Carolina-grown rice is still preferred to potatoes. Country music, centered in Nashville, Tennessee, is still preferred on the region's radio stations. Yet the New South is being radically transformed. The South has, for the first time since it was settled by whites mostly of British extraction and blacks extricated from their homelands to be New World slaves, become a preferred destination for immigrants of all kinds. The tired, pastoral, slow Old South has given way to a New South of broad diversity and opportunity that is on the go. America's corporate megaculture is as much part of the New South as any other region. Northerners have flocked to the Sunbelt for jobs and warmer weather in what is now a diversified southern economy. Even African Americans whose families earlier forsook the black codes and hopelessness of the Old South have begun returning. The internal migration to the South, at the expense of northern cities, has been so extensive as to endanger the famed southern accent in the booming southern cities. The South has finally become integrated into the rest of the nation.

The city of Atlanta, left in flames after the Civil War, is the symbol and the proof of southern renewal. All roads in the South seem to lead to Atlanta, whose metropolitan population grew over 38 percent from 1990 to 2000 and whose skyscrapers put to rest the stereotype of the Old South and the Atlanta of *Gone with the Wind*. Atlanta, with over 4,600,000 people, was the center of America's civil rights movement and is now America's ninth largest metro area, with more than 1,000 international businesses located there.[5] The Coca-Cola Company, whose trademarks have worldwide recognition, has long been headquartered in Atlanta. Many southerners consider a Coke a suitable if not preferable alternative to a morning cup of coffee. Coke became so ubiquitous in the South that many southerners still use the word "Coke" to refer to any soft drink. Entrepreneur Ted Turner, who founded Turner Broadcasting Company, made Atlanta a cable-broadcasting center with CNN and affiliated networks. The Hartsfield-Jackson Atlanta International Airport is one of America's busiest, with over 83,000,000 passengers passing through it each month.[6]

While Atlanta is the South's inland hub, the South also enjoys a number of important seaports. Norfolk and Newport News, Virginia, are situated at the mouth of Chesapeake Bay. On down the Atlantic coast, Wilmington, North Carolina, Charleston, South Carolina, and Savannah, Georgia, are major ports. Charleston, a planned city dating from 1680, and Savannah have managed to preserve the feel and architecture of the Old South. Florida has two major seaports on the Atlantic: Jacksonville and Miami. Jacksonville, a financial capital, has the distinction of being America's largest city in terms of area—841 square miles. Miami can be said to be one of America's international cities, but with a decided southern orientation. It is the point of entry for Caribbean and South American tourism and immigration. Miami, with a heavy influence of Cuban culture, has become a center of Spanish language broadcasting and Hispanic fashion in America. Miami has also experienced a large Haitian immigration.

Miami's beaches in Florida are an American paradise for travelers. Getty Images/ PhotoDisc.

Florida real estate was the subject of skeptical humor even before the Marx brothers made fun of it in their 1929 movie *The Cocoanuts.* Yet buying "some swamp land in Florida" turned out to be a good investment for most. Florida beaches are among the best in the world, and there are miles and miles of them. Retirees have flocked to south Florida from the cold North. About 18 percent of Florida's population is age 65 or older. Orange groves in central Florida have been diminishing to make way for tourist attractions that draw international clientele. Orlando is now a golfing mecca that is also home to Walt Disney World Resort, the Universal Orlando Resort, Sea World Orlando, Discovery Cove, and Cypress Gardens. Tourist dollars fuel Florida's economy and make a state income tax anathema to Florida legislators.

Tampa is a major port on Florida's Gulf Coast, which features Busch Gardens among its many tourist attractions. Mobile, Alabama, New Orleans, and Houston are other important ports along the Gulf of Mexico. With the exception of these cities, the Gulf Coast is generally populated sparsely. Fishing has traditionally been a major enterprise in the small towns along the coastline. The discovery of oil and natural gas deposits in the gulf, however, have made the energy industry and related industries the basis of most of the coast's economy. Refineries and chemical and paper plants surround the coast from Mobile to Corpus Christi. Unfortunately, the hot and humid Gulf Coast, which rises little above sea level, has a continuing history of being ravaged by hurricanes. When the 2005 hurricane season knocked out part of the Gulf Coast's energy exploration, refining, and transportation capabilities, the entire nation felt the squeeze of higher fuel prices and shortages.

The Gulf Coast from Mobile through Louisiana shared a very different history from the interior South. Mobile and New Orleans were French cities, which meant that Roman Catholicism took root there from the earliest colonial times, rather than the evangelical Protestantism that flourished in most of the South. By 1820, French Jesuits were operating a Roman Catholic college in Mobile. Along the coast and most notably around New Orleans, French, Spanish, white, black, and native cultures created an ethnic jambalaya unlike anywhere else in America or, for that matter, in the world.

The east Texas cities of Houston and Dallas are major cultural and financial centers whose tall buildings reflect the gleaming Texas sun. Thanks in great part to the television series *Dallas,* we tend to think of big oil and big cattle when we think of this part of Texas, but agriculture and industry have

The Alamo in San Antonio, Texas remains a symbol of liberty and freedom even today. Getty Images/PhotoDisc.

built these gigantic and growing cities, too. The Dallas–Fort Worth metropolitan area is the fifth largest in America; Houston's is the eighth largest. In
Texas, we begin to see a transition from southern culture into southwestern
culture, and not just in the substitution of boots for dress shoes and Stetsons
for baseball caps. In the cities of Houston and Dallas, the white population is
about 50 percent, and the African American population is about 25 percent,
but over one-third of each city's population claims a Hispanic or Latino heritage. In San Antonio, a city of 1,200,000 people about 200 miles southwest
of Houston, the white population approaches 68 percent, the African American population is less than 7 percent, and 59 percent of the population are of
Hispanic or Latino origin.

### The Midwest

The states of Ohio, Michigan, Indiana, Wisconsin, Minnesota, Illinois,
Iowa, Nebraska, North Dakota, South Dakota, Kansas, eastern Colorado, and
parts of Missouri and western Pennsylvania make up America's Midwest, its
breadbasket. Chicago is its center. The influence of the many Germans who
settled in Ohio, Illinois, Missouri, and Wisconsin, the Swedes and Norwe-
gians in Wisconsin and Minnesota, and southern African Americans in the
larger Midwestern cities can still be felt. Chicago has the largest Polish population of any city outside of Poland. Huck Finn and Tom Sawyer were, in a
sense, born on the Mississippi River. Midwesterners are down-to-earth folks
who speak plainly and straightforwardly in the preferred accent of the national
media. Midwesterners will tell you they have no accent. The Midwest is steak
and potatoes country.

If it is true that southerners would have to go through Atlanta even to get
to heaven, Midwesterners would have to go through Chicago. Incorporated
as a town with a population of 350 in 1833, it was a city of over 4,000
people four years later. Now with a population of nearly 3,000,000 living on
228 square miles of land, Chicago claims the world's busiest airport, O'Hare
International, the world's largest convention center, McCormick Place, the
world's largest food festival, the Taste of Chicago, and the world's biggest
parochial school system, which is run by the Roman Catholic archdiocese of
Chicago.

Chicago's geographical location in the middle of the country and its
29 miles of lakefront on Lake Michigan helped to make it a transportation
hub and a gigantic manufacturing and industrial power. Long the nation's
second city to New York City, Chicago has typified the trend among large
Midwestern cities of losing population as southern, southwestern, and western cities continue to grow. Chicago lost its second city status to Los Angeles
in the later twentieth century, but the years of New York–Chicago rivalry

caused Chicagoans to start counting everything in sight to prove theirs was no tiny toddlin' town. They counted 148,000 manholes and 47,330 fire hydrants on 3,780 miles of streets. They found 4,300 miles of sewer mains, 4,290 miles of water mains, and even 6,400 bike racks. Chicago's 30,000,000 visitors each year could enjoy 560 parks, 200 live theaters, 49 museums, and more than 7,000 restaurants and 200 annual parades.[7]

The Midwest includes what is commonly called *America's industrial heartland* or, perhaps somewhat pejoratively, the *Rust Belt*. The fact is that in the Midwest, manufacturing and farming live closely together. In addition to Chicago, the cities of Cleveland, Ohio, Pittsburgh, Pennsylvania, Milwaukee, Wisconsin, Cincinnati, Ohio, and Detroit, Michigan, grew to become large manufacturing centers. The Ohio River Valley and the Great Lakes helped to create these industrial cities, empowered by the needs of local agriculture. Pittsburgh means steel; Detroit means automobiles; Milwaukee means beer; Kansas City means beef; and St. Louis is the gateway to the West.

The Midwest is also called *Middle America* and includes the Corn Belt, filled with small towns separated by lots of open space. The towns are populated with people who have solid and independent values. Hot summers and cold winters combine with rather flat land and generally good soil to create some of the most abundant agricultural land in the world. Corn, wheat, and soybeans are the major crops. Raising hogs and cattle augment income from grain farming. There is extensive dairy farming in Wisconsin and Minnesota above the plains. Wisconsin produces about 50 percent of the cheese in America. Fruit orchards dot the western Great Lakes. The family farm is disappearing, but the Corn Belt is still about 80 percent farmland, notably in places like Illinois and Iowa.[8]

The Midwestern states of Kansas, Nebraska, South Dakota, and North Dakota lie in the Great Plains. The plains extend from Texas up into Canada, with eastern boundaries that roughly straddle the western limits of Louisiana, Arkansas, Missouri, Iowa, and Minnesota. Portions of eastern New Mexico, Colorado, Wyoming, and much of Montana also lie within the plains. The High Plains stretch from south Texas into southern Nebraska. Tornadoes and tremendous thunderstorms rule this area, which is hot in summer and cold in winter. Buffalo herds once roamed these grassy prairies. Not even the Indians much settled there. Ranching became the thing—hard winter wheat in the south and spring wheat in the north plains. In the north, barley and oats are major second crops, along with sunflowers.

### The West

The West covers a lot of territory: the interior states of Wyoming, Montana, Utah, Idaho, and western Colorado; the Pacific Northwest states of Oregon,

Washington, and Alaska; Hawaii; and most of California. The interior states of the West are perhaps most emblematic of the American pioneer tradition. They have small populations that are largely white and non-Hispanic. Wyoming, for example, is typical of the area, with a little over 500,000 people, 89 percent of whom are non-Hispanic whites. The land does not give way to an easy existence, but the people there seem to have a certain open and welcoming friendliness that leaves no room for pretension. Wyoming gave women, equal toilers on the frontier, the right to vote in 1869. The Rocky Mountains rise out of the Great Plains in Wyoming, and the Continental Divide cuts directly through it. Although raising cattle and sheep and growing a few crops have always been essential parts of Wyoming life, agriculture lags behind mining and mineral extraction in Wyoming's economy. Wyoming is the nation's largest coal producer. Its national parks—Yellowstone and Grand Teton—and its national monuments—Devil's Tower and Fossil Butte—help to place tourism second in importance to the state's economy. Millions of acres of national forests are also located in Wyoming. Wyoming is truly the land where the antelope roam.

Montana, stretching to 559 miles east to west along the Canadian border and 321 miles north to south, calls itself Big Sky Country. Its western third lies in the Rocky Mountains, where the Continental Divide descends; the remaining part of the state lies in the Great Plains. Around 65 percent of Montana is occupied by ranches and farms whose major products are wheat and beef. Twenty-five percent of the state is covered by forests, thus making the timber industry important to the local economy, but tourism is second only to agriculture. Glacier National Park is an important destination, but Montana has over 17,000,000 acres of public land and seven Indian reservations. Montana also contains immense coal deposits.[9] Idaho, on the western side of the Continental Divide, is filled with scenic rivers and streams that make whitewater rafting a simple pleasure.

Utah has some of the nation's highest peaks but is better known for the Great Salt Lake, a briny remnant of an ancient freshwater lake, and the desert next to it. For most pioneers, Utah held little promise for settlement. For the members of the Church of Jesus Christ of Latter-day Saints, however, Utah became the Promised Land on earth after a long and arduous exodus from persecution in Illinois.

### California

California is larger in area and has a larger gross domestic product than most nations. Like the northeast coast's megacity, the area between Santa Barbara and San Diego is California's answer, a blur of cities and suburbs that seem to make one gigantic metropolis with almost imperceptible boundaries.

California is a land of beautiful coasts along the Pacific Ocean, mountains, broad valleys, southeastern deserts, and northern forests. The Coast Ranges line the coast along fault zones that make California prone to earthquakes. The Central Valley, which is east of the ranges, is agriculturally rich. The valley is a distinct geological feature that was formed between the Coast Ranges and the rugged Sierra Nevadas by drainage of the Sacramento and San Joaquin rivers. More than 430 miles long and, on average, 50 miles in width, thanks to the damming of rivers and streams and irrigation, the valley is one of America's richest agricultural regions. The abundance of crops grown there include almonds, barley, corn, cotton, grapes, oats, pistachios, rice, sorghum, sugar beets, sunflowers, tomatoes, walnuts, and wheat.[10] Railroads and the discovery of oil also fueled the valley's growth and the development of its cities—Bakersfield, Fresno, Merced, Stockton, Sacramento, Chico, and Redding. North of the Central Valley is a plateau that contains volcanoes, notably Mount Shasta and Mount Lassen. Northern California gets more precipitation than the south, where irrigation is needed to support agricultural crops. In fact, water for Los Angeles is supplied through two aqueducts. The 1913 aqueduct is 223 miles long; the 1970 aqueduct is 137 miles long. Fires in dry Southern California, where there are major oil fields, are sometimes driven by strong winds. The Imperial Valley in Southern California can grow crops all year. Grapes are grown around San Francisco in California's famed wine country; flowers are grown in the Lompoc Valley; oranges and lemons are grown around the Los Angeles Basin. Specialty crops add to the fresh cuisine of California.

Los Angeles and San Francisco are California's two main urban hubs. They are very different cities. Los Angeles, America's second largest city, with 3,800,000 people and a metro population of almost 13,000,000, is a coagulation of cities connected by freeways with no real center. The manmade port of Los Angeles–Long Beach is the major West Coast import-export point. While Hollywood and the entertainment industry give it its glitter, Los Angeles retains its affinity with the Southwest. Although the Asian population is 10 percent of the total, some 47 percent of the population claims Hispanic, mostly Chicano, heritage; 58 percent of the people do not speak English at home; and 41 percent were born outside of the country. The Los Angeles *barrio,* a word that simply means "neighborhood," has an area of 193 square miles and a population of almost 2,000,000 people.

San Francisco is a more traditional city of a bit more than 750,000 people and a metro population of 4,100,000. San Francisco's Hispanic population is only about 14 percent, in sharp contrast to Los Angeles. Its Asian population, however, is nearly 31 percent. The San Francisco Bay area, home to Silicon

Valley and award-winning wines, is one of America's most scenic places, with an excellent harbor that is a gateway for Asian immigration.

### Hawaii

Hawaii, an archipelago of volcanoes that stretches west from the big island more than 1,800 miles, has long been an entry point for Asian immigration. Only about 114,000 of its 1,263,000 inhabitants are native islanders. Asians outnumber whites five to three. Hawaii, the big island, is two-thirds of the landmass. Nearly all the population lives on the eight main islands: Hawaii, Oahu, Maui, Kauai, Lanai, Molokai, Niihau, and Kahoolawe. The state controls most of the land, about 80 percent. Hawaii is in the middle of nowhere: some 3,600 miles from Tokyo and 2,100 miles from San Francisco. Kilauea and Mauna Loa are the most famous volcanoes on the big island. With a consistently temperate climate, tourism is a central economic force. Hawaiian music, the hula, and the luau have long been a staple of American culture that is constantly reinforced in film and on television. When mainland Americans think about Hawaii, they typically picture the big blue waves offshore—surfing is the state individual sport—and recall the tastes of pineapples, Kona coffee, and macadamia nuts.

### The Pacific Northwest

The three states of the Pacific Northwest are home to about 10,000,000 Americans. Portland, Oregon, and Seattle, Washington, are the main cities, characterized by white populations of over 70 percent. Both have good harbors, and both are industrial centers. There is high rainfall along the rugged coast that produces tall evergreens—Douglas firs, red cedar, and Sitka spruce—and the valleys created between the Coast Ranges and the volcanic Cascades, the Willamette in Oregon and the Puget Sound lowlands in Washington, provide agricultural opportunities. East of the Cascades, which make up two-thirds of Oregon and half of Washington, the climate is rather arid. The Columbia River provides needed irrigation as well as hydroelectric power. Like the dams on the Mississippi River, the 11 dams on the Columbia, including Bonneville and Grand Coulee, are further tributes to American can-do engineering in the conquering of nature.

Lumber and the fur trade built the Pacific Northwest, isolated as it once was on the northwest tip of the country, but Boeing and Microsoft now help to sustain it. The spirit of independence that relative isolation promoted can still be felt there. It is as if the Pacific Northwest were its own separate country. It could produce everything from apples to milk and cheese, hops to spearmint, and even grapes to grow its own wine industry. Wheat is a major crop in the hilly Palouse of Washington, and farming is a major undertaking

Alaska is one of America's many natural treasures, full of national parks, lakes, and glaciers. Mt. McKinley, found in Alaska, is North America's tallest mountain. Getty Images/PhotoDisc.

in the Columbia Plateau on the Oregon-Washington border. Even with the diminution of the importance of the salmon business, the Pacific Northwest nonetheless has created its own cuisine based on the fresh foods available there. It is an environmentally friendly place where strangers are welcome, but not asked to stay.

Alaska, the largest state in the United States in terms of land, is popularly thought to be the land of Eskimos, which, of course, it is. Yet today, these native people account for only about 22 percent of the state's sparsely populated territory. Whites constitute some 71 percent of the total population, and the city of Anchorage contains some 40 percent of the state's entire population. While the fishing and oil and gas industries are very important to the Alaskan economy, the vast majority of Alaska's people are engaged in the service sector. Alaska is a gorgeous yet forbidding land. Tourism is a major summer industry as visitors come to the Land of the Midnight Sun to see the wonders of its many national parks and preserves, its thousands of lakes and glaciers, and its hundreds of islands. Mt. McKinley in the Alaska Range reaches 20,320 feet, the highest elevation in the United States. Alaska truly is America's Last Frontier.

### The Southwest

The Southwest includes the states of New Mexico, Arizona, and Nevada as well as southern interior California, west Texas, and parts of Oklahoma. The Rio Grande River is one of its defining characteristics. Flowing south out of snow-packed mountains in Colorado, the Rio Grande cuts through New Mexico and, north of El Paso, Texas, forms a 1,250-mile border with Mexico as it makes its way southeasterly to the Gulf of Mexico near Brownsville.

The Falcon Dam above Mission and the Amistad Dam above Del Rio have helped to mitigate the severe flooding that had been common downstream. In New Mexico, the reservoirs formed by the Elephant Butte and Caballo dams provide sources for irrigation. The Rio Grande remains the lifeblood of this part of the region, one of the few available sources of water to sustain human, animal, and plant life.

The plains, mountains, deserts, rivers, and canyons of the generally arid Southwest provide some of America's most dramatic landscapes and vital natural resources. The plains that stretch northwest beyond the Texas border from San Antonio and Dallas through Midland and Lubbock are cowboy country and home to immense herds of cattle, even some of the famous Texas longhorn cattle, on gigantic ranches. It is also oil country. Texas continues to be a major oil and natural gas producer, especially since the development of resources off the coast in the Gulf of Mexico. Oil built both Midland and Houston.

New Mexico calls itself the Land of Enchantment with good reason. Its eastern plains, punctuated by the Carlsbad Caverns to the south, give way to the red Sangre de Cristo (blood of Christ) Mountains in the north and the San Andres Mountains west of the Pecos River as it wends southward. The White Sands National Monument southwest of Alamogordo appears as mounds and mounds of sugar dunes, but it is really gypsum. On the western side of the Rio Grande, the Jemez Mountains and the Black Range cozy up to the Continental Divide, which roughly parallels the Rio Grande. As the desert continues from the southwestern part of the state, forests of pines and firs lie along the hills to the Black Range and the Mogollon Mountains. The northwestern New Mexico desert includes Indian lands and the otherworldly Bisti Badlands Wilderness Area.

In New Mexico, perhaps more than in any other southwestern state, the mix of native, Mexican, and Anglo cultures has coexisted for so long that it is often impossible to identify which culture contributed what. New Mexico had the greatest number of Hispanic settlers of all the old Spanish territory America took after the Mexican War. Evidence remains of their adobe homes as well as the pueblos of the natives. Beans, corn, and chilis are the basic staples of the cuisine of both cultures. In fact, red chilis are one of New Mexico's major crops. Four tribes have reservations of over 400,000 acres in New Mexico: the Jicarilla Apache, the Keresan, the Mescalero Apache, and the Zuni. Although the Anglo culture predominates overall, it developed its own distinctive southwestern flavor.

Arizona is the Grand Canyon State. The Colorado River cuts across northwestern Arizona to the Nevada line, then to the Hoover Dam, where it flows south eventually to form Arizona's border with California. The Grand

Canyon is perhaps America's best-known, most photographed and painted natural wonder, but Arizona is filled with natural wonders. Giant saguaro cacti populate the southeast. The Canyon de Chelly on the Navajo Reservation in northeast Arizona is as breathtaking as the Grand Canyon. The Petrified Forest east of Holbrook and the Painted Desert above Flagstaff are uniquely beautiful. The burgeoning city of Phoenix is surrounded by desert, copper mines, and Indian reservations. There are 18 federal reservations in the state. The Navajo Reservation is by far the largest, occupying nearly 14,000,000 acres. The Tohono O'Odham (Papago) Reservation is almost 2,800,000 acres; the San Carlos Reservation of the Apache tribe is 1,800,000 acres; the Fort Apache Reservation is 1,600,000 acres; and the Hopi Reservation is 1,500,000 acres. The rest are considerably smaller.

Nevada is situated in the ancient seabed called the *Great Basin.* It is extremely dry, with a landscape that sometimes resembles Mars with scrub brush. Yet the Great Basin National Park shows off the natural beauty of the basin, and Lake Tahoe's forests and clear water are jolting contrasts from the desert. Silver and gold made Nevada; the gambling and tourism industries sustain it. Glittering Las Vegas rises out of the desert on borrowed water, promoting itself as a place where what happens there, stays there—as if the

Known around the world for its beauty, the Grand Canyon is only one of the southwest's precious sites. Getty Images/PhotoDisc.

tourists were prospectors who had just hit the mother lode and came to town to have a night on the town. The Wild West lives on.

### The Appalachians and Ozarks

Of special note are two cultural regions that lie within the larger regions. They are notable for their traditionally isolated mountain culture. The Appalachian Mountains are a series of what the locals call hills that stretch from northeastern Alabama to southern New York. They encompass western portions of North Carolina and Virginia, northern Georgia, eastern Tennessee and Kentucky, southeastern Ohio, all of West Virginia, and central and northeastern Pennsylvania. The Blue Ridge Mountains form the eastern boundary. The Central Valley then gives way to the Appalachian Plateau, with the Allegheny Front to the east of the valley. The Shenandoah Valley provides the only viable agricultural land in Appalachia. Coal mining in southeastern Kentucky, West Virginia, Pennsylvania, and western Virginia has provided a means of income for this otherwise poor area of small farms, but at no small cost to the health and safety of the miners. The Appalachians began to be populated in the 1730s by English, Scottish, and Welsh settlers. They were later joined by the Scotch-Irish from Ulster. Their enthusiastic Protestant religion proliferated into tens of sects just among Baptists. The Appalachians became involved in the Great Awakening that began in the 1740s and lasted for about 80 years. Camp meetings—tent revivals were a mainstay of Appalachia by the early 1800s—and the emotive gospel music, featuring Old World fiddles, merged with bluegrass and became what we call today country music. The Ozarks were settled largely by Appalachian people who migrated westward. The Ozarks extend from central Missouri through northern Arkansas and into eastern Oklahoma and mark the only significant hills in America's midsection. Ozark culture features many of the same characteristics as Appalachian culture, and both have preserved folk crafts and music from an earlier period.

## THE PEOPLE

There are about 300,000,000 people in the United States now, ranking it third behind China and India, each with populations of more than 1,000,000,000 people. However, the population density of China is 359 per square mile, and of India, 914 per square mile. In the United States, on the other hand, there are only 82 people per square mile, well below the world figure of 125. This is attributable not only to the vastness of the country, but also to its generally temperate climate save for interior and northern Alaska. Russia, for example, has almost twice the landmass of the United States, but much of the land is uninhabitable, thus leaving it with only 22 people per square mile. Canada, with about the same area as the United States, has only nine people per square mile.

California is the most populous state, with 35,484,000 people (228 per square mile), followed by Texas, with 22,119,000 (84.5 per square mile); New York, with 19,190,000 (407 per square mile); Florida, with 17,019,000 (316 per square mile); and Illinois, with 12,654,000 (228 per square mile). New Jersey is the most crowded state, with 1,165 people per square mile, and Rhode Island is a close second, with 1,030 people per square mile. Wyoming has the least population of all the states at 501,000, with only 5.2 people per square mile. Alaska has the most wide open spaces, with only 1.1 persons per square mile.

The legacy of spaciousness can be found in Americans' personal sense of distance, which is comfortable at about two feet. Getting any closer would cause visible unease and be considered an affront, if not an assault, most likely resulting in an angry request that the offending party "get out of my face" and "stop breathing my air" before pushing and shoving begins. Yet while Americans enjoy having room to roam and a personal sacrosanct space, the vast majority live in urbanized areas.

The new millennium finds 19,450 incorporated places in the United States with a total population of nearly 180,000,000. Nine of those places are cities of more than 1,000,000 people, which are home to 23,300,000 people. New York City, the largest of them, with over 8,000,000 citizens, has 26,403 people per square mile. Sprawling Los Angeles, with 3,800,000 people, has a population density of 7,877 per square mile, but Chicago's 2,800,000 people are packed into the city at the rate of 12,633 per square mile. Houston's 2,000,000 citizens have 3,372 neighbors in every square mile, but Philadelphia's 1,500,000 citizens have 11,234. Phoenix (1,400,000), San Diego (1,300,000), San Antonio (1,210,000), and Dallas (1,200,000) round out the list of America's largest cities, all with population densities of more than 2,700 per square mile.[11]

Fourteen million Americans live in the 22 cities with populations between 500,000 and 1,000,000. More than 40,000,000 live in the 214 cities with populations of 100,000–500,000. Almost 28,000,000 live in the 397 cities with population between 50,000 and 100,000. Small-town America, however, is very much alive. Nearly 52,000,000 Americans live in the 18,143 cities and towns with populations of less than 25,000. Of those cities and towns, 16,683 have populations under 10,000 and are home to about 10 percent of all Americans.

The cities alone do not tell the whole story of where and how most Americans live. An entirely different kind of automobile-enabled culture has developed in the suburban areas that surround America's great cities. When the suburban and other areas that are dependent largely on core cities are considered as metropolitan areas, a clearer picture emerges. The metropolitan area of New York City, which includes parts of New Jersey and Pennsylvania, swells to 18,600,000 people, more than twice the number in the city itself. The Los Angeles metropolitan area, with 12,800,000 people, is more than three times the population of the city alone. Chicago's metropolitan area has 9,300,000 inhabitants, Philadelphia's has 5,800,000, and Dallas's has 5,600,000. These are America's largest five metropolitan areas, topping the list of 50 metropolitan areas with populations of more than 1,000,000.

Today, 79 percent of Americans live in urbanized areas—more than half of them in urbanized areas of over 1,000,000. The urban populations of California, Hawaii, Massachusetts, Nevada, New Jersey, and Rhode Island exceed 90 percent. Only about 2 percent of Americans live on farms.

So who are these Americans? America is now more racially and ethnically diverse than at any time in its history. Nearly 2 percent of the population claims the heritage of two or more races. Of those claiming a single race, whites still comprise the majority at over 75 percent. African Americans are a little over 12 percent of the population, American Indians and Alaska natives a bit under 1 percent, Asians 4.2 percent, and 2 percent claim some other race. Over 14 percent of the total population of any race claim Latino or Hispanic heritage.[12] Fifty percent of Hispanics are Mexican in origin; 36 percent live in California, with large contingents of Cubans in Florida, and others in Illinois, Texas, and New York. Of whites, most claim a British ancestry, but about 22 percent are of German descent, and 18 percent are of Irish descent.

The mix keeps changing. Around 1,000,000 legal immigrants are admitted each year, 70 percent of them relatives of U.S. citizens. In 2002, for example, of the 1,063,700 admitted immigrants, 174,200 came from Europe; 342,100 from Asia; 60,300 from Africa; 404,400 from North America, of whom 219,400 were Mexican; and 74,500 from South America. The number one destination for Mexican, Indian, Chinese, Filipino, and Vietnamese immigrants was California. Most Cubans went to Florida. New immigrants have tended to cluster in the large cities—Los Angeles, San Francisco, New York, Chicago, and Houston, for example—where others of the same heritage are already ensconced. However, cities such as Las Vegas, Atlanta, Salt Lake City, and Minneapolis have growing Hispanic populations. Asian populations are growing in Denver, Seattle, Boston, Detroit, and Miami. In addition to this legal immigration, estimates are that there are 7,000,000 unauthorized immigrants living in the United States: 4,808,000 from Mexico, with sizable numbers also from El Salvador

(189,000), Guatemala (144,000), Colombia (141,000), and Honduras (138,000). Of these 7,000,000 unauthorized immigrants, 2,209,000 were in California; 1,041,000 were in Texas; and 489,000 were in New York.

About 12 percent of the people in the United States were born elsewhere. Not surprisingly, 49,600,000 people, 18.7 percent of the U.S. population five years old and older, speak a language other than English at home. While some native-born Americans find this situation alarming, corporate America has welcomed these new consumers, especially those who speak Spanish, now America's second language. Spanish can be heard frequently in Los Angeles, San Antonio, and Miami, but all over America, packaging has suddenly appeared in Spanish and English, voting ballots may be obtained in Spanish, and bilingual signs have sprung up in retail stores, even in suburbia.

It is not just a platitude that America is a land of immigrants. It always has been and continues to be a destination for refugees and those seeking a better life. The real story about America is not its growing and changing population, but its ability to assimilate new immigrants into the American dream. To be sure, the process is seldom quick and sometimes difficult. Somehow though, the once undesirable neighborhoods of America's biggest and oldest cities segregating Italians, Irish, Jews, African Americans, Chinese, Puerto Ricans, and Poles became centers for the pursuit of happiness American style.

America's public education system, designed at the outset to teach citizenship as well as reading, writing, and arithmetic, is perhaps one of the unheralded causes of this transformation. As America expanded westward, land was set aside for schools, grade school through college. Today, the United States is a highly educated nation: 186,500,000 Americans (83.9%) who are at least 25 years old are high school graduates, and 27 percent have bachelor's degrees or further higher education.

Americans like to think they live in a classless society. No one is better than anyone else—everybody puts his pants on one leg at a time. Americans do not bow, curtsey, or nod their heads when they meet friends or strangers. With a firm grip and a handshake, Americans look into the eyes of the people they meet and immediately begin a new relationship on an equal, first-name basis. Yet the self-confidence and independence this behavior connotes is also the power behind the innovation and inventiveness that Americans cherish, and entrepreneurial risk taking can lead to incredible wealth. Bill Gates of Microsoft, Michael Dell of Dell Computer, and Sergei Brin of Google are to the computer age what Andrew Carnegie, J. P. Morgan, and John D. Rockefeller were to the industrial age. There are about 70 personal computers for every 100 Americans.

Sometimes politicians running for office can find just the right slogan that resonates with a fundamental belief nearly everyone holds closely. Bill

Clinton promised good things to those who work hard and play by the rules, much like a preacher promising heaven to those who pray and keep the 10 Commandments. Most Americans believe that hard work, whether backbreaking physical labor or long hours at the office (some 45,000,000 people list their occupation as managers or professionals, the largest single occupational category), is the path to the American dream. It is understood that salaried employees who work only 40 hours a week will not move up in the organization. Doing the minimum shows no initiative. The good things hard work is expected to bring are financial independence, which is tantamount to personal independence, new homes, new cars, nice vacations, and a lifestyle of choice. Americans seem to enjoy showing off the bounty of their success. A big house, a big car, season tickets to football games—the things money can buy—tell everyone "I made it." It is as if there were an imaginary ladder of success Americans try to climb, and near the top rung, money talks.

Clinton cleverly juxtaposed the notion of work and play. Americans work hard and play hard, too, as we shall see, but what absolutely galls most Americans is anyone who tries to get ahead by cheating. Playing by the rules at work, at play, and in life is a basic expectation. What the rules are is not particularly important, and they are always subject to change. The idea that someone who was undeserving would get something for nothing is, however, almost too much to bear. This was viewed as the problem with the welfare system; people who could have worked were getting checks for not working—not playing by the rules. On the other hand, Americans pour out their hearts and willingly open their wallets for people who cannot help themselves or are victims of disasters. American generosity is legendary. Millions of dollars from individual Americans have gone to survivors of tsunamis, earthquakes, and terrorist attacks. Likewise, millions of Americans volunteer in various social and religious organizations to help the less fortunate.

You do not have to be rich to participate in the American dream. Readily available credit allows dreams to come true. Americans are carrying $9,709,000,000 in personal debt. It starts for many with college. The median educational loan for graduates is $16,500. The average amount financed for a new car is more than $24,000. The average household has credit and car loan debt of $18,700. Then there is the mortgage on the house. Americans carry more than $7 trillion in mortgage debt. Payment of debt accounts for 13.6 percent of Americans' after tax income, but only about 5 percent fail to keep up with their payments. Easy credit is an invitation to a life of hard work.

Recent surveys have shown that the vast majority of Americans view themselves as hard working, inventive, and honest. A majority of Americans also view their compatriots as greedy and not religious enough. One in five Americans, on the other hand, thinks America is too religious. Nearly half view the country as violent, and over one-third view their fellow Americans as immoral and rude.[13] Hard work, inventiveness, and honesty are core American values that have persisted over time and are elemental to the formation of American character. These values are also expectations that Americans have for each other and certainly for its newest citizens.

It is not surprising that Americans are often viewed by others as too big for their britches. Americans' expectation for things being done in the American way, whatever that may be, appears as arrogance. In fact, the American penchant for efficient use of time—gulping down fast food, always on time for appointments—seems to have created a robotic society tuned to the clock as if in the last two minutes of a football game. When expectations are not met—if a traffic jam causes one to be late, for example—Americans feel a certain stress that may manifest itself as haughtiness. Yet as self-reliant problem solvers, they also believe that whatever caused the system to go awry can be fixed.

We will see in more detail later that Americans are generally a religious people, and America is home to perhaps 150 or more religious groups. There is a diversity of religious values and beliefs among Americans, but that religion plays a role in building American character is indisputable. Neither can it be disputed that violence is part of everyday American life, which seems to contradict the religious and civic values that hold the nation together. In 2003, for example, 1,381,000 violent crimes were known to police across America: 17,000 murders; 93,000 forcible rapes; 413,000 robberies; and 858,000 aggravated assaults. Over 10,400,000 property crimes were also reported. Ninety percent of the violent crimes occurred in large metropolitan areas. Handguns were the weapons used in more than half of the murders.

The official language of the United States of America is ... well, there is no official language. That is probably a good thing because if Congress declared an official language, most Americans would refuse to speak it. Government and government motives have always been viewed with a certain suspicion, and any attempt to regulate language would probably be considered a violation of cherished individual rights. Thus, in a sense, there are some 300,000,000 dialects of American English in the United States. The fact is, however, that language may be a clue to what region a person grew up in or lives in. It also may hint at social class, age, education, and ethnicity. When Americans hear expressions like these, they can usually size up the speaker's background:

Was you goin' to town?

Like eeeeyoooo, that's gross!

They are vacationing in Warshington!

The delegation arrived in Cuber to see Castro!

How ya'll doin'?

Leave the paper on the stoop!

He's all hat and no cattle!

Are you going to the shore this weekend?

Do she have the book?

So, yous wanna go get a cheesesteak?

That maht could work!

You betcha!

Let's get a grinder for lunch!

I've got to red up the house already!

I asked for a soda, not a Coke!

Dame un bipeo later!

The machine's all tore up!

Go out to the bahn and check on the horses.

Dose doyty boyds are nesting right under my window!

Broadly considered, there are only two general dialects in the United States, northern and southern, each with numerous variations. The general northern dialect is spoken in all areas of the country outside the Old South of the Confederacy. Greatly influenced by the language of New England, further dialects of the general northern dialect developed with westward expansion. The Great Lakes dialect is spoken from Syracuse to Milwaukee, and its nasal *A*s can be heard in Chicago, Detroit, Buffalo, and Cleveland. The North Midland dialect, with full *R*s pronounced, stretches from south Jersey and northern Maryland across most of Ohio, Indiana, Illinois, Iowa, Missouri, Nebraska, and eastern Oklahoma. The western dialect, also with general northern dialect roots, is relatively new in linguistic history terms and is mixed with regional sounds. Subsets or subdialects of the western dialect include the Southwest, the Pacific Northwest, central and northern California, and the interior western states. The general southern dialect has only two divisions. The southern dialect is spoken in the southeast from Maryland south to Florida and in the lowlands of Georgia, Alabama, Mississippi, Louisiana, and east Texas. The South Midland dialect is spoken in the highlands and inland from southern Ohio through the Texas panhandle.[14]

Such broad classifications hardly do justice to the variety of the American language. Ethnic groups bring their own flare to the language—African Americans, Cajuns, Chicanos—and America's major cities, notably Boston, New York, and San Francisco, have developed a distinctive patois. Teenagers of all ethnic groups continue to make and remake their own languages. Yet even in the face of this complexity and diversity, it has been argued that Americans' mobility and the constant, flat sounds of so-called standard American over radio and television will wipe out regional linguistic variations. Linguistic boundaries may change and blur, but the fact remains that people in Boston do not sound anything like people in New Orleans. What is really important to the fabric of American life, however, is that Bostonians and New Orleanians, Texans and Michiganders, can all understand each other. Any Englishman will tell you that there is an American accent.

## THE PAST

### The Natives and European Exploration

The earliest immigrants to America began arriving perhaps 30,000 years ago from Asia over a land bridge that connected Siberia with the North American continent. Archaeological evidence also suggests that indigenous populations in South America migrated northward. By the time Europeans discovered this New World at the end of the fifteenth century, there were anywhere from 1,500,000 to 6,000,000 natives in the continental United States and probably around 75,000,000 in the entire New World. Migrations to North America and within the continent continued for thousands of years. These immigrants spread from the west to the Atlantic Ocean. There was a substantial migration from established Mexican cultures northward into the Mississippi Valley and beyond through which the cultivation of maize spread. They created empires, trading routes, and a great number of distinct languages and cultures. They were artists, artisans, farmers, hunters, and traders who raised families in religious traditions with social values.

The complexity of the native cultures was lost on early European explorers. Indeed, we still live with Christopher Columbus's confusion that he had found India and therefore named these American natives Indians. These explorers were confronted by people who spoke languages unintelligible to them, who were naked, who were suspicious of their motives, and who approached them carefully. One voyager chronicled his astonishment that the women could swim and run faster than the men. Women athletes had been discovered. The explorers referred to themselves as the Christians and to the naked natives as savages.

These European attitudes informed what quickly became a European race to claim whatever riches the New World had to offer. To the minds of the civilized Christian Europeans, the natives owned no claims to the land. Christopher Columbus, sailing for Spain, discovered America in 1492, but never saw what would become the United States. John Cabot made claims for England to North America in 1497. The Spanish, however, seemed to have a leg up on the British. Juan Ponce de Léon explored the coasts of Florida in 1513. After Cortés conquered the Aztecs and Mexico in 1522, Spanish explorers went north from there and from Cuba. Cabeza de Vaca explored the Gulf Coast from Florida to the southwest from 1528 to 1536. Hernando de Soto explored what would be 14 states from Florida to Michigan and west between 1539 and 1542. Francisco Vásquez de Coronado explored the southwest from 1539 to 1541 and discovered the Grand Canyon. Juan Rodriguez Cabrillo explored California in 1542. In 1565, the Spanish established the first city in the future United States, St. Augustine, Florida. Sirs Walter Raleigh and Humphrey Gilbert did not establish Roanoke Island, the lost colony, until 1585. Jamestown, established in 1607, was England's first successful settlement.

France, the Netherlands, and Sweden were also in the race. France commissioned Giovanni de Verrazanno to seek the fabled Northwest Passage in 1524, but it was Jacques Cartier who established French North American claims in 1535. The Spanish eliminated French settlements in Florida. In 1673, Louis Joliet and Jacques Marquette explored the upper Mississippi River, and in 1698, Sieur de LaSalle explored Lake Michigan and the upper Mississippi River. Sieur de Bienville established New Orleans in 1698, and a year later, Sieur d'Iberville was the first European to enter the Mississippi River from the Gulf of Mexico.

Henry Hudson made a claim for the Netherlands for all the land from the river named for him to Albany in 1609, but about 30 years later, the Dutch government issued a patent to the New Netherlands Company for the area between Virginia and New France. Sweden established a colony near Wilmington, Delaware, in 1638, but the Dutch took it from them in 1655. Nine years later, however, the Dutch surrendered New Amsterdam to the English owing to a bit of English brinksmanship. New Amsterdam became the English colony of New York, and the Dutch were out of business in North America.

By 1700, England's colonies, hugging the Atlantic coast, were surrounded by French territory to the north and west and Spanish territory to the south. New France was an immense land that extended from Newfoundland and Nova Scotia all the way to Lake Superior, southward down the Mississippi to the Gulf of Mexico, with eastern borders along the English colonies. Wars would make dramatic changes. England took Nova Scotia and Newfoundland from France in the 1713 Treaty of Utrecht, which ended Queen Anne's War. England found itself pitted against France and Spain in the French and Indian War that lasted from 1756 until 1763 and thus is also known also as the Seven Years' War. With England's victory, in part thanks to its American colonists, the so-called First Treaty of Paris in 1763 gave England all of New France as well as the Floridas, which had been owned by Spain.

Even with England's tremendous victory, the war did not settle the so-called Indian question. Settlers were moving into Indian territory rapidly and ceaselessly. King George III tried to stop them by drawing the 1763 Line of Demarcation along the backbone of the Appalachian Mountains, a line which settlers were forbidden to cross. It did not work. The great chief Pontiac rebelled against the constant encroachment of the Europeans onto native lands from 1763 until he was defeated in 1766.

### The Birth and Development of the United States

When the next Treaty of Paris was signed on September 3, 1783, ending the American Revolutionary War, the United States' borders suddenly stretched to the Mississippi River. England was out of the South as Spain had allied with France and the colonies and repossessed the Floridas. When the Constitution replaced the Articles of Confederation, which had not been approved until 1781, George Washington became the nation's first president in 1789. He became the leader of 3,893,874 Americans, of whom 694,207 were slaves, according to the 1790 census. The new nation set out on its own, no longer under British control, but with the legacies of having been British citizens: a Protestant Christian religion, common law, democratic institutions, statements of rights, the English language, and English manners and customs.

Already in 1780, Congress envisioned new states in the new territory. States began ceding their land claims to the federal government. In 1785, Congress provided funds for surveys to lay out townships in 36 numbered subdivisions of one mile each. Lot 16 was reserved for public schools. No land was to be sold for less than $1 an acre. The 1787 Northwest Ordinance set into operation the development of the states of Ohio, Michigan, Illinois, Indiana, and Wisconsin. Selling land would help the bankrupt federal government. In 1796, Congress approved the selling of one square mile (640 acres) for $2 an acre. In 1800, you could buy 320-acre plots for $2 an acre on four years of credit. In 1804, 160-acre plots went for $1.64 an acre. In 1820, 80-acre plots went for $1.25 an acre.

President Thomas Jefferson just wanted to buy New Orleans. Control of that port city was vital to American commerce. Much to his surprise, Napoleon was willing to sell not only the port city, but also all of Louisiana Territory, which Spain had quietly ceded to France. For a purchase price of $15,000,000, the United States got 800,000 square miles of land, which would include the future states of Louisiana, Arkansas, Missouri, Iowa, Nebraska, South Dakota, and parts of seven other western states.

The United States continued to tidy up its borders. In 1818, the United States and England agreed to a 49 degree latitude northern border and joint occupation of Oregon country. In 1819, the United States paid Spain $5,000,000 for Florida and established a southwest boundary that cut Spain off at the 42nd parallel, thus with no claim to the Pacific Northwest. In return, the United States gave up the Texas Gulf Coast. Mexico became America's new neighbor in 1821 when it became independent of Spain. The Republic of Texas, independent of Mexico since 1836, was annexed in 1845 at its behest. In 1846, the United States and Britain signed an agreement to settle the Oregon country border along the 49th parallel, which permitted establishment of the states of Washington, Oregon, Idaho, and parts of Montana and Wyoming.

The treaty settling the Mexican War in 1848 gave Texas its Rio Grande border as well as south and west Texas. The United States received California, Arizona, the Oklahoma panhandle, and the southwestern corners of Kansas and Wyoming. In just 60 years since Washington took office, the United States stretched from sea to sea. Yet as the United States reached the long-sought dream of what some thought to be its manifest destiny, the year 1848 also marked the stirrings of a revolution in America.

Women had steadily been making headway along the avenues long closed to them. They were gradually getting legal control of their own property in marriage, and teaching grade school had become an acceptable calling. Education beyond elementary school was beginning to open up—Mount Holyoke College became the nation's first women's college in 1837. Women were beginning to emerge as leaders in education, social issues, literature, and journalism, but they lacked civil rights equal to men's as well as the equal opportunities men enjoyed. In 1848, delegates to the first Women's Rights Convention assembled in Seneca Falls, New York. In the convention's "Declaration of Sentiments and Resolutions," the delegates declared that men had established "absolute tyranny" over women, and the facts proved it. Men did not permit women to vote, and women were forced to live under laws in which they had no voice. Married women were "civilly dead," and men had usurped women's rights to their own property and wages. Men had taken the good jobs for themselves and left to women only poorly paying positions. Men had blocked women from educational opportunities and created a different "code of morals" for women. Perhaps most appallingly, men had tried to destroy women's confidence in themselves, lessen their self-respect, and make them "willing to lead a dependent and abject life."[15] This was the first volley in a continuing struggle for civil rights, which, like the African American struggle for basic rights, would have a long and continuing history. White men were not interested in letting people unlike themselves into their private club.

The westward expansion of the United States took place within the framework of sectional controversy, which was explicitly played out in the U.S.

Senate. Southern senators had long tired of what they saw as the attempts of northern senators to usurp power by limiting the expansion of slavery and the southern way of life. The southerners felt left behind politically. Northern senators, many of whom believed the existence of slavery in the United States was in itself an abomination, also were disgusted by the fact that southern political power in the House of Representatives was propped up by the constitutional provision that slaves be counted as three-fifths of a person in the decennial census. (Native Indians were not counted at all because as members of separate nations, they were not citizens. Women were counted on both sides, but not allowed to vote or even hold property in most states.) This meant that southerners could claim greater representation based on a population with no right to vote. Thus, as the South stagnated in a largely rural, plantation economy with little urbanization and poor transportation, the North was bursting with new populations and growing industry, and excellent transportation routes had developed to market it products.

The great Senate compromise that allowed new states to enter the Union traded slave states for free states once the old Northwest Territory entered the Union with slavery banned. The Civil War, fought from 1861 to 1865, ended that compromise and, more importantly, gave former slaves freedom and voting rights, at least constitutionally. Reality was quite a different thing. Black slaves from the West Indies and Africa were some of the very first Americans, having been imported in large numbers in the early 1700s and present early in the preceding century. The importation of slaves into the country ceased in 1808 (this was another compromise that helped to pass the Constitution), and thus the African American population became indigenous. Yet African Americans' efforts to enjoy the fullness of American citizenship remain a continuous struggle. America and Americans cannot be fully understood without considering what is popularly called the *race question*. While no American alive today can imagine that people of any color were once bought and sold as property in this nation conceived in liberty, neither has any American been untouched by this legacy.

The Civil War was horrific. The 1860 census counted 31,400,000 Americans. Over 3,800,000 troops (2,800,000 Union soldiers; 1,000,000 Confederate soldiers) had served in the war by its end, and 558,052 were killed (359,528 Union soldiers; 198,524 Confederate soldiers). More than 412,000 soldiers were wounded and survived.[16] Families were decimated and divided. Much of the South was left in ruins. The conclusion of the war left two major questions: what would become of the suddenly freed former slaves, and how would the South be repatriated into the Union? Congress, for its part, outlawed slavery and created the Freedmen's Bureau in 1865. The bureau was to provide education, food, clothing, and advice to the freed slaves.

It was also to distribute confiscated land, but this proved mostly a futile effort. Widely hated in the South, the bureau did, however, provide the only educational opportunities available to African Americans at that time in the South. The bureau was also helping African Americans negotiate contracts for their labor, an entirely new concept for former slaves, and the bureau also began recording the legal marriages of the former slaves, also something new. By 1872, however, the Freedmen's Bureau was gone.

President Andrew Johnson, like his predecessor Abraham Lincoln, wanted to bring the Southern states back into the Union quickly, requiring only that 10 percent of a seceded state's voters take an oath of allegiance to the Union and accept the prohibition of slavery before a new state government be created, which would then be recognized as legitimate. Johnson acted quickly to use Lincoln's formula to bring in some states and then issued his own somewhat more difficult 10 percent solution. The recognized states then began to pass the infamous Black Codes, which placed African Americans into second-class status by law, without the institution of slavery yet still without the right to vote. In reaction, Congress passed the 14th Amendment to the Constitution in 1866, which was adopted in 1868. This constitutional amendment declared "all persons born or naturalized in the United States," notably former slaves, to be citizens. Furthermore, it provided that no state "shall make or enforce any law which shall abridge the privileges or immunities of citizens of the United States." The amendment also forbad states to "deny to any person within its jurisdiction the equal protection of the laws," yet it stopped short of explicitly giving African Americans the right to vote. That would not come until 1870 with adoption of the 15th Amendment to the Constitution.

The political squabbles among Congress, the president, and recalcitrant state governments led, in 1867, to Congress's placing the old Confederate states, with the exception of Tennessee, under military rule in five districts. Under military jurisdiction, all of the 10 formerly rebellious states were readmitted to the Union by 1870, and new governments under new and better constitutions were in place three to four years after readmission. It was not until 1877, however, that all the military districts in the old Confederacy were closed. Thus ended the Reconstruction of the South. The federal government gave up any effort to reform southern racial thinking or enforce the laws it had passed to assure African American equality. Left to their own devices, southern states developed Jim Crow laws that entrenched racial segregation, disenfranchised African Americans, and encouraged racial injustice.

Following the Civil War, the United States continued to expand its territory. The 1867 purchase of Alaska from Russia for $7,200,000 increased U.S. territory by 20 percent. Pro-American revolutionaries tossed out the royals in Hawaii in 1893, and it was annexed to the United States in 1898. Thus, at the dawn of the twentieth century, the American states as we know them today were secured. Hawaii and Alaska both officially entered the Union in 1959. The country was populated and settled. Homesteading, except in Alaska, ended in 1935.

The U.S. Constitution was constantly reinforced as new territories petitioned for statehood. State constitutions had to be written and approved by Congress, and nothing in a state constitution could be antithetical to or contradict the federal document. The voters in a prospective state had to vote in favor of the state constitution and vote in favor of joining the Union. The state constitutions, therefore, are often reiterations of the U.S. Constitution, setting up three equal branches—executive, legislative, and judicial—as checks and balances and adopting the liberties expressed in the Constitution's first 10 amendments, the Bill of Rights. Even at a time when *We the People* meant white men, aristocratic or common, the values of American constitutional democracy spread across the nation, eventually creating 50 united, sovereign republics. Thus, for Americans, the Constitution, the Declaration of Independence, and the Bill of Rights are revered living documents. They together form the foundation for understanding how Americans think of themselves and live in a nation of laws.

### American Indian Policy

The 1783 Treaty of Paris that gave the land east of the Mississippi River to the new United States of America also by default gave the United States all of the land in that area belonging to the native Indians. They, too, were living in a new country, but with no voice.

Indian tribes were treated from the start as separate nations, and thus the president was responsible for dealing with them as part of his foreign policy. The early presidents enjoyed their status as so-called great white fathers. President Washington laid out what the policy objectives would be: peace, Indian happiness, and their attachment to the United States. President James Monroe acknowledged in 1821 that the federal Indian policy had failed. He noted that Indians had been treated "as independent nations, without their having any substantial pretensions to that rank."[17] A War Department report found that there were 129,266 Indians then in the states and territories of the United States and that their land claims totaled 77,402,318 acres.[18] Something had to be done.

Indians would be given the Great Plains, thought worthless to European whites, and Congress gave the War Department power to negotiate treaties, to be ratified by the Senate, and eastern Indians were to be moved into a place where they could live peaceably with western Indians. Between

1825 and 1841, numerous treaties were made and ratified, and the Indian frontier formed around the western borders of Louisiana, Arkansas, and Missouri, east almost to Illinois, and including what would be most of Iowa and southern Wisconsin. With the passage of the Indian Removal Act in 1830, getting the natives out of white settlements east of the Mississippi River became official U.S. policy. Yet no matter the nicety of the treaties, many natives had no desire to move. In the winter of 1838, the army forcibly removed 15,000 Cherokee from their homeland in northwestern Georgia to Indian Territory over the Trail of Tears at the cost of some 4,000 Cherokee lives. Seminoles, who waged a long, ill-fated war; Chickasaw; Creek; and Choctaw took different trails to the same end. In 1823, the Supreme Court declared that Indians had occupancy rights but no ownership rights to their land.

By 1840, the Indians were secured in lands away from settlers, but only 10 years later, they were being squeezed by both westward and eastward expansion, united by railroads. There were around 83,000 northern Plains Indians—Santee, Yankton, Oglala, Teton, Sioux, Northern Cheyenne, Arapahoe, and Crow. There were about 65,000 southern Cheyenne, Arapahoe, Navajo, and Apache living in Colorado, the Southwest, and the central Rockies. The Five Civilized Tribes removed earlier from the Southeast—Cherokee, Choctaw, Chickasaw, Creeks, and Seminoles—shared the southern plains with the Comanche, Kiowa, and Pawnee tribes. These numbered 75,000. After the Civil War, Congress acted to restrict Indian lands even more. As the Indians revolted, the government sought to limit them to an Indian Territory in the future state of Oklahoma.

In 1871, Congress took nationhood status away from the tribes. Oklahoma was organized in 1890 as two entities: Oklahoma Territory and Indian Territory. By this time, the millions of buffalo that had roamed the West and had provided the basis for Plains natives' lives even after the Civil War were reduced to only about 1,000 by wholesale slaughter. In 1898, tribal courts were abolished. On March 3, 1901, the Indians in Oklahoma became U.S. citizens by act of Congress. Oklahoma became the 46th state in 1907. The United States pursued a number of Indian policies, including the 1887 Dawes Act, which allowed allotment of reservation land to Indians to turn them into something like white farmers. On June 2, 1924, all native-born Indians became U.S. citizens thanks to their war service. In 1934, the Wheeler-Howard Act (Indian Reorganization Act) reversed Indian policy and negated the Dawes Act, while promoting Indian customs, and gave tribes the right to organize themselves with constitutions and bylaws into tribal councils. It was extended to Alaska and Oklahoma Indians in 1936. By 1947, 195 tribes or groups were operating under the act.

In 2001, there were slightly over 4,000,000 American Indians and Alaska natives, including over 180,000 Latin American Indians, in the United States. In rounded numbers, the largest tribes are the Cherokee, with 730,000; Navajo, with 298,000; Choctaw, with 158,000; Sioux, with 153,000; Chippewa, with 150,000; Apache, with 97,000; Blackfeet, with 86,000; Iroquois, with 81,000; Pueblo, with 74,000; Creek, with 71,000; Eskimo, with 55,000; and Lumbee, with 58,000. All other tribes have populations of less than 50,000, including the Cheyenne, Chickasaw, Colville, Comanche, Cree, Crow, Delaware, Kiowa, Menominee, Osage, Ottawa, Paiute, Pima, Potawatomi, and so on.[19] By far the largest and the only reservation/trust land with over 100,000 Indian inhabitants is the Navajo Nation Reservation and Off-Reservation Trust Land in Arizona, New Mexico, and Utah, which has about 174,000 Indian inhabitants.

### Immigration and Migration

We have seen that the United States developed primarily out of English culture and tradition. In 1780, 75 percent of Americans were of English or Irish descent. Germans and Dutch were a distant second and third of the population. The nineteenth century, however, brought streams of immigrants to America. The potato famine in Ireland during the 1840s brought Irish to the United States at a peak rate of over 100,000 per year. German immigrants swelled the population after the failure of the liberal 1848 Revolution. German immigration was also encouraged by the Union government, in need of soldiers during the Civil War. Promises of free land fueled the numbers willing to fight for the North. About 1,000,000 Asians—Chinese, Filipinos, Japanese, Indians—came to the United States in the last half of the nineteenth century and beginning of the twentieth century, but their numbers were dwarfed by the migration of Europeans. Jews began migrating to the United States from eastern Europe during the last quarter of the nineteenth century to escape religious persecution. Continued persecution in western Europe, most notably in Hitler's Germany, brought more Jews to the United States.[20]

At the beginning of the twentieth century, there were 76,212,168 Americans. Of these, 10,431,276 were born elsewhere. Imagine building a national identity out of 1,167,623 people from Great Britain; 1,615,459 Irish, who did not like the British; 1,134,744 Scandinavians, Swedes being the largest group; 104,197 French and 2,663,418 Germans, who were usually at war with each other back home; 484,027 Italians; 145,714 Hungarians; 383,407 Poles; 423,726 Russians; 81,534 Chinese; 24,788 Japanese; 11,081 Cubans; and 103,393 Mexicans, with smatterings of people born in India, Portugal, Czechoslovakia, Turkey, Austria, Greece, Belgium, and even Luxembourg.[21]

Although the number of Asian immigrants was rather small, especially in comparison to the number of Europeans, U.S. policy beginning in 1924 excluded Asian immigration and encouraged maintenance of the same mix of people who had already come into the country. Chinese were not allowed into the United States for almost 20 years. Country immigration quotas were abandoned in 1965 for hemispheric quotas, which in turn were abandoned in 1978 for a total worldwide ceiling. Those who apply for immigration visas first now have the best chance of getting them. Preference is given to immigrants with family already in America and with job skills needed in the United States. Political refugees may have special status. More than 1,000,000 immigrants received permanent residential status under various refugee acts between 1991 and 2000. Of these, 426,555 came from Europe, primarily the Ukraine and the Soviet Union/Russia. Another 351,347 came from Asia, more than half of them from Vietnam, and following in order thereafter from Laos, Iran, Thailand, and Iraq. North Americans numbering 185,333, all but about 40,000 Cubans, came into the United States with refugee status. Over 51,000 Africans came in, most of them to escape the human disasters in Ethiopia and Somalia. They were joined by 5,857 South Americans.

As part of the State Department's Diversity Visa Program, 50,000 visas are issued annually to people from countries underrepresented in the immigrant pool. While Russians, Indians, Canadians, Mexicans, Filipinos, Poles, Pakistanis, and several other nationalities are excluded from this program, America is now receiving small numbers of immigrants from Africa, South America, and elsewhere who are not otherwise subject to refugee acts.

Between 1892 and 1954, more than 12,000,000 immigrants entered the United States just from Ellis Island.[22] Yet while immigrants from abroad poured into America, two other incredible migrations were taking place inside the country.

In the space of 80 years, from 1890 to 1970, African Americans forsook the rural South for northern and western cities. More than 6,000,000 people sought freedom from overt racism and a better life in industrial cities that provided jobs. This grassroots migration fundamentally transformed African American culture into an urban phenomenon. Not until the 1970s did African Americans begin to return to the South as racial barriers diminished, and the general population movement was away from northern cities into a quickly developing Sunbelt. The ongoing Mexican migration into the United States is likewise having transforming effects on Mexican-American culture.

Whites, too, were migrating. Migration out of the southwestern agricultural plains began in earnest by 1910 and continued through the 1970s. While the initial migration from this area has been attributed to increased farming efficiencies and a general westward expansion of the population seeking new opportunities, especially in California, a combination of events following the 1929 stock market crash caused another burst of migration to California and elsewhere. As the American economy languished in depression, farm prices plummeted. On top of that, rain virtually ceased in the 1930s, giving rise to the dust storms that gave the area of north Texas, the Oklahoma panhandle, western Kansas, southeast Nebraska, southeastern Colorado, and extreme eastern New Mexico the appellation the Dust Bowl. Some 300,000–400,000 Okies made their way to California in a seemingly endless caravan that was documented in literature, film, and photographs. Not all the migrants were impoverished and carrying all their belongings on a rickety old farm truck, but these were the pictures Americans saw, pictures that violated their beliefs in an abundant land and the promise of prosperity.[23]

### The Twentieth Century

At the dawn of the twentieth century, the United States was in full possession of its mainland territory and the outlying territories that would eventually add two new states, but the business of American democracy remained quite unfinished. In fact, it was just getting started. The federal government had granted generous right of ways and land to promote the building of railroads that would unite East with West. The first line was completed in 1869 when the rails of the Union Pacific coming from Omaha, Nebraska, met the rails of the Central Pacific coming from San Francisco in Ogden, Utah. In 1883, the Northern Pacific line from Duluth, Minnesota, to Seattle was completed. The Southern Pacific route from New Orleans to Los Angeles was finished in 1884, and the Atchison, Topeka, and Santa Fe line from Atchison, Kansas, to Los Angeles and San Francisco was completed in the same year.

With these railroads and others, American manufacturers and industrialists had a truly national market. Vast fortunes were made in rails, oil, steel, banking, and finance. Robber barons to some and philanthropists to others, these multimillionaires made their money in a laissez-faire, capitalist economy with few constraints. Government regulations were few, there were no income taxes (an income tax was inaugurated in 1861 by the Union to help pay for the Civil War, but it was abandoned in 1872), and there was not even a national bank to regulate money supply or modulate economic booms and busts. (Andrew Jackson, who considered all banks to be evil, vetoed a bill to recharter the Second Bank of the United States in 1832.) Income taxes were reinstated in 1913, the same year the Federal Reserve banking system was created. Wage earners, with meager benefits, were expected to save their money for the bad times. Unemployment insurance and assured old age pensions became a reality only in 1935 with the passage of the Social Security Act. After the failure of Reconstruction, the American laissez-faire system was not perceived to have responsibility for social change or social welfare. Franklin Roosevelt and his New Deal would change all that in the depths of the Depression.

The road to the United States becoming an industrial powerhouse that could also feed the world was not a straight line up the chart. To be sure, after the Civil War and into the twentieth century, the United States was growing in leaps and bounds in virtually any imaginable category, from territory and population through industrial and agricultural production. However, the unregulated American economy was given to excessive speculation and violent downturns. Called *panics,* these trying economic downturns occurred in 1819, 1837, 1857, 1873, 1884, 1893, and 1907. The Panic of 1819 was caused by easy credit for buying and speculating on land. When things got out of control, the Bank of the United States, which had once helped to fund the speculation with easy money, began calling in some loans, and the bubble finally burst, leaving the country in a depression for about four years. When President Jackson decided to end another burst of land speculation in 1836 by requiring that federal lands had to be paid for in specie (coin), rather than in worthless paper, he precipitated the Panic of 1837 that lasted a good seven years and resulted in a dramatic deflation of commodity prices and unemployment throughout America's cities. The relatively short Panic of 1857, which was preceded by another speculative boom in land and railroad stocks, again saw prices for stocks, bonds, and commodities drop. The Panic of 1873, which lasted until 1879, was caused by banks making extremely liberal loans to rapidly expanding American businesses, particularly railroads. Banks, many of which lent their reserves and even borrowed funds as well as their assets, failed, and thousands of businesses went bankrupt. The short Panic of 1884 was again caused largely by poor banking practices.

The Panic of 1893 illustrated how tenuous the U.S. financial system really was. The stock market crashed early in the year, and foreigners sold out their positions, which caused an increased demand for gold, on which the U.S. currency was based de facto. (The gold standard became official in 1900.) As a result, the U.S. Treasury gold reserves were depleted to as little as $55,000,000. The proper reserve was understood to be $100,000,000. Financier, banker, and industrialist J. P. Morgan rescued the U.S. Treasury by purchasing a privately placed bond issue, the proceeds from which the Treasury would use to increase gold reserves to stabilize the dollar. Morgan later made a tidy profit on the bonds when they were sold publicly. This severe panic lasted three years and ended the future of hundreds of banks and thousands of businesses. The short Panic of 1907 was more of the same.

It had become abundantly clear that the American dream could sometimes be a nightmare. Entire fortunes could be wiped out in an instant. For those without fortunes, there was no protection at all. Workers turned to labor unions, which began to be formed after the Civil War, in the search for higher wages, better benefits, and better working conditions. Labor management–owner relations would be particularly difficult through the industrialization of the country. The great titans of American industry, the fittest who had survived, did not expect to have demands placed on them by underlings.

America had long been content to exert its hegemony only in North and South America, calling up the tradition of the 1823 Monroe Doctrine, which was a warning to European powers that the era of colonization and intervention in the Americas was over. Indeed, Americans had enjoyed a long period of isolation from the world. They were suspicious of old Europe and its endless wars. Americans were likewise suspicious of a large standing army and, in fact, did not possess one. America did, however, have a navy. The Spanish-American War showed it off to the world. Suddenly, the United States found itself an imperial power, much to the disappointment of the large anti-imperialist contingent at home. Cuba, Puerto Rico, and eventually, the Philippines (for a $20,000,000 payment to Spain) came into American hands. President McKinley supported the 1899 treaty that gave the Philippines to the United States in the belief that Americans had a divine obligation to civilize and Christianize the Filipino people. When Teddy Roosevelt, a former secretary of the navy, became president after McKinley's assassination, he liberally utilized America's gunboats to enforce so-called democracy in the New World.

World War I marked America's transformation into a recognized world power. There can be no debate that sheer numbers of American soldiers turned the tide for the Allied forces, which, before the Americans arrived, were hunkered down in vicious trench warfare along battle lines that were not moving. Curiously, however, in spite of President Woodrow Wilson's Preparedness Campaign, the United States was quite unprepared to mount a major war effort. It was not until May 1917 that the Selective Service Act authorized a temporary increase in troops. More than 4,700,000 Americans finally served in the war. About 350,000 were African Americans, who found themselves mostly doing menial tasks in the segregated military.[24]

The American government itself, kept rather small during the age of hands-off capitalism, was not capable of directing the war effort alone. Military procurement practices were slow and even contradictory. Wilson formed the War Industries Board, made up of volunteer businessmen, labor leaders, and other notables, to manage the purchase, production, and distribution of materials for civilians and the military. While the military bridled at civilian involvement in its affairs and industrialists both feared doing business with the government (they correctly believed they would be stuck with overcapacity when the war ended) and found government regulation of their business to be socialistic, if not totally un-American, America's first attempt of government-industry cooperation was a success. This lesson was put to good use during World War II.

The Roaring Twenties were ushered in by what proved to be the first of many so-called red scares in twentieth-century America, when the government began rounding up anarchists and communists after the war. There was never any evidence of a Bolshevik plot against America, but the godless Communists would continue to be a bugaboo that could be called out to scare the citizens of an otherwise secure country. This scare came and went quickly as the economy expanded and America set out on a new foot, but was very content to look inward. This new world power would not be part of the League of Nations. Women now had the right to vote. The work that women's rights advocates Susan B. Anthony and Elizabeth Cady Stanton had begun when they founded the National Woman Suffrage Association in 1869 paid off over the following years in getting women the vote in a number of states, but in 1920, their dream of the 19th Amendment to the Constitution finally came true.

As white flapper girls and college kids in raccoon coats sought to redefine the new era on their own terms, Harlem, New York, burst forth as the center of a new, urban African American culture. The Harlem Renaissance featured African American poetry, literature, and an intellectual life like never before seen. The sounds of jazz and the blues even brought whites to Harlem. Men in top hats and women in ermine and pearls would go to sing "Minnie the Moocher" with Cab Calloway, who was dressed to the nines. They went to hear Eubie Blake's music and Duke Ellington's elegant compositions. The Harlem Renaissance was an announcement that a new African American culture had arrived that was very much American. In fact, so American was it that white musicians and bandleaders liberally borrowed the African American music they heard to play for their white audiences.

The 1920s also marked the beginning of one of America's most failed experiments: Prohibition. In 1919, the 18th Amendment to the Constitution had been adopted. This amendment prohibited "the manufacture, sale, or transportation of intoxicating liquors within, the importation thereof into, or the exportation of thereof from the United States and all territory subject to the jurisdiction thereof, for beverage purposes." The Woman's Christian Temperance Union (WCTU), founded in 1874, and the Anti-Saloon League, founded in 1893, together were powerful forces in the movement to ban alcoholic beverages. The WCTU effectively operated through churches, and its members traversed the country asking children to "take the pledge" that they would never drink alcohol. They were influential in getting alcohol banned in some states and localities. So effective was the WCTU that the public often conflated the WCTU with the women's rights movement. This confusion

Women carrying placards reading "We want beer" protest during an anti-prohibition parade in New Jersey in the early 1930s. © AP Photo.

may actually have delayed passage of the bill granting women the right to vote. Women's voting rights had, in the end, proved less controversial than prohibiting alcohol. The Anti-Saloon League, founded by men, also worked through churches, but its goal was always antialcohol legislation. Until Prohibition ended in 1933 with the passage of the 21st Amendment, which repealed the 18th Amendment, Americans made home brew and bathtub gin and drank publicly at speakeasies, where illegal alcohol was readily available.

If nothing else, Prohibition left a colorful history of federal agents chasing Mafia bootleggers and gangsters in their automobiles with machine guns blazing. If fact, all Americans began chasing each other in their automobiles. A revolution had taken place. In 1895, only four automobiles were registered in the entire country. By 1920, there were over 8,000,000.[25] Henry Ford and his Model-T were primarily responsible for this revolution that would fundamentally change America. Ford's manufacturing techniques, which employed mass production assembly lines, actually brought the prices of automobiles down. In 1920, a brand-new black Model-T cost about $450. Americans took to them like ducks to water, leaving Ford with more than 40 percent of the automobile market and creating the demand for new and better roads.

By 1930, there were more than 26,500,000 cars registered in the United States, but America's carefree ride through the 1920s came to a screeching halt on October 29, 1929. The stock market crash that day ended another speculative bubble in overpriced securities, and the economy began a vicious downward spiral. Soon, thousands of banks and businesses were under water. Unemployment, which stood at 3.2 percent in 1929, was almost 25 percent by 1933. Those lucky enough to keep a job found their wages decreased. Agriculture prices collapsed so severely that farmers began to revolt in frustration. The vaunted American consumer, whose income had steadily risen through the 1920s, suddenly could no longer consume, which further decreased demand and the need for production. Borrowers could not repay banks. The Federal Reserve could not handle a monetary crisis of this proportion. Charitable organizations did not have the resources to assist the new poor. Corporate profits dissipated. Once proud working Americans found themselves in breadlines.

Franklin Roosevelt was elected president in 1932. His can-do attitude and optimism bolstered the hopes of Americans for recovery, yet in 1940, the nation's economy was scarcely better than it had been in 1929. Unemployment was still over 14 percent. Roosevelt inflated the currency by abandoning the gold standard and created government agencies—derisively called *alphabet agencies*—designed to put Americans back to work. Between 1933 and 1935, the Federal Emergency Relief Administration provided over $3,000,000,000 for relief funds and temporary jobs. True to the American belief that work brings rewards, very little money was spent on direct welfare expenditures, except to feed people. Even in the Depression, getting something for nothing was anathema to Americans—jobs were the answer, and Roosevelt said as much. In 1935, the Works Progress Administration (WPA) took over relief efforts. Lasting until 1943, the WPA put people to work on public improvement, educational, and artistic projects. At one time, more than 3,000,000 Americans were working for the WPA. The Civilian Conservation Corps and the National Youth Administration were designed to provide work for young people. Farmers got help with commodity prices, and the Rural Electrification Administration brought electricity to rural America. The Tennessee Valley Authority brought electricity to downtrodden Appalachia. The Securities and Exchange Commission was to clarify investment trading regulations and corporate finances for investors. The National Labor Relations Board, created by the 1935 National Labor Relations Act, oversaw the act's provisions that allowed for union organization and collective bargaining. In 1938, the Fair Labor Standards Act, for the first time in American history, set a minimum wage and progressive stages toward a 40-hour workweek.

The surprise Japanese attack on Pearl Harbor on December 7, 1941, brought America fully into World War II and out of the Depression. That Americans died in a sneak attack galvanized the country behind the war effort. Isolationists and anti-imperialists threw in the towel. More than

16,300,000 Americans served in the military during the war. Over 400,000 Americans died, and another 670,000 were wounded.[26] As war production geared up on the home front, women like never before entered the workforce, in part replacing men who were overseas. They were epitomized in the famous "Rosie the Riveter" poster. Scientists were organized into two major secret research projects to develop radar and the atomic bomb. The entire country was mobilized for the war effort—no sacrifice was too small to support the boys at war or to maintain the nation's security. Posters on the fences of defense plants and military installations reminded workers of their responsibility: "What you see, what you hear, when you leave, leave it here."

Some wartime paranoia about spies and the protection of war secrets may be understandable, but army lieutenant general John L. DeWitt, Commanding General of the Western Defense Command and Fourth Army, mixed paranoia with racial stereotypes and in so doing began one of the most egregious episodes in American history. He wanted President Roosevelt to designate military areas from which Japanese aliens, Japanese American citizens, alien enemies other than Japanese aliens, and other suspicious persons would be excluded. Claiming that the Japanese race was an enemy race and that even

Many Japanese-Americans were gathered and placed in internment camps following the attack on Pearl Harbor. Here, detainees are lined up outside a cafeteria. National Archives and Records Administration.

those who were supposedly Americanized in second and third generations had undiluted racial strains, the Japanese had to be kept from sabotaging infrastructure and defense plants, causing damage in populous areas, and signaling from the coastline. He counted 112,000 so-called potential enemies of Japanese extraction—14,500 in Washington, 4,000 in Oregon, and 93,500 in California. In asking the secretary of war to implement his plan, DeWitt noted menacingly the fact that at the time of his writing to the secretary on February 14, 1942, no Japanese plots having been uncovered was proof that they were under way.[27]

Only five days later, Roosevelt approved the military areas DeWitt wanted. Then, on March 18, the president signed Executive Order no. 9102, which established the War Relocation Authority (WRA) and placed it under the Office for Emergency Management in the Executive Office of the President. The director of the WRA was given authority to evacuate such persons as necessary, provide for "the relocation of such persons in appropriate places," and provide for their needs and supervise their activities. Thus began the internment of Japanese aliens and citizens in the western halves of Washington, Oregon, and California as well as the southern third of Arizona under the WRA. The WRA set up 10 relocation centers and a refugee shelter in New York. Over 110,000 Issei and Nisei, who left some $200,000,000 in assets behind, were moved through assembly centers into relocation centers during World War II. The majority were American citizens. Some Japanese were permitted to live outside of the centers, but not in military areas, and resettled in the Midwest. The WRA was disbanded in 1946. In America, racism always trumped civil rights, as America's African American and native citizens knew so well.

The America that emerged victoriously from World War II was a changed place. Women had attained a new status during the war. Not only were they home front heroes in wartime production, but they also had a new status in the military. President Roosevelt signed the act forming the Women's Auxiliary Army Corps (WAAC) on May 15, 1942. As the name implied, however, the WAAC was not an official part of the army; its purpose was to train women to do jobs that free men up to fight the war. By the end of the war, about 200,000 women had served in the corps in more than 150 noncombat positions. Unlike the regular segregated army, African American women were fully integrated into the WAAC and given equal opportunities. Forty of the first 450 officer candidates selected were African American women. On July 1, 1943, Roosevelt signed an act establishing the Women's Army Corps, granting the former WAAC full military status.

African American men and women returned home as victorious heroes of the war to de facto discrimination in the North and de jure discrimination in the South. This fact helped to fuel the movement for civil rights, but it would be the federal government that took the first step. In July 1948, President Harry Truman issued two executive orders. Executive Order no. 9980 created the Fair Employment Board to oversee the end of racial discrimination in federal employment. Executive Order no. 9981 created the President's Committee on Equality of Treatment and Opportunity in the Armed Services, which was to desegregate the military. By October 1954, the last all–African American military unit had been disbanded. This, of course, did not necessarily mean that discrimination had ended. Even before America entered the war, Roosevelt had issued Executive Order no. 8802 in June 1941 to avert a threatened protest march of 100,000 African Americans on Washington, D.C. The order outlawed discrimination in defense industries and government service.

With Europe completely decimated, the United States could not return to the comfortable isolation it once had. It had used the atomic bomb for the first time in Hiroshima on August 6, 1945, and three days later on Nagasaki, leaving tens of thousands of Japanese dead and wounded. The Japanese surrendered, and the United States was the world's only nuclear power. America found itself in an uneasy alliance with Soviet Russia, which was unwilling to give up most of the territory it had liberated from Germany. By 1949, Russia had the bomb, too, and the Cold War was well under way. Thus the United States led the Western effort to contain Communism at any turn. To the dismay of the old isolationist faction that had killed the United States' entry into the League of Nations, the United States joined the United Nations (UN), albeit with a permanent seat on the Security Council that gave it veto power over any international actions of which it did not approve.

The Cold War was more than a number of protracted military engagements fought by stand-ins for the United States and Russia. The two superpowers set out on a course of deterrence based on mutually assured destruction; that is, if you use nuclear weapons first, we will bomb you into oblivion. Massive nuclear arms buildups took place to the extent that any efforts at limiting weapons by treaty took place in the language of reducing overkill capacity. Thus, even as the boom of the late 1940s and 1950s progressed—affordable, generic housing developments sprung up all over the nation, babies were being born in unprecedented numbers, the economy was humming, the GI Bill made college accessible to millions of veterans—there was a pall over the nation. The threat of nuclear war was real. Schoolchildren were regularly drilled for that eventuality. Teachers instructed their students that at the sound of a special alarm, they were to immediately and in total silence stand up from their wooden desks, get down on all fours in a ball under their desks, and cradle their heads in their arms until further notice. The kids had another way of putting it: get under your desk and kiss your behind good-bye.

Senator Joseph McCarthy, a Republican from Wisconsin, fed on this fear. In a 1950 speech, he claimed to have evidence that there were 205 known Communists working in the State Department. Until he was censured by the Senate in December 1954, he ruined scores of lives and careers in a witch hunt for Communists and Communist sympathizers in politics, government, the entertainment industry, and the military. He was so bold even to take on President Eisenhower, the hero of World War II. This Red Scare, like the scare of the 1920s, soon dissipated with his demise, but it demonstrated the power that the fear of alien, godless Communism held in America, a fear that permitted people's rights to be abandoned in the name of liberty.

On the surface, though, America looked like a happy, innocent place filled with smiling white teenagers in souped-up jalopies lined up at diners for burgers and fries. They were listening to rock 'n' roll on their car radios, the newest sensation. Elvis Presley was the symbol for this enthusiastic, wild music. Some claimed his music to be satanic, even though its roots were in African American gospel music and blues. When Ed Sullivan, the host of the country's then most popular variety show and a must for family viewing on Sunday nights, had Presley on his show, he assured Americans that Elvis was a good boy. Rock 'n' roll was here to stay, no matter what parents thought of it.

Beneath the surface of the supposedly placid 1950s, the fight for African American civil rights was intensifying. The National Association for the Advancement of Colored People, first convened in 1909, decided to pursue legal avenues as well as social action to further the rights movement. In 1940, the association created its Legal Defense and Education Fund, which began to have successes in the courts. In 1946, white election primaries were declared unconstitutional, and so was segregated interstate bus travel. More favorable rulings followed, and in 1954, the Supreme Court decided in *Brown v. the Board of Education of Topeka* that segregation in public schools was unconstitutional. President Eisenhower punctuated this landmark ruling when he used federal troops to enforce integration at Central High School in Little Rock, Arkansas, in 1957. In that year, Dr. Martin Luther King Jr., whose father and namesake had been leading civil rights protests since the 1930s, began the Southern Christian Leadership Conference (SCLC) to coordinate nonviolent protests against discrimination, using African American churches as bases of operation.

The SCLC and other civil rights organizations kept the pressure up into the 1960s with sit-ins at lunch counters, freedom rides through the South,

A group of people hold signs and carry American flags, protesting the admission of nine African-American students to Central High School in Little Rock, Arkansas, 1957. Courtesy of the Library of Congress.

boycotts, marches, and demonstrations. Even though King was adamant that nonviolence be the hallmark of the movement, civil rights workers and leaders were killed and wounded in their pursuit of freedom. Civil rights work was not for the timid or faint of heart. The Kennedy administration was sympathetic to the movement. Kennedy, like Eisenhower, had to federalize state guard troops, this time at the University of Alabama in June 1963, to enforce integration. The drive for civil rights was moving inexorably forward, even through the drama of the Cuban missile crisis and the first commitment of troops to Vietnam. The Soviet menace was still very much alive, and the Kennedys were good Cold Warriors.

In August 1963, the civil rights movement came together with a march on Washington, D.C. Some 250,000 people showed up in support of African American civil rights and pending legislation to enforce them. Martin Luther King delivered his famous "I Have a Dream" speech in front of the Lincoln Memorial. Scarcely three months later, John Kennedy would become the victim of assassination in Dallas, Texas. His successor, Lyndon Johnson, himself a supporter of African American civil rights, cajoled Congress, in which he had long served and accumulated unprecedented power as a senator, to pass the 1964 Civil Rights Act in honor of the dead president. This act prohibited discrimination in public establishments, including schools, based on race, color, religion, or national origin. It went beyond African American and white to address human issues. The subsequently passed Voting Rights Act of 1965 mostly reinforced previous legislation, but it announced that the practices that had been used to prevent African American from voting would no longer be tolerated.

Backed by law, the civil rights struggle continued. It became, thanks to Martin Luther King, inexorably united with the peace movement. Already in 1965, the Students for a Democratic Society had organized an antiwar protest in Washington, D.C., that drew up to 50,000 protesters. The Vietnam War escalated, and many Americans could see no end to it. By 1968, more than 525,000 American troops were fighting there, and young men were being drafted into what looked like a purposeless war. The old saw that Communism had to be contained even in Southeast Asia no longer seemed relevant to American interests at home. Fatalities rose. The My Lai massacre on March 16, 1968, in which American troops killed 300 innocent villagers, was taken by protesters as proof of American brutality. Then, on April 4, Martin Luther King Jr. was assassinated in Memphis, Tennessee. The rule of law that Americans cherished seemed to have vanished. African Americans rioted. College campuses broke out in protests. On June 5, Robert Kennedy, who had tried to calm the nation after King's killing, was himself assassinated after winning the California presidential primary.

President Johnson, who by all rights should have been heralded as a hero of the civil rights movement as well as the movement to get health care to the aged (Medicare) and better education to children, was thoroughly discredited for his handling of the Vietnam War. Even his closest advisors abandoned him, and he chose not to run for president in 1968. Richard Nixon, on the other hand, had been vice president for Eisenhower's two terms and claimed to have the expertise to be president and a plan to end the Vietnam War that he could not reveal. The 1968 Democratic Convention in Chicago, which nominated Johnson's vice president, Hubert H. Humphrey, known as the Happy Warrior, had the unhappy experience of being painted with Johnson's war legacy. The convention turned into a brawl on the streets between out-of-control protestors and the police.

With Nixon's election, the chaos became even worse. There was another peace protest in Washington, D.C., in November 1969 that brought 500,000 protestors into the capital. On May 4, 1970, Ohio guardsmen panicked during a war protest, killed four students, and wounded nine others. Campuses around the country went up in flames, Reserved Officers Training Corps (ROTC) campus offices being a favorite target. Publication of *The Pentagon Papers* in 1971 revealed the lies the military made to put a good face (from their point of view) on the war. Nixon had grown used to seeing protestors outside the White House. In March 1973, he essentially declared victory and pulled out the last of the American troops from Vietnam. In 1975, the South Vietnamese surrendered to the Communist North Vietnamese. The last memory most Americans have of the Vietnam War is pictures of helicopters leaving the grounds of the American embassy in Saigon with marine embassy guards knocking Vietnamese allies off the runners of the helicopters as they tried to get out. Nevertheless, some 140,000 Vietnamese settled in the United States after the war.

Nixon called this peace with honor. Returning veterans of the war were accorded no honor; they were just as likely to meet with derision from a divided nation. Americans had never lost a war. The country that had beat Japan once, Germany twice, and stopped the spread of Communism in Korea was bested by a tiny Asian country of determined guerilla fighters. The OPEC oil embargo in October 1973, which left Americans in gas lines and in the dark, intimated that Americans were no longer in control of their own destiny. There seemed to be a crisis in America's self-confidence. The resignations of Nixon's corrupt vice president, Spiro T. Agnew, and then of Nixon himself for impeachable offenses added to this crisis. President Jimmy Carter beat Gerald Ford, Nixon's handpicked successor, in the 1976 election as America turned away from Republican problems and sought a new vitality in the Democrats. Carter, however, appeared only to wonder in amazement over what he called the malaise that had spread over the country. Carter added to the national malaise when he donned his sweater, sat by a fireplace, and told America to conserve energy. His inability first to rescue and then to free hostages from the American embassy in Iran, a payback from Iranian revolutionaries for America's having propped up the corrupt and repressive regime of Shah Reza Palahvi for years, again gave Americans the feeling of powerlessness. The country was looking for a leader who could restore America's confidence in itself.

Throughout this turmoil, the women's rights movement carried on. The 1963 Equal Pay Act required that employers could not use sex as the basis for differential wages. The Civil Rights Act of 1964 had prohibited discrimination based on race, color, religion, or national origin, but it did not explicitly prohibit discrimination based on sex. In this sense, the legislation dealt a blow to the movement. However, women's advocates did get something out of it. Women suddenly appeared in Title VII, which concerned employment practices again. It became an unlawful employment practice to fail to hire, or to hire or fire anyone with respect to compensation, terms, conditions, or privileges of employment, based on that person's race, color, religion, sex, or national origin. (The Cold War being still very much alive, it was still expressly lawful to discriminate in employment against members of the Communist Party of the United States or members of any Communist organization required to register with the government.) The 1964 act also established the Equal Employment Opportunity Commission to oversee the application of the law.

This was not enough. Feminists and their supporters wanted women to have the constitutional protection that was afforded to people of diverse races, colors, religions, and national origins. The National Organization for Women (NOW) was founded in 1966 to promote women's issues and further the cause. Finally, in 1972, the year in which feminist Gloria Steinem's *Ms.* magazine first went on the newsstands, Congress passed what was to be the 27th Amendment to the Constitution—the Equal Rights Amendment. The wording was quite simple: "Equality of rights under the law shall not be denied or abridged by the United States or any state on account of sex."[28]

Thirty-eight states had to pass the amendment for it to become part of the U.S. Constitution, and Congress had allowed seven years for that to happen. It appeared at first that easy passage by the states lay ahead, but roadblocks soon developed. Many conservative religious groups considered the ERA an affront to motherhood that would take women from their homes and children. Some critics argued that equal rights would mean unisex toilet facilities, or bathrooms, as they are called in America. These and other specious arguments began to take hold as America's taste for reform soured, and many Americans wanted to return to traditional American values. The ERA was in trouble. In July 1978, NOW organized a rally that brought 100,000 ERA supporters to Washington, D.C., in support of extending the 1979 deadline for ratification. Congress responded positively, but on June 30, 1982, the ERA died. Only 35 states had ratified it, and the new president, Ronald Reagan, and his party did not support it. In spite of the continuing efforts to introduce new ERA legislation, American women, unlike women in the European Union and a number of countries, have no constitutional guarantee of equal rights.

In January 1981, a new sheriff came to town on a high note—the release of the hostages in Iran. The affable Ronald Reagan paraded into Washington, D.C., behind a Hollywood smile that hid his determination to bring in the old and throw out the new. Declaring that the federal government was the problem, not the solution, he envisioned a new day in America—a strong America with a strong defense, less government regulation that strangles business and entrepreneurship, less government spending, and lower taxes. This was a return, in conservative thinking, to the primordial America that had been abandoned in the 1960s and 1970s. In 1982, he cast the Cold War in simple theological terms: the Soviet Union was the Evil Empire. This was a battle between good and evil, and America would again be strong and win. America's enemies would be rendered harmless, and children could sleep well at night with Fortress America protected by the Strategic Defense Initiative, the so-called Star Wars defense that would obliterate enemy weapons in space before they could reach the United States.

Americans remained, however, vulnerable to terrorist attacks. More than 200 marines were killed in their barracks in Lebanon in 1983. Then, when Iranian terrorists in Lebanon took seven American hostages, Reagan approved a plan to trade arms for the hostages, somehow convincing himself that he was not negotiating with terrorists, which he had publicly vowed never to do. It was then discovered that some of the money the Iranians had paid for arms to fight Iraq had been secretly diverted to the Contras in Nicaragua, who were trying to overthrow the Communist-supported Sandinista regime. Congress had passed legislation twice restricting any aid to the Contras. Some lesser heads rolled when all this came public, and Reagan's popularity took a temporary nosedive. By this time, it was apparent, however, that the Soviet Union was imploding. In 1985, Soviet leader Mikhail Gorbachev opened the Evil Empire to democracy and, eventually, dissolution. When the Berlin Wall came crashing down amid wild celebration in 1989, Reagan was hailed as the hero who ended the Cold War. Now there was only one superpower.

Reagan's political legacy was kept alive by his vice president, George Herbert Walker Bush, who was elected president in 1988. The United States, with a beefed up military, could freely police the world. When Iraq's Saddam Hussein invaded oil-rich Kuwait and annexed it in August 1990, the United States, working through the United Nations, set a deadline for Iraq to exit Kuwait. Iraq ignored the deadline, and military targets were unmercifully bombed the next day. With Iraq still intransigent, the U.S.-led Operation Desert Storm decimated Iraqi troops in the space of four days. More than half a million American soldiers fought in that short war. Bush emerged a war hero all over again. (He had fought and earned medals in World War II.) America had won another war, and quite handily, too, but Saddam Hussein remained in power. It seemed at the time that Bush would easily win reelection, but he made one critical error. He had pledged Reaganesquely not to raise taxes: "Read my lips. No new taxes." Then he raised taxes. It was political suicide.

Democrat William Jefferson Clinton took full advantage of Bush's misstep. Dubbed "the comeback kid" during the presidential campaign, Clinton deftly survived accusations that he was a draft-dodging, pot-smoking womanizer to win the 1992 election. He was quite a change from the stately Reagan and the rather anodyne George Bush. Clinton brought a youthful vitality to the office, reminiscent of the Kennedy years. He also brought a new agenda.

In the first days of his administration, he set out to tackle the issues of gays in the military and national health care. His wife, Hillary, by her own admission not one to sit at home and bake cookies, was put in charge of the Task Force on National Health Care Reform. Extending basic civil rights to gays in the military, or anywhere else, and so-called socialized medicine were absolutely anathema to the political Right. The battle lines that would characterize Clinton's presidency were drawn, and Clinton lost the first two battles. Congress and the nation were clearly divided.

In 1994, the Republicans took over the House of Representatives, and their leader, Newt Gingrich, pledged to stand by the tenets of his Contract with America, which was a reiteration of the conservative mantra against big government. In spite of squabbles over federal budgets, which resulted in the unheard of closing of the government twice in 1995, Clinton and Congress managed to approve two deficit reduction acts, the second of which included tax cuts. Clinton also acquiesced in signing a welfare reform bill in 1966 that put a five-year limit on receiving aid. Annual deficits, which had ballooned with Reagan's defense expenditures, were turned to surpluses by 1998. A growing economy also contributed to the surpluses. Clinton easily won reelection in 1996.

Clinton's ignominious behavior with a White House intern and his lying about it circuitously got him impeached. Investigating the Clintons became a Washington pastime, and the seemingly endless investigation into an Arkansas land deal turned up nothing illegal, but the investigation continued. When the special prosecutor, Kenneth Starr, found out that Clinton had had oral sex with intern Monica Lewinsky, Clinton's sexual behavior suddenly came under investigation. Clinton denied under oath that he had sexual relations with Lewinsky. Evidence said otherwise. Conservative Republicans in the House, many taken there in the Regan landslides, sanctimoniously went about drawing up impeachment articles. Four articles were brought against Clinton, but the House passed only two, accusing Clinton of perjury and obstruction of justice.

Clinton's popularity was quite high when the U.S. Senate convened as a court, with the chief justice of the Supreme Court presiding, on January 14, 1999, to consider the impeachment articles passed by the House. No Americans alive then had ever witnessed an impeachment trial. This was the only such trial of the twentieth century and only the second in American history. For his part, Clinton believed the entire impeachment proceeding to be politically motivated. The Senate trial ended on February 12, and Clinton was still president.

Clinton was said to have an amazing ability to separate his personal problems from his job. Through all the political and personal allegations and investigations and the Senate trial, the business of the nation had to go on. Saddam Hussein, left in office as president of Iraq after the Gulf War, remained nettlesome. Clinton ordered missile attacks on Iraq in 1993 for hatching a plot to kill former president George Bush on a victory lap through Kuwait; in 1996 for actions against the Kurds; and in 1998 for refusing to allow UN weapons inspectors into the country. Clinton involved himself in the miasma of Middle East peace talks. He sent Americans into Somalia with UN troops in 1993 on a humanitarian mission. He sent troops to Haiti in 1994 to maintain democracy there. He ordered the bombing of Serbia in 1999 to prevent so-called ethnic cleansing. Clinton also had to deal with terrorist attacks on Americans abroad. Osama bin Laden was believed to be the power behind the bombings of U.S. embassies in Tanzania and Kenya in 1998. In 2000, terrorists bombed the USS *Cole* off the coast of Yemen. Clinton generally followed a foreign policy that was inclusive, placing value on acting in concert with international organizations and allies and that portrayed the use of American power as bettering the condition of mankind.

It was said of Clinton that you either loved him or hated him. On the whole, Republicans hated him. He had snookered them at every turn and survived as a popular figure. He became the perfect foil for the political Right to raise money and to energize its constituency, which abhorred Clinton's dalliances and violently disagreed with his pro-choice (proabortion), profeminist, progay, internationalist ideas. The presidential election of 2000 pitted George W. Bush, son of George H. W. Bush, whom Clinton had beat in 1992, against Clinton's vice president, Al Gore. Gore tried to distance himself from Clinton the man but embraced his policies and took some credit for his successes. George Bush ran as a so-called compassionate conservative and a born-again Christian who thought Jesus Christ was the greatest philosopher. If there was any doubt that the divided Congress, whose tradition of comity had been destroyed, was an indicator of the cultural divisions in the country at large, that doubt ended with the election.

On November 7, 2000, Americans went to the polls expecting to know the outcome of the election later that evening. It eventually became clear, however, that the entire election would hinge on the vote in Florida. The votes of that state were important because Americans do not elect their presidents by popular vote. A vote for a presidential candidate is, in reality, a vote for an elector pledged to that candidate. That elector then goes to the Electoral College to cast one vote for a candidate, presumably, but not necessarily, for the candidate to which he or she is pledged. The number of electors is in proportion to each state's population, as determined by the decennial census. The winner needed 270 electoral votes for election, and Florida had 25 votes. (Some states divide electors proportionally by the votes candidates receive.

Florida was a winner-take-all state, so whichever candidate won the popular vote would get all the state's electoral votes.)

A legal spectacle ensued when Bush seemed to have won Florida by just a few hundred votes. Democrats wanted a recount in four south Florida counties. Republicans, of course, did not. Federal district courts were petitioned, and the Florida Supreme Court also got into the act. This went on into December. On December 13, the U.S. Supreme Court, itself divided 5–4, effectively ended any more recounting of ballots, and Gore conceded defeat. Bush got Florida's 25 electoral votes, which gave him 271 to Gore's 266. The official vote count in Florida was 2,912,790 for Bush and 2,912,253 for Gore, a difference of only 537 votes. Gore, however, had won the popular vote with 50,989,897 votes (48.38%) to Bush's 50,456,002 (47.87%) votes. Thus, with 543,895 more popular votes than Bush, Gore was the loser.[29]

Bush told the nation he would work hard to earn its trust. *Trust* was a key word because many Americans thought he had stolen the election. With no clear mandate to govern, Bush's presidency got off to a slow start. The terrorist attack on September 11, 2001, however, provided Bush with a voice and a theme: he would be a wartime president. At this time of stress and bewilderment, the nation rallied behind its leader, who declared war on terrorism. The search for Osama bin Laden—wanted dead or alive—took on the language and feel of an Old West sheriff and his possie searching the desert for a notorious stagecoach robber.

The first offensive in the war on terrorism was against Afghanistan scarcely three weeks after the 9/11 attack. A coalition, mostly American, bombed and invaded that country, a known location of terrorist training camps, and by mid-November, the ruling Taliban forces, which took over when the Russian occupation failed, had forsaken the capital city of Kabul. By March, the war was over, and the coalition forces set about installing a new government, propping it up with on-the-ground military support. Osama bin Laden was still on the loose.

On March 19, 2003, the United States, with a few minor coalition partners, invaded Iraq. It was said that Saddam Hussein was hiding weapons of mass destruction, but none was found. The Bush administration has since tried to put the U.S. occupation of Iraq in terms of the second offensive after Afghanistan of the War on Terror. Some critics have charged that it was not faulty intelligence or terrorism (Islamic fundamentalists did not much like Saddam Hussein either) that caused the United States to invade Iraq, but rather Bush's simple desire to avenge Hussein's plot to kill the elder Bush. Other critics have claimed that the real issue was oil.

President Bush declared the Iraq War over on May 1, 2003, yet Americans continued to die there. While Bush handily won a second term in 2004 by emphasizing his role as a war president (Americans would not dump a war president in the midst of a war), and as terror alerts seemed to be coming out of Washington with increased rapidity as the election approached, the nation was tiring of a war that appeared to have no clear purpose or end. Iraq was looking a lot like Vietnam. When Hurricane Katrina struck the Gulf Coast in August 2005, Bush seemed, at first, aloof from the tragedy, and his government's emergency management team was plainly incompetent. Suddenly, Bush did not look much like a leader, as criticism came his way from every direction. His approval rating began to plummet.

In an apparent attempt to regain his stature, Bush gave a speech on the War on Terror on October 6, 2005. Borrowing a term from Ronald Reagan, he equated radical Islam with evil. He went on to say that the struggle against this evil was much like the struggle against Communism. The extremist, radical Muslims wanted to build an Islamic empire "from Spain to Indonesia." As far as Iraq was concerned, "there is no peace without victory. We will keep our nerve and win that victory."[30] Harkening back to Reagan's morality play did not garner Bush much support. When it came to light that the government had been listening to citizens' telephone conversations without court warrants in the name of the War on Terror, Bush supported this abrogation of personal rights and thus appeared to have gone beyond the line Americans traditionally had drawn between personal rights and government power. By the middle of 2006, the majority of Americans were not with him. The War on Terror, in which the Bush administration had tried to include the war in Iraq, became not only a military quagmire, but it also was bankrupting the country. Enormous annual budget shortfalls were securing America's place as the world's largest debtor nation, leaving the United States economically dependent on foreign nations to fund its debt. The once self-assured American public looked to the future with uncertainty and trepidation.

The November 2006 midterm elections were a clear repudiation of Republican support for the war in Iraq. This long war seemed to have no endgame. Furthermore, there were signs that the Republican coalition was breaking apart. Fiscal conservatives were upset with the gigantic federal deficits pushed higher by the Bush administration. The social and religious conservatives that had become the Republican base were shaken by the revelation that Jack Haggard, a minister who was president of the 30,000,000-strong National Association of Evangelicals and a participant in the weekly conference calls from the White House to its important constituents, sought illegal drugs and had a relationship with a male prostitute. Republican scandals abounded. War hero Representative Randy "Duke" Cunningham of the 30th Congressional District of California resigned in disgrace for taking outrageous amounts of bribes from defense contractors. Representative Bob Ney of Ohio's 18th

Congressional District also resigned in disgrace, tainted by money he had taken in the notorious Jack Abramoff influence peddling scheme. Abramoff was a lobbyist with close ties to the Bush administration. Voters had had enough of an unpopular war and rampant religious and financial dishonesty. Democrats were swept into power in the U.S. House, Senate, and many state houses.

## THE PRESENT

The wealth and debt of the United States bring unimaginable numbers into play. Its gross domestic product was $10,383,000,000,000 in 2002, exceeding all of Europe together. Its stock market capitalization exceeded $14,000,000,000,000; Japan's was less than one-fourth of that. Wealth begets power. The United States' military budget was $399,100,000,000, eclipsing Russia's in second place at $65,000,000,000. However, the United States has been adding to its national debt with annual budget deficits of around $400,000,000,000. Paying interest on the debt has become a major budget item. On March 13, 2006, the U.S. public debt stood at $8,270,385,415,129.52.[31] To put all this in a celestial perspective, the maximum mileage from the earth to the sun is only 94,500,000.

The United States is the world's leading corn and wheat exporter. It produces about 25 percent of the world's beef, veal, and poultry, and it leads the world in consumption of those products. The United States is also among the world's top three producers of coal, natural gas, petroleum, cement, sulfur, aluminum, gold, phosphate rock, lead, and copper. This kind of magnificent abundance coupled with high worker productivity created an American belief in self-sufficiency that manifested itself politically as a persistent streak of isolationism, which continues even today in the midst of the global economy and international misadventures. Yet in this world economy, the United States finds itself a net importer of goods as the wealthy (by world standards) American consumer happily gets more bang for the buck by purchasing cheaper goods made abroad.

Let's examine a snapshot of twenty-first-century America.[32] The typical American enters the world a strapping 7.33 pounds. By adulthood, the typical American woman is 63.8 inches tall, weighs 163 pounds, and measures 36.5 inches at the waist. The typical American man is 69.3 inches tall, weighs 190 pounds, and measures 39 inches at the waist. Americans are big people. Unfortunately, however, American prosperity has its downside. Estimates are that 64 percent of adults are overweight, and 30 percent of those are obese. Fifteen percent of America's teenagers and children age 6–12 are also overweight. In spite of Americans' love affair with sports, 59 percent of adults in the United States do not engage in vigorous leisure physical activity or exercise, and fully one-third of high school students fail to perform the physical activity recommended for their age group.

The median age of all Americans is 36.2 years. Some 20,000,000 are under five years old, but over 34,000,000 are 65 years old and above. There are already 1,600,000 seniors living in the nation's 18,000 nursing homes. As the post–World War II baby boomer generation nears retirement age, traditionally at 65 years of age, the number of senior citizens will rise dramatically. American women can expect to live, on average, to 79.9; men, to 74.5. About 2,440,000 Americans die each year. Heart disease and cancer are the leading causes of death, accounting for over half of all deaths.

Over 145,000,000 (about 66%) of Americans 16 and over are in the labor force. Most women work. The female labor force participation rate exceeds 70 percent. The full-time workweek is usually 40 hours, eight hours Monday through Friday. Surprisingly, even though the United States is a major world exporter of agricultural products, less than 2 percent of the nation's civilian workforce is engaged in agriculture and forestry. Employment in the manufacturing and industry sectors together is less than half the employment in the service sector. It is said that the majority of America's teenagers have worked in the food service sector, often setting out on a quest for personal independence in the form of a car.

In 2001, Americans traveled 1,938,000,000 passenger miles in their 135,921,000 cars. They vied with 761,000 buses and 92,939,000 trucks. They traveled over 3,982,000 miles of highways, 902 miles of which were in urban areas, and 592,246 bridges, 48,492 of which were in Texas. Nearly 76 percent of Americans drove to work alone and had, on average, a commute of 25.5 minutes, or nearly an hour a day in the car. The typical American household made 2,171 annual vehicle trips: 479 to and from work; 458 shopping; 537 other family or personal business; and 441 social and recreational trips. Sadly, there were also more than 18,000,000 motor vehicle accidents that resulted in 44,000 deaths. Twenty-two of every 100,000 licensed drivers can expect to die in a traffic accident. Drivers in Montana have the greatest chance of dying on the road, with 2.6 deaths per 100,000,000 vehicle miles traveled.[33]

Most Americans (67.1%) own their own homes; the others rent. The average size of families is 3.18 persons, and their median income is $53,692. The average household size is 2.60, with a median income of $44,692. The 73,754,171 owner-occupied homes in the United States have a median value of $151,366. Homeowners with mortgages can expect to have monthly costs of $1,212; those without mortgages can expect to have $345 in monthly expenses. Home to Americans is as much a concept as it is a place. In the last five years of the twentieth century alone, 112,852,000 Americans (43%) moved to a different home. More than 65,000,000 of them remained in the same county and 25,000,000 in the same state, but more than 25,000,000 moved into a different state. Mobility is a key characteristic of American culture that serves to break down regional variation.[34]

The American economic system allows for and even encourages a wide gap between the richest and the poorest. There is, therefore, class in America, but it tends to be defined primarily by wealth (and education). It is difficult to define the boundaries between upper class and middle class, and middle class and lower class, and efforts to make such definitions miss the point. The point is that whatever class lines may exist can be easily crossed. This is a basic tenet of American beliefs. First generation in America Jewish comedians who had made it, for example, shared a shtick about how poor they were growing up: "My family was so poor that my brother and I had to share a pair of shoes. We each had one!" Pulling oneself up by one's own bootstraps brings social acceptability, if not adulation. In that sense, America is classless—Americans control their own destiny. Some 9,500,000 Americans are self-employed. American society holds hope, therefore, for the 37,000,000 Americans who live below the poverty level, 13,000,000 of them children, and the 40,600,000 Americans who have no health insurance.[35]

For all the hurry in Americans' lives, they are generally affable people who enjoy a good joke, even perhaps a ribald one, and value an active social life. Their affability and casual manner ("Hi ya, pal, glad to meet ya!"), however, may leave those from other cultures with a certain empty feeling. Americans are known the world over for their ability to engage in small talk—the weather, sports, television shows, clothes—on social occasions. Politics and religion are taboo subjects, except among very close friends and family. Americans carefully guard their own private individual beliefs, and they do not expect to argue about them publicly.

## NOTES

1. U.S. Bureau of the Census, *Statistical Abstract of the United States: 2005,* http://www.census.gov. Unless otherwise noted, this is the source of statistical data throughout this chapter.

2. A word about miles, and, for that matter, acres, is necessary here. The United States adopted its measurement system from the British forefathers of the original colonies, and Americans view kilometers, hectares, or any such metric system nomenclature as foreign. Thus, as foreign terms, most Americans do not know what a kilometer or a hectare is—that a mile equals 1.609 kilometers or that an acre equals 0.405 hectares—and certainly any discussion of distances and areas in those terms

would yield the innocent, good-natured question, "You're not from around here, are ya?" which is not really a question, but rather a conclusion, and requires no response.

3. NYC Company Inc., "NYC Statistics," http://www.nycvisit.com.

4. The League of American Theatres and Producers Inc., "Broadway Season Statistics at a Glance," http://www.LiveBroadway.com.

5. City of Atlanta Online, "History," http://www.atlantaga.gov.

6. Hartsfield-Jackson Atlanta International Airport, "Operating Statistics," http://www.atlanta-airport.com.

7. City of Chicago, "Chicago by the Numbers," http://egov.cityofChicago.org.

8. Stephen S. Birdsall and John Florin, "An Outline of American Geography; Regional Landscapes of the United States," in *The Agricultural Core,* http://usinfo.state.gov.

9. Montana Historical Society, "The Economy," http://www.montanahistorical society.org. See also "The Setting."

10. Los Angeles Department of Water and Power, "The Story of the Los Angeles Aqueduct," http://wsoweb.ladwp.com.

11. It is estimated that Phoenix has since surpassed Philadelphia in population.

12. U.S. Census Bureau, "Fact Sheet: United States, 2004 American Community Survey, Data Profile Highlights," http://factfinder.census.gov.

13. Pew Research Center, Pew Global Attitudes Project, "U.S. Image Up Slightly, but Still Negative," press release, June 23, 2005, http://pewglobal.org.

14. See *Columbia Guide to Standard American English* (New York: Columbia University Press, 1993); and Evolution Publishing, "Linguistic Geography of the Mainland United States," http://www.evolpub.com.

15. U.S. Department of State, "Basic Readings in U.S. Democracy," http://usinfo.state.gov. See also "Seneca Falls Declaration (1848)."

16. U.S. Civil War Center, U.S. Department of Defense Records, "Statistical Summary—America's Major Wars," http://www.cwc.lsu.edu/cwc/other/stats/war cost.htm.

17. The Avalon Project at Yale Law School, "Second Inaugural Address of James Monroe," March 5, 1821, http://www.yale.edu.

18. U.S. Senate, *American State Papers,* 18th Cong., 2d. sess., 1825, 543, http://www.loc.gov.

19. These are self-reported data available in the *Statistical Abstract of the United States: 2005.*

20. See U.S. Information Agency, "One from Many," in *Portrait of the USA,* http://usinfo.state.gov.

21. U.S. Census Bureau, Table 4, in *Technical Paper 29,* March 9, 1999, http://www.census.gov.

22. "One from Many."

23. James N. Gregory, *American Exodus: The Dust Bowl Migration and the Okie Culture in California* (New York: Oxford University Press, 1989), 6–11.

24. "Statistical Summary"; Library of Congress, "World War I and Postwar Society, Part I," in *African American Odyssey,* http://www.loc.gov.

25. U.S. Census Bureau, *Historical Statistics of the United States: Colonial Times to 1957* (Washington, DC: U.S. Government Printing Office, 1960), 462.

26. "Statistical Summary."

27. See Dillon S. Myer, *Uprooted Americans: The Japanese Americans and the War Relocation Authority during World War II* (Tucson: University of Arizona Press, 1971).

28. National Organization for Women, "Equal Rights Amendment," http://www.now.org.

29. Federal Election Commission, "2000 Official Presidential Election Results," http://www.fec.gov.

30. The White House, Office of the Press Secretary, "Fact Sheet: President Bush Remarks on the War on Terror," October 6, 2005, http://www.whitehouse.gov.

31. Bureau of the Public Debt, "The Debt to the Penny," http://www.publicdebt.treas.gov.

32. U.S. Census Bureau 2004 American Community Survey & National Center for Health Statistics, "Fast Stats A to Z," http://www.cdc.gov. The following data are taken from these sources.

33. *Statistical Abstract of the United States: 2005.*

34. "Fast Stats A to Z."

35. U.S. Census Bureau, "Poverty: 2004 Highlights," http://www.census.gov.

## BIBLIOGRAPHY

Birdsdall, Stephen S. *Regional Landscapes of the United States and Canada.* 6th ed. Hoboken, NJ: John Wiley, 2005.

Blum, John M., et al. *The National Experience: A History of the United States.* 8th ed. Fort Worth, TX: Harcourt, Brace, Jovanovich, 1993.

Branch, Taylor. *Parting the Waters: America in the King Years, 1954–1963.* New York: Simon and Schuster, 1988.

Chafe, William Henry. *The Unfinished Journey: America Since World War II.* 5th ed. New York: Oxford University Press, 2003.

Donald, David Herbert, Jean H. Baker, and Michael F. Holt. *The Civil War and Reconstruction.* New York: W. W. Norton, 2001.

Fite, Gilbert C., and Jim E. Reese. *An Economic History of the United States.* 3rd ed. Boston: Houghton Mifflin, 1973.

Flexner, Eleanor. *Century of Struggle: The Women's Rights Movement in the United States.* Rev. ed. Cambridge, MA: Belknap Press of Harvard University Press, 1975.

Jeydel, Alana S. *Political Women: The Women's Movement, Political Institutions, the Battle for Women's Suffrage and the ERA.* New York: Routledge, 2004.

Johansen, Bruce E. *The Native Peoples of North America.* 2 vols. Westport, CT: Praeger, 2005.

Johnson, Paul. *A History of the American People.* New York: HarperCollins, 1997.

Jordan, Winthrop D. *White over Black: American Attitudes toward the Negro, 1550–1812*. New York: W. W. Norton, 1977.

Lemann, Nicholas. *The Promised Land: The Great Black Migration and How It Changed America*. New York: Vintage Books, 1992.

Morrison, Samuel Eliot, Henry Steele Commager, and William E. Leuchtenburg. *The Growth of the American Republic*. 7th ed. 2 vols. New York: Oxford University Press, 1980.

Patterson, James T. *America's Struggle against Poverty, 1900–1985*. Engl. ed. Cambridge, MA: Harvard University Press, 1986.

Pritzker, Barry M. *Native Americans: An Encyclopedia of History, Culture, and Peoples*. Santa Barbara, CA: ABC-CLIO, 1998.

Ratner, Sidney, James H. Soltow, and Richard Sylla. *The Evolution of the American Economy: Growth Welfare and Decision Making*. New York: Basic Books, 1979.

Reimers, David M. *Still the Golden Door: The Third World Comes to America*. 2nd ed. New York: Columbia University Press, 1992.

Sitkoff, Harvard. *The Struggle for Black Equality, 1954–1980*. New York: Hill and Wang, 1981.

Sowell, Thomas. *Ethnic America: A History*. New York: Basic Books, 1981.

tenBroek, Jacobus, Edward N. Barnhart, and Floyd W. Matson. *Prejudice, War, and the Constitution: Causes and Consequences of the Evacuation of the Japanese Americans in World War II*. Japanese American Evacuation and Resettlement Series. Berkeley: University of California Press, 1954.

vann Woodward, C. *The Strange Career of Jim Crow*. 3rd rev. ed. New York: Oxford University Press, 1974.

Wilson, Kenneth G. *Columbia Guide to Standard American English*. New York: Columbia University Press, 1993.

# 2

# Religion and Thought

*Benjamin F. Shearer*

In God We Trust.

—The U.S. $1 bill

...and God bless America.

—President George W. Bush

THE OPPORTUNITY FOR religious freedom brought immigrants to America long before the United States became an independent nation. The early immigrants—English, German, Dutch, French—brought their religious convictions and their churches with them to America, as have millions of later immigrants. America proved the perfect place for religious beliefs to evolve and blossom in distinctly American ways.

Freedom of religion is a fundamental American principle, guaranteed in the First Amendment of the Constitution, which prohibits Congress from establishing a state religion or prohibiting the free exercise of religious beliefs. In the course of time, however, the notion of the separation of church and state, even older in origin than Thomas Jefferson's use of the term, became the Amendment's legal foundation, in no small part owing to nativist fears of Roman Catholicism. The separation of church and state, firmly placed into the legal lexicon by a 1947 Supreme Court case, has proved, however, a sticky operational concept.[1] In an overwhelmingly Christian nation, the courts preside over the constant tug and pull on the wall that is to separate religion from government.

Americans' firm conviction that religion is a matter of personal belief that cannot be regulated in any way by any government gives religion a unique place in American culture. Churches enjoy tax-exempt status as charitable institutions. More important, however, religious beliefs also enjoy freedom from public criticism. Religious beliefs and ideas are considered sacrosanct—they may be publicly expressed without consequence. It is a fact of American social life that religion is a subject to be avoided. Americans generally dislike engaging in informal discussions with no hope of easy solution or compromise. No matter one's personal views, no American would consider a public denunciation of anyone else's religious beliefs. Americans are somehow able to embrace Christians, Jews, Muslims—people of any belief—in their broad definition of what it means to be American, although non-Christians, often grossly misunderstood, have had a difficult struggle for inclusion. When religious beliefs find political positions, however, those political positions are open to public discourse and debate.

Religious beliefs, though considered a private matter, bleed into the public consciousness and culture of America. There is no law that creates a wall of separation between personal religious thought and public action. Americans by and large believe that God is leading the United States, imbuing it with democratic values and the wealth and beauty of its natural environment, and that America has, therefore, the obligation to bring God's democratic and

The back of an American one-dollar bill, which is just one of several places where one can find the words "In God We Trust." © Gramper | Dreamstime.com.

Christian values to the world. Indeed, the hallmark of the predominant Protestantism in America is democratic church structures built on the voluntary
association of individuals who, on their own initiative, have transformed
themselves into true believers.

God is in the daily commerce and discourse of all Americans. Abraham
Lincoln first put the motto "In God We Trust" on American money during
the depths of the Civil War. The Cold War put it there for good—America
was doing God's work against godless Communism. Presidents since Calvin Coolidge have been lighting the national Christmas tree, and no modern presidential speech could end without invoking God's blessing on the
country. Efforts to make the Christmas tree ceremonies that take place in
thousands of political jurisdictions each year more inclusive by referring to
a so-called holiday tree are labeled pejoratively as political correctness and
receive howls of protestation from conservative religious leaders for taking
the Christian, Jesus-centered character out of Christmas. Preachers permeate
television and radio airwaves. A sneeze in a crowded room draws a chorus of
"God bless you."

## OVERVIEW OF RELIGION IN AMERICA

Freedom of religion in America precludes asking anyone about personal
religious beliefs, whether in job interviews or even in the decennial federal
census. The federal government has never collected data on religious adher-
ence. Determining numbers of members of denominations or churches is,
therefore, dependent on surveys by various organizations or the denominations
themselves. The fact that different religious groups count different things
(baptized vs. active members, for example) further confounds efforts to understand American religion through numbers. Nevertheless, a look at the big
picture is instructive.

Most Americans believe in God; only around 2 or 3 percent of the population are agnostics or atheists. The United States is about 80 percent Christian;
data from independent surveys vary from over 76 to 82 percent. Around
13 percent of Americans are nonreligious or secular, and about 2 percent are
Jewish. No other religions—Greek Orthodox, Russian Orthodox, Islam, Hin-
duism, Buddhism, Druidism, Sikhism, Scientology, Deism, Taoist, New Age,
or Native American—are believed to approach 1 percent of the population.[2]

The 10 largest religious bodies in the United States are the Roman Catholic Church with 67.8 million; the Southern Baptist Convention, with 16.2
million; the United Methodist Church, with 8.2 million; the Church of Jesus
Christ of Latter-day Saints, with 6 million; the Church of God in Christ
(Black Pentecostal), with 5.5 million; the National Baptist Convention, USA,

with 5 million; the Evangelical Lutheran Church of America, with 4.9 million; the National Baptist Convention of America, with 3.5 million; the Presbyterian Church (USA), with 3.2 million; and the Assemblies of God (USA), with 2.8 million. The largest 25 denominations in the United States account for over 148 million people.[3]

Evangelical Protestants (Baptists, Reformed and Confessional churches, nondenominational Christians, Pentecostals, Churches of Christ, etc.) equal the Roman Catholic population at about 25 percent. Mainline White Protestant churches (Methodists, Lutherans, Presbyterians, Episcopalians, and Congregationalists) are about 22 percent of the population. African American Protestants, in African American churches that were created by African Americans in the atmosphere of slavery and segregation, make up about 8 percent of the population.

It is a sad fact of American life that white and African American people could not worship together equally as God's children. Racism permeated every niche of society. On the other hand, owing to the enterprise of early African American religious leaders, African American churches were founded that would become the bedrock religious and social foundation of African American society. The African American churches were legally untouchable and totally independent thanks to the First Amendment. They were also de facto the only African American institutions in America—places where African American culture could flourish, places where African Americans could find pride and independence, places where African Americans were in charge. The Reverend Martin Luther King coordinated the civil rights movement through African American churches. Today, African American churches continue their proud traditions and work for the economic empowerment of the African American population.

American Protestant churches have been divided by race as well as by biblical interpretation. Evangelicals, who believe in a literal, strict interpretation of the Bible but, unlike Fundamentalists, allow for miracles beyond the Bible, have generally shunned social action in favor of personal salvation. Evangelicalism has therefore been inherently individualistic in seeking in its adherents the personal transformation that allows them to accept Jesus Christ as their Lord and personal Savior. As a result, evangelicals generally remained aloof from the social and political landscape of the country, until their political power was unleashed by conservative activists. The mainline Protestant churches are not as likely to insist on literal biblical interpretation and have emphasized the importance of social action as a means toward salvation. It was these churches, therefore, especially beginning in the early twentieth century, that actively developed charitable enterprises to serve the poor and disenfranchised and became active in political and social issues and movements.

Fundamentalism, as much a creed as a state of mind, has been a constant force against modernism in American life, even though it was thought many times to have vanished. The name derives from the publication between 1910 and 1915 of *The Fundamentals: A Testimony to the Truth* in 12 volumes. Fundamentalists are evangelicals who believe in the religious, scientific, and historical truth of the Bible: Jesus Christ's divinity, virgin birth, atonement for mankind's sins by death on the cross, and resurrection from the dead and the return of Jesus Christ on Judgment Day to judge the living and the dead either for eternal bliss or eternal damnation.[4] Fundamentalists also believe in Bible prophecy.

Armed with biblical truth, fundamentalists have been persistent, if not militant, guerilla warriors in the fight to make their vision of a Christian America come true. This vision harkens back to an America that existed only ideally, but before exegetes questioned the literal meaning of the Bible, before women questioned their traditional roles, before gay rights was a topic of discussion, before evolution became an accepted theory, and before abortion was legalized. Fundamentalists believe they are preserving traditional American values that so-called liberal churches, liberal politicians, and modern American culture have helped to erode. They have enjoyed being outsiders who can pick and choose their battles emboldened by independence and unencumbered by church bureaucracies. They have successfully employed print and broadcast media to get their message out and revivals to convert the nonbelievers. A simple, understandable America prepared for Judgment Day is especially appealing in times of social change and uncertainty. Waves of revivalism swept the country during the Roaring Twenties, during World War II, and in the Vietnam War era.

The American religious landscape is changing rapidly at the turn of the twenty-first century. The Roman Catholic Church continues to grow in absolute numbers with the influx of traditional Catholics from Mexico, even as it closes churches in the inner cities of the Northeast and Midwest. The number of Roman Catholics would be growing even more, but Evangelical Protestantism has made inroads into that population. Over 30 percent of Mexicans coming into the United States are believed to be evangelicals, even though they may maintain traditional Roman Catholic practices and, indeed, may return to Catholicism. The membership in mainline Protestant churches appears to be dwindling in comparison to the burst in evangelical numbers. Americans also seem to be attracted to nondenominational, Bible-based megachurches with congregations of more than 20,000.

There can be no doubt that America is in the midst of another wave of religious awakening. It is evangelical, if not sometimes Pentecostal. It is black and white and multicolored. It is largely Protestant. Americans want traditional

American values, not a tax code–sized volume of church canons. It is New Testament; it is simple; it is salvation from uncertainty, social disconnection, and the vagaries of terrorism.

## AMERICA'S LARGEST RELIGIOUS DENOMINATIONS

### The Roman Catholic Church

As the nation's single largest denomination since 1852, Roman Catholicism is a potent religious, political, and social force. The American Church is divided into 33 provinces, each with an archbishop who may or not be a cardinal. There are 281 active bishops in 195 American dioceses, as bishop's ecclesiastical jurisdictions are called. The Church counted 19,081 parishes, 44,487 priests (some 9,500 are retired), 5,568 brothers, 74,698 sisters, and almost 14,000 permanent deacons in 2003. Priests may be diocesan (sometimes called parish priests or secular priests) or members of religious orders. There are 150 religious orders in the United States, and 14,772 of the priests belong to religious orders. Only the deacons are permitted to marry, but, like the priesthood, only men may be admitted. In addition to various charitable activities, the Church also has 585 Catholic hospitals, 7,142 elementary schools, 1,374 high schools, and 230 colleges and universities all over the country.[5]

Today, about 39 percent (25 million people) of the Catholic population is Hispanic, and by 2020, that percentage is expected to reach more than 50 percent. Since 1960, over 70 percent of the growth in the number of Roman Catholics is attributable to the national influx of Hispanics in the population. There are approximately 2.3 million African American Catholics, and about 25 percent (500,000) of the Native American population are baptized Roman Catholics.[6]

Parishes were especially important to the immigrant Roman Catholic Church. Because parish churches were neighborhood churches, and urban immigrants segregated into neighborhoods with others of the same cultural backgrounds, parishes became the hub of social and cultural as well as religious activities. Friday night fish fries with alcoholic beverages and gambling were typical social activities. Bingo games became associated with the Roman Catholic Church. The Catholic Youth Organization provided athletic competition. So strong was the cultural influence of the parishes in heavily Roman Catholic northeastern cities like Philadelphia that when Philadelphians meet each other to this day, no matter their religion, they identify themselves by the parish in which they grew up.

Roman Catholic parishes in 2000 averaged 3,254 members, or 1,269 households. The average non–Roman Catholic congregation averaged only

303 members. Roman Catholics donated $5,864,000,000 to their parishes in Sunday collections during 2002, 90 percent of which remained in the parishes to be used for parish undertakings.[7] Even though about 68 percent of American Roman Catholics are registered in parishes, there is evidence that parish life is no longer what it once was. Around 40 percent of American Roman Catholics think the parishes are too large. Whereas nearly 75 percent went to Mass weekly in the 1950s, that number has now shrunk to 34 percent. In spite of Church rules, three-fourths of Roman Catholics believe one can be a good Catholic without going to church every week.[8]

The American Protestant democratic tradition has always stood in stark contrast to the Roman Catholic Church's nondemocratic tradition, a fact that helped to fuel nativists' fear of a papal takeover of the country as Catholics from Ireland, Italy, Poland, and Germany poured into the country. The Roman Catholic hierarchy—the pope, cardinals, bishops, and priests—has not only guarded against the introduction of doctrinal heterodoxy but has also systematically maintained clerical supremacy in decision making, even down to the appointment of priests to parishes. American Roman Catholics, accustomed to voting for their political leaders, have had no vote on who their parish priest may be, no less on any matters of doctrine. Seventy-two percent of Roman Catholics now want a say in selecting their parish priests.[9] American Roman Catholics are increasingly at odds with the Church's teachings and practices. Sixty-nine percent want to see the Church abandon its prohibition of artificial birth control; 65 percent want priests to be able to marry; and 60 percent want women to be permitted to become ordained priests. Even on the critical issue of abortion, 33 percent of Catholics believe it should generally be available, and 44 percent believe it should be available with further restrictions. It is not surprising, then, that 82 percent of American Roman Catholics believe they can disagree with the pope and still be good Catholics and that 72 percent believe that their consciences should supersede Church teaching.[10] American Roman Catholics seem to have adopted the Protestant majority's belief in the priesthood of believers, in which individual conscience is supreme. The picking and choosing of which Roman Catholic teachings to reject or accept has been called *cafeteria Catholicism,* and it has become so rampant that some Church leaders believe a line needs to be drawn—either be a Roman Catholic, or not.

With majorities of American Roman Catholics believing they could be good Catholics without adhering to their Church's positions on abortion, marriage, divorce, birth control, weekly Mass attendance, and 23 percent even thinking that they could be good Catholics without believing that Jesus Christ rose from the dead, the need for dedicated priests could not be greater.[11] The Roman Catholic priesthood in America, however, had been in a crisis mode from several directions and for a long time. The average age of American priests is 61. Only 500 new priests were ordained in 2003. As population in general has grown, and the Roman Catholic population in particular has increased, the number of priests has declined. The Church has tried to make up for this decline by developing its lay deaconate program and programs to train lay catechetical teachers, youth ministers, and lay ministers. A 2000 study of the problem found that 2,386 parishes shared a pastor and 2,334 had no resident pastor. Four hundred thirty-seven parishes were receiving pastoral care from someone other than a priest. In the United States in the 1950s, there was one priest for every 650 people. By 1999, the ratio had inflated to 1:1,200. In the West, where the Hispanic population was exploding, the ratio was 1:1,752.[12]

If the shortage of vocations to the priesthood was a serious problem, the increasing and steady revelations that priests had long been sexually abusing children was a crisis of faith of much larger proportion. By 2002, the American public at large was outraged at the way the Roman Catholic Church was handling the scandals; 45 percent of all Americans were dissatisfied, and 25 percent were angry. A week after Pope John Paul II met with American cardinals in Rome in April 2002 about the scandal, 58 percent of Roman Catholics believed the pope had not done enough about it. Sixty-two percent of Roman Catholics were not pleased with the way the American hierarchy was dealing with the crisis. Eighty-three percent of Roman Catholics wanted to see law enforcement called in when church leaders learned of alleged child abuse by priests.[13]

In June 2002, Bishop Wilton D. Gregory, president of the United States Conference of Catholic Bishops, addressed his fellow bishops on the sexual abuse scandals. He called it "a very grave crisis," noting that the bishops, singly and as a group, had worked on the sexual abuse issue since 1985, listened to victims and consultants, and finally adopted principles in 1992 to be followed when sexual abuse was alleged. Gregory acknowledged that the work the bishops had done was "overshadowed by the imprudent decisions of a small number of Bishops" during the past 10 years. He confessed that it was the fault of the bishops that sexually abusive priests were allowed to remain in positions that allowed them to abuse again; that law enforcement was not called in; that fear of scandal permitted abuse to continue; and that victims were sometimes treated as adversaries. He apologized for all the bishops and resolved to change the way things would be done in the future.[14]

The Conference of Bishops created the National Review Board for the Protection of Children and Young People to study the problem. In February 2004, the board reported its findings: 4,392 priests (4%) had been accused of molesting minors between 1950 and 2002, and the Church had spent over $500,000,000 in dealing with the reported 10,667 accusations. Eighty-one percent of the victims were male; 2,000 children under 11 years old had been abused by pedophile priests; 78 percent of the allegations involved children 11–17 years old. Allegations of abuse of minors rose in the 1960s, peaked in the 1970s, and occurred all over the country.[15] With release of the report, Bishop Gregory assured that the bishops had put a system in place to respond at once to abuse allegation, assist victims, and take offenders out of the ministry.[16]

The anger of most Roman Catholics was directed at the bishops, rather than at the clergy in their parishes, where priests continued to earn high marks throughout the unfolding of the scandal. In fact, between 2001 and 2002, Sunday giving in the parishes rose 4.8 percent. In 2002, America's 15.9 million registered, active Roman Catholic households gave the Church, on average, $455. Parishes are heavily dependent on Sunday collections for their revenues. Typically, parishes spend 42 percent of their revenues on salaries and the remaining 58 percent on plant and program expenses. The United States Conference of Catholic Bishops, through which the bishops exercise their pastorate for the nation, also asks Roman Catholics to support other activities through special annual collections. Money is collected to aid the Roman Catholic Church in central and eastern Europe, to fund Catholic Relief Services and migration and refugee services. The Catholic Campaign for Human Development uses donations to fight the root causes of poverty in America. There is a collection for Roman Catholic home missions, black and Indian missions, and the Church in Latin America. Peter's Pence is a collection to enable the pope to respond to aid requests by those who have been victims of war, oppression, and natural disasters. Other collections support world evangelization, third world food projects, institutions in the Holy Land, and Catholic University of America, which was founded by the American bishops. Unlike other denominations, the Roman Catholic Church nationally does not give direct financial support to Roman Catholic colleges and universities other than Catholic University.[17]

The work of the Roman Catholic Church in America is furthered by some 135 national organizations and hundreds of local lay groups. The Knights of Columbus is the largest such group, with 1.6 million members. The members of this fraternal society donated $128.5 million to charities in 2002 and performed 60.8 million hours of volunteer service. The Knights of Peter Claver and Ladies Auxiliary, with 45,000 members, serve the specific needs of African American Catholics and annually donate hundreds of thousands of dollars and hours of service. The Society of St. Vincent de Paul's 102,000 members visit homes, hospitals, day care facilities for the aged, and prisons.

Their donations and services were valued at $335 million in 2002. These and many other organizations like the Jesuit Volunteer Corps vitally involve the laity in fulfilling the Church's missions to serve others.[18]

The Roman Catholic Church in America, through the teachings and pronouncements of the United States Conference of Catholic Bishops, has taken the position that the "separation of church and state does not require division between belief and public action, between moral principles and political choices, but protects the right of believers and religious groups to practice their faith and act on their values in public life." Faithful citizens who "bring their moral convictions into public life," therefore, "do not threaten democracy or pluralism but enrich them and the nation." In regard to abortion— "always intrinsically evil"—the bishops counseled Roman Catholics in public positions that "acting consistently to support abortion on demand risks making them cooperators in evil in a public manner."[19] In concert, of course, with the Vatican, the American bishops have been a steady voice in speaking for the sanctity of all life, not just the unborn. Thus they have reminded the faithful that human cloning, euthanasia, assisted suicide, the death penalty for capital crimes, and targeting civilians in war all violate that fundamental principle. Furthermore, Catholics have the obligation to protect family life, pursue social and economic justice, serve the poor and the helpless, care for the environment, and work to eliminate poverty all over the world.[20] The bishops have also supported an amendment to the Constitution that would define marriage as a union between a man and a woman, arguing that while they decried the "unjust discrimination, harassment or abuse" against homosexuals, homosexual unions are "inherently non-procreative" and therefore cannot have the status of marriage.[21]

### Baptists

#### The Southern Baptist Convention

The first Baptist church in America was founded in 1638 in what would become Rhode Island. An offshoot of English Puritanism, Baptists shunned any state-sponsored religion and believed that baptism should be performed only on those who had proved their faith. In 1707, the Philadelphia Baptist Association was formed, which included churches in Pennsylvania, Delaware, and Rhode Island, and also included churches in Connecticut, Maryland, Virginia, and New York. At the time of the American Revolution, there were about equal numbers of Anglicans and Baptists in the colonies, but their numbers were smaller than those of Congregationalists and Presbyterians. By 1800, however, Baptists were the largest denomination in the United States, its numbers having swelled with new black and white members after the Great Awakening, which spread conversion through the country from the 1730s into the 1770s.

In 1814, Baptists formed the General Missionary Convention, but it was divided between North and South over the slavery issue in 1845. Thus was born the Southern Baptist Convention, today the largest of America's Baptist groups, the single largest Protestant and evangelical group, and the largest religious body in the country after the Roman Catholic Church. Contrary to what its name implies, the Southern Baptist Convention is much more than a regional church. Although the heaviest concentrations of Southern Baptists remain in the Old South, churches have been established throughout the country, including in the Northeast, Midwest, mountain states, and Southern California. Between 1952 and 1990 alone, over 8,500 new churches were established in the United States.[22]

The Southern Baptist Convention is not just an American church. Southern Baptists take the call to evangelize the world very seriously. Since 1846, its International Mission Board has sent over 15,000 missionaries all over the world.[23] At the close of 2005, the board had 5,036 field personnel under appointment and 6,797 student volunteers working abroad. In 2005 alone, overseas baptisms totaled 459,725. Membership came to 7.3 million in 108,713 overseas churches. In 2005, Southern Baptists contributed $133.9 million in support of the annual International Mission Study and Lottie Moon Christmas Offering, in addition to $22.9 million for world hunger and disaster relief.[24]

Southern Baptists hold the Bible to be divinely inspired by a triune God and without error. The Bible always trumps any statement of belief. Jesus Christ is God the Son incarnated in a virgin birth, who died on the cross to redeem mankind from sin and will return in glory to judge the world. Salvation is possible only for those "who accept Jesus Christ as Lord and Saviour." Because each person is accountable to God—called *soul competency*—there is no salvation outside of a person's relationship with God. Good works or church attendance will not bring salvation. Personal faith in Christ as Lord is a requirement of salvation, which involves regeneration, justification, sanctification, and glorification. Regeneration is "a work of God's grace" that, with repentance, changes the heart and results in a new birth as the sinner turns to God and commits to Jesus Christ. Justification is "God's gracious and full acquittal ... of all sinners who repent and believe in Christ." Sanctification sets the believer apart to God's purposes and enables "progress toward moral and spiritual maturity." Glorification is "the final blessed and abiding state of the redeemed." Once accepted by God, true believers filled with God's grace never fall away from the state of grace, even though they may occasionally go astray.[25]

Southern Baptists accept the priesthood of all believers, which means true believers have the same rights as ordained ministers to interpret scripture and talk with God. Only men, however, are permitted to be pastors. Each local congregation is autonomous of the state and general conventions and operated through democratic processes. Southern Baptist congregations observe Sundays as days of public and private worship and devotion and *Christ's two ordinances* (called *sacraments* by some denominations): baptism by immersion in water and the Lord's Supper. The members of the congregations are expected to support evangelism and mission activity and an adequate system of Christian education, in which teachers' freedom is limited "by the preeminence of Jesus Christ" and by "the authoritative nature of the Scriptures." Fifty-two colleges and universities, two Bible schools, and one academy are members of the Association of Southern Baptists Colleges and Schools. Congregation members are also to exercise good stewardship by contributing "cheerfully, regularly, systematically, proportionately, and liberally for the advancement of the Redeemer's cause on earth."[26]

The Southern Baptist faith has retained the long Baptist support for the principle of the absolute separation of church and state. It also supports cooperation among New Testament churches for justified ends. The Convention's teachings on social issues are "rooted in the regeneration of the individual by the saving grace of God in Jesus Christ." Good Christians have the duty to seek peace and pray for the "reign of the Prince of Peace," to "speak on behalf of the unborn" and to "provide for the orphaned, the needy, the abused, the aged, the helpless, and the sick." They should also "oppose racism, every form of greed, selfishness, and vice, and all forms of sexual immorality, including adultery, homosexuality, and pornography." In regard to family matters, the Southern Baptist Convention holds that "God has ordained the family as the foundational institution of human society." Because both husband and wife are created in God's image, both are of equal worth in the eyes of God. The husband, however, has the "God-given responsibility to provide for, to protect, and to lead his family." The wife "is to submit herself to the servant leadership of her husband" and she has "the God-given responsibility to respect her husband and serve as his helper in managing the household and nurturing the next generation."[27]

### National Baptist Convention, USA Inc.

The National Baptist Convention, USA, is a historically African American church with reported membership of 5 million adherents and 33,000 churches, making it America's sixth largest religious body and the largest of the African American Baptist churches.[28] This convention traces its origin to

1886 in the movement ongoing since the 1830s of African American Baptists to separate from white conventions and form their own cooperative organizations. The movement was replete with regional conventions, consolidations, and schisms. By 1916, the National Baptist Convention, USA, emerged.

An important concept to the Convention is the Baptist tradition and ideal of voluntary membership; that is, the Convention exerts no control, theological or otherwise, over its members. These are matters for local churches. The Convention's task is help the membership effectively realize goals on which they all agree. A board of directors governs the national convention. Every fifth year, a president is elected by member churches at Annual Session. The president and various officers are members of the board of directors as well as the presidents of the 62 constituent state conventions, representatives of the convention's boards and auxiliaries, and 29 members at large. The convention's 10 boards and auxiliaries deal with such matters as Christian education, evangelism, missions, and music. There is also a Woman's Auxiliary.

The National Baptist Convention, USA, is not theologically innovative; that is, it adheres to traditional Baptist beliefs in grace as a gift from God available to all who will believe, repentance and justification, regeneration (being born again), and sanctification. It holds the Bible to be the divinely inspired truth without error and to hold God's plan for salvation and the standards for human conduct. Two sacraments are recognized: baptism by immersion and the Lord's Supper. Mankind divides into the righteous and the wicked in death and thereafter, awaiting the end of the world, when both the living and the dead will be judged to heaven or hell.[29]

### The National Baptist Convention of America Inc.

The National Baptist Convention of America came from the same roots as the National Baptist Convention, USA. In 1895, three African American Baptist conventions merged into a single entity to unify domestic and international goals, taking the name the National Baptist Convention of the United States of America. This made it the largest African American church in America. In 1915, however, the unity of the group was destroyed over a debate about ownership of its Publishing Board. Thus two separate groups emerged. Efforts to come back together, notably during Annual Session in 1988 to protest apartheid, failed. The National Baptist Convention of America, which had remained unincorporated since the 1915 split, finally was incorporated in 1987 with headquarters in Shreveport, Louisiana. Doctrinally, the two churches have no differences.

The National Baptist Convention of America has about 3.5 million members and more than 8,000 churches in the United States. The United States' eighth largest church, it is active in religious publishing and education and is committed to evangelism at home and abroad. Missions are supported in the Caribbean, Panama, and Ghana. The Convention is also committed to freedom of religion, civil liberty, social justice, and equality.[30]

### Other Baptist Churches

The voluntary nature of Baptist conventions and associations, leaving local churches autonomous, is a democratic tradition that has made Baptists susceptible to divisions and regroupings. In 1988, the National Missionary Baptist Convention of America split from the National Baptist Convention of America Inc., not because of doctrine, but because of its publishing board and other earthly matters. This historically African American convention ranks as the 12th largest religious body in America, with 2.5 million members.[31]

The Progressive National Baptist Convention Inc., also with about 2.5 million members, was formed late in 1961 out of the National Baptist Convention Inc. Ostensibly fighting over the tenure of convention leaders, whose nearly lifetime elections to office kept the convention on a traditional foundation, the real issue was civil rights. The progressives wanted their convention to be fully involved in the movement for human and civil rights and exhibit the fullness of Baptist and American democracy in the election of its leadership. They were happy to give Dr. Martin Luther King Jr. a home in an African American Baptist denomination. To this day, the Progressive National Baptist Convention actively supports and advocates for complete human liberation through voter registration drives, affirmative action, and African American economic empowerment. All church leadership positions are open to men and women. The convention squarely stands for fellowship, progress, and peace.[32]

American Baptist Churches USA claims to be "the most racially inclusive body within Protestantism" and will soon have no racial or ethnic majorities. The United States' 20th largest denomination, with 1.43 million members and about 5,800 congregations, the American Baptists are the northern remnant of the 1845 split over slavery that created the Southern Baptist Convention. It was incorporated in 1907 as the Northern Baptist Convention, renamed the American Baptist Convention in 1950, and took its current name in 1972. American Baptists, who favor ecumenical ties, have always been actively involved in direct social outreach, including the civil rights movement, the empowerment of women, and a number of ecological and social justice issues.[33]

The Baptist Bible Fellowship International (BBFI) is ranked 22nd of America's largest denominations, with 1.2 million members. Located in Springfield, Missouri, with its flagship Baptist Bible College, BBFI was officially organized in 1950, but its roots lie in the 1920s. A group of Baptist preachers were alarmed that modernism was creeping into the Baptist Church, and they wanted to return to the fundamentals. This independent, fundamentalist Baptist group claims more than 4,000 churches across the country that support their missionary work.[34]

## Methodists

### The United Methodist Church

The United Methodist Church is the third largest religious body in the United States and the largest of the mainline Protestant and Methodist denominations, yet it has less than half the members of the United States' largest evangelical denomination, the Southern Baptist Convention. Curiously, as the Church has lost membership in the United States, declining now to 8.2 million from 10.7 million in 1970, it has more than tripled its international membership to 1.5 million in the same period. In the United States, there are almost 45,000 clergy members and over 35,000 local churches; 1,050 people are involved in the Church's global ministries, with 120,000 volunteers working in 100 countries.

The U.S. church is organized into five jurisdictions, in which there are 50 Episcopal areas, 63 annual conferences, and 520 districts. Bishops are elected by the conferences from among conference elders (ordained ministers). The first woman bishop was elected in 1980, and there are currently 15 active women bishops. Women clergy have been ordained since 1956, and they now number over 12,000. A General Conference is convened every four years, its members elected by the annual conferences in equal numbers of lay and clergy delegates. This body makes official church pronouncements and updates *The Book of Discipline,* which contains all the Church's theological and other positions. The United Methodists have built an extensive educational system that includes 10 universities, 82 four-year colleges, and 8 two-year colleges, along with 13 theological schools and 10 precollegiate schools. In fulfillment of their belief in doing good works for society, the Methodists also have 120 community service ministries; 83 hospitals and health care systems; 78 children, youth, and family services; and 297 ministries for the aged. In 2001, local churches gave over $5 billion for all the Church's programs.[35]

Methodism, as a movement inside of the Church of England based on the teachings of John and Charles Wesley, did not organize separately until George Washington was president. There were few Methodists in the American colonies—fewer than 7,000 in 1776. By 1850, however, there were over 1.6 million Methodists, and by 1890, over 6.2 million.[36] The growth of Methodism in America was nothing short of phenomenal, even after black congregations separated from the main church in 1816 and 1821 and pro-slavery southern Methodists broke away to form their own church in 1845. The northern and southern branches were not reunited until 1939, but the black congregations remain separate. The United Methodist Church of today was formed in 1968 when the Methodists united with the Evangelical United Brethren Church.

The United Methodist Church affirms basic Christian beliefs in a triune God; the fall of mankind; and salvation through Jesus Christ, who died and rose from the dead to atone for sin and who will come to judge the living and the dead. It accepts the authority of the Bible on matters of faith and recognizes the sacraments of baptism and the Lord's supper. The Holy Spirit brings redemptive love, and faith in Jesus Christ brings forgiveness, recon-ciliation with God, and transformation. The United Methodist Church is overtly ecumenical, believing in "the essential oneness of the church in Christ Jesus." The Methodists are not so much concerned with doctrine other than it affects discipleship, as with implementing "genuine Christianity in the lives of believers." Wesleyan teaching lends the gentle message to Methodism that God created a good world with the intention that mankind be holy and happy. God's prevenient grace prompts us to please God and seek repen-tance and faith. With repentance comes justifying grace, forgiveness, and a true change of heart. This new birth brings sanctifying grace, which leads to Christian perfection, a state in which love of God and others fills the heart. In Methodist theology, faith and piety are not enough. They must be ac-companied by the performance of good works and discipline. Thus salvation "always involves Christian mission and service to the world," and "love of God is always linked with love of neighbor, a passion for justice and renewal of the life of the world."[37]

The Social Creed adopted by the United Methodist Church and contained in *The Book of Discipline* acknowledges the "blessings of community, sexual-ity, marriage and the family" and affirms the duty to preserve and enhance the natural world. Furthermore, it affirms human and property rights for all people, including minorities of all kinds, and world peace, and expresses belief in collective bargaining, "responsible consumption," and "the elimina-tion of economic and social distress."[38]

The United Methodists' charism is to be involved in social action, rather than living separately from the world. Thus the Church has taken a number of positions on social issues. The Church has, for example, opposed capital punishment and recognized the right to civil disobedience on the demands of conscience. It has opposed human cloning but approved human gene thera-pies that cannot be passed on to others when used to alleviate suffering. It has opposed military service and supported ministry to conscientious objectors.

It has supported equal rights for homosexuals, although self-proclaimed active homosexuals cannot become ordained ministers or be appointed to Church positions because homosexuality violates Christian teachings. It has rejected differing social norms for men and women and has supported a law to define marriage as the union of a man to a woman. The Church has opposed late-term abortion, and while not approving abortion of any kind, it has supported legal abortion in conflicting circumstances when it may be justified.[39]

### The African American Methodist Churches

Racism, not theological difference, caused African American Methodists to form their own congregations under their own initiative. The African Methodist Episcopal Church (AMEC) traces its beginnings to a black mutual aid society that was founded in 1787 in Philadelphia by former slave Richard Allen. He became pastor of Bethel AMEC in 1794 and succeeded later in establishing the AMEC as an independent organization. Today, AMEC has 2.5 million followers in the United States, and its successful missionary activities have helped it to establish congregations in 30 countries.[40] The African Methodist Episcopal Zion Church (AMEZ), now with 1.43 million members, was first organized in New York City in 1796. Its first church, Zion, was opened in 1800 while still part of the white Methodist establishment. By 1821, however, AMEZ became independent, and James Varick was ordained its first black bishop in 1822.[41]

### The Church of Jesus Christ of Latter-day Saints

The fourth largest church in America, with nearly 6 million members in the United States and a worldwide membership exceeding 12 million in 26,670 congregations and with over 330 world missions, the Church of Jesus Christ of Latter-day Saints (LDS) is one of the world's fastest growing religions, yet it is also perhaps the most misunderstood. Many Americans think the LDS is not even a Christian church, a confusion generated in part by the LDS claim that it is not a Protestant church and by the public habit of referring to Latter-day Saints (their preferred title) as Mormons.

In fact, however, the LDS believes itself to be the restored church of Jesus Christ, which had been rent asunder first by the Roman Catholic Church and then by various Protestant movements. The early Christians were the first saints, and owing to God's revelations to the prophet Joseph Smith that he would restore God's church on earth, the new church would be composed of latter-day saints. Smith is said to have had revelations directly from God, father and son, beginning in 1820, when he was only 14 years old. In 1823, a resurrected prophet who lived in America around 420 C.E. first

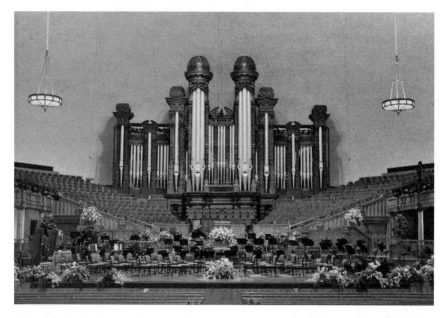

The inside of the Mormon Tabernacle in Salt Lake City, Utah. © Karimala | Dreamstime.com.

appeared to Smith. In 1827, this prophet, Moroni, led Smith to a hillside outside Palmyra, New York, where he had buried the gold plates on which the prophet Mormon had condensed the ancient history and religious beliefs of the Western Hemisphere. By 1830, Smith had translated and published *The Book of Mormon* and established the Church of Christ in Fayette, New York. In 1838, the church took its current name, based on new revelation.

As God's chosen, Smith and his church set out on a mission to build the perfect society, Zion, away from the sinful world. They went to Ohio, Illinois, and Missouri, finding themselves outcasts yet still gaining converts wherever they went. Smith was killed in 1844 by a local mob in Carthage, Illinois, outside the LDS settlement in Nauvoo. Brigham Young led most of the Latter-day Saints from Missouri to Utah in 1847, where they began a successful colonization effort. (Some Latter-day Saints remained behind in Independence, Missouri, and formed the Reorganized Church of Jesus Christ of Latter-day Saints, now called the Community of Christ, with about 250,000 members.)

The LDS wanted to create a theocracy, with church leaders in charge of all activities. This was to be a society built on cooperation, rather than competition; group activity, rather than individual prowess; and the stewardship of resources for the common good of all. In 1848, the LDS created the provisional state of Deseret, with church leaders in civil positions, and unsuccessfully sought statehood. Utah would not become a state until 1896, and suspicion of LDS beliefs and practices was the reason. Most suspicious was the early Mormon acceptance and encouragement of polygamy, which seemed to violate basic Christian doctrine concerning marriage and the family and certainly violated basic American values as understood by the politicians who would legislate on Utah statehood.

LDS beliefs held the Church outside the mainstream of Catholic or mainline and Evangelical Protestant thinking. In LDS parlance, all non-LDS believers are gentiles, including Jews. The God of the LDS is three persons with a single purpose, but separate beings. The LDS president is considered a prophet, who speaks directly with God, but all saints are also entitled to revelation. The LDS accepts the Bible and *The Book of Mormon* as divinely inspired scripture as well as *Doctrine and Covenants* (revelations since the founding of the Church) and a selection of Joseph Smith's writings, the *Pearl of Great Price.* Life is considered a test—human beings had once lived in the spirit world with God, but, with no memory of that spirit existence, were given physical bodies to prove themselves worthy to return to God. LDS doctrine holds further that marriages and family relationship, when *sealed* in the temple, last throughout eternity. Furthermore, because physical death does not mean automatic judgment to heaven or hell, relatives may have family members baptized or their marriages sealed in the temple to ensure their eternal bliss. Thus genealogy is important to the LDS.

Being a Latter-day Saint is not just adhering to doctrine, but it is also a lifestyle. Latter-day Saints are expected to live by the highest standards of honesty and integrity (that is why billionaire Howard Hughes wanted Latter-day Saints as his accountants), obey the law, and avoid premarital sex and extramarital affairs. The Church opposes all kinds of immoral behaviors, including gambling, pornography, and abortion (with certain exceptions). Latter-day Saints are also expected to tithe to the church 10 percent of their income, fast for two meals one day a month, and use that money to help the poor, do missionary work, and serve the church, all the time following Joseph Smith's 1833 health code. This code, the World of Wisdom, forbids the use of alcohol, tobacco, tea, and coffee and the misuse of drugs.

The structure of the church and its support organizations make for a tightly knit community of believers. The LDS is notably nonclerical. Local congregations, called *wards,* are presided over by unpaid bishops with fixed terms. *Stakes* are groups of wards. Males begin the three orders of priesthood at age 12. By 18, they may be affirmed the highest order, Melchizedek priesthood, which has in ascending order the offices of elder, high priest, patriarch, seventy, and apostle. The church is governed by the First Presidency (the president and two counselors) and the 12 Apostles. On a president's death, the man who has been an Apostle the longest ascends to the presidency. The Seventies—there are now five groups of them—implement the policies of the First Presidency and the Apostles. Saints have the right to vote to uphold officers and administrative proposals. Latter-day Saints meet in meetinghouses or chapels ordinarily to worship. Temples, of which there are over 700 worldwide, are used for the administration of ordinances.

The LDS operates an educational system with seminaries, institutes of religion, and the three campuses of Brigham Young University. It has an extensive Sunday school program for members 12 and older. Its Young Men and Young Women organizations for ages 12–17 provide social, cultural, and religious programs. The Primary operates nurseries on Sundays and assists parents in teaching the Gospel to children age 3–11. Furthermore, LDS families have a pair of priesthood holders visit them once a month for home teaching.

While more than half of the population of Utah remains Latter-day Saints today, the LDS was forced to abandon its communitarian ideals outside the confines of the Church, in which they still survive. The price of statehood was the acknowledgment of competitive capitalism, the selling of Church-owned businesses, and the decoupling of the church from the state. The Manifesto of 1890, the Church's pronouncement that it would no longer tolerate polygamy, was the beginning of that process. Acceptance of polygamy by the LDS had been a major stumbling block to statehood. It would not be until 1978, however, that African American men would be accepted into the priesthood. Women are still excluded from the priesthood.[42]

### The Church of God in Christ Inc.

The fifth largest church in the United States is the historically African American Pentecostal Church of God in Christ, with about 5.5 million members and 15,300 local churches. It was founded and organized by Elder Charles Harrison Mason, who was born in 1866 near Memphis, Tennessee, to a Missionary Baptist family. He and a small band of fellow elders were swept up by the revivalism sweeping the country and especially by the three-year revival taking place in Los Angeles. By 1897, the name of the Church was chosen. By 1907, it was organized by Mason, the Chief Apostle, and a tabernacle was built in Memphis in 1925. Today, the Church is governed through the Chief Apostle, the General Board, and the state jurisdictional bishops, who are elected by the General Assembly from the ordained elders.[43]

The members of this church believe in a triune God; that Christ, born to a virgin, died to atone for human sin; and that the Holy Ghost (Holy Spirit) brings the plan of salvation to earth, empowering believers to serve the world. The Bible is the only authority on all matters. Human nature is sinful and depraved because Adam ate the forbidden fruit and condemned his progeny to an unholy state. The Holy Ghost redeems human beings through repentance, faith, justification, regeneration, sanctification, and baptism. Baptism in the Holy Ghost follows rebirth (the personal act of repentance is salvation) and is accompanied by speaking in tongues. The Church believes in three ordinances (sacraments): baptism (by immersion), the Lord's Supper, and feet washing. Devils or demons and evil spirits of the spiritual world can be embodied in humans and cast out in the name of Jesus by believers. Divine healing is also practiced by the Church, and miracles can and do occur still, as believers wait for Christ's Second Coming.[44]

### Presbyterian Church (USA)

The Presbyterian Church (USA) is the largest of the Presbyterian churches in the United States, claiming 2,363,136 members in 2004 in 11,019 congregations throughout the nation. It is headquartered in Louisville, Kentucky. Although the first American presbytery dates back to Philadelphia in 1706, the American Presbyterian Church experienced a tremendous number of schisms and mergers through the centuries, including a division in 1861 between North and South as the Civil War commenced, which was healed only in 1983 with the reunification of northern and southern branches in the creation of the Presbyterian Church (USA).

The Presbyterian Church bases its beliefs on the Reformed theology of John Calvin as taken to Scotland by John Knox. Primary among these beliefs are the sovereignty of God, predestination (God elects people for service and salvation), faithful stewardship of creation, the two sacraments of baptism (infant baptism recommended, immersion not required) and the Lord's Supper, and seeking social justice while living in accord with God's message. Predestination is perhaps the most controversial Presbyterian belief, for it means that God chooses certain people for salvation, and there is no way to know who, other than oneself, has been elected for salvation. If God has not selected you, you are powerless to do anything about it. Calvin's original doctrine has later been tempered with the understanding that belief in Jesus Christ signifies election by God, and Christ has provided salvation enough for everyone.

Calvin introduced democracy into church governance in direct contradistinction to Roman Catholic clericalism. Presbyterians elect lay people, who are ordained as elders to work with ministers to govern a local church. The group of governing elders and ministers is called a *session*. Presbyteries are groups of churches; synods are groups of presbyteries; and the General

Assembly oversees the entire church. The first American General Assembly was held in 1789. Today, there are 21,194 ordained ministers and 101,324 elders in 16 regional synods and 173 presbyteries. As early as 1930, women were ordained as elders in one of the churches, which eventually united with the present-day Church. By 1956, women were ordained as ministers. When the factions finally united, women had long been accepted into the ministry. Today, 29 percent of active Presbyterian ministers are women.

The Presbyterian Church (USA) is active in worldwide evangelization and spent $125 million on national and international mission work. In the United States, there are 11 Presbyterian Church seminaries, 7 secondary schools, and more than 65 colleges and universities related to the Church. Yet even as the work of the Church progresses, its membership fell 12.5 percent between 1994 and 2004. The average size of a Presbyterian congregation is 214 members; the median size is 109. Attendance at worship services averages 52 percent. Church membership is 92 percent white. Annual individual contributions to the Church averaged $936 in 2004.

The Presbyterian Church (USA) has taken stands on a number of important social issues. In regard to abortion, the Church has called for "an atmosphere of open debate and mutual respect for a variety of opinions." There was a consensus, however, that abortion should not be used merely as a birth control or gender selection option; that the health of the mother should be a mitigating circumstance at all times; that no law should limit access to abortion; and that no law should completely ban abortion. The Presbyterian Church (USA) has welcomed homosexuals into its community and decried any kind of discrimination against them but condemned homosexuality as a sin. Admitted, openly homosexual persons may not be ordained as elders, deacons, or ministers. The Church opposes capital punishment and state-sanctioned gambling, favors gun control, and is true to conflicting beliefs of its past constituent groups, supports personal decisions not to drink alcoholic beverages, but supports responsible drinking for those who do choose to drink alcohol.[45]

### Lutherans

#### The Evangelical Lutheran Church in America

The Evangelical Lutheran Church in America (ELCA) is the seventh largest church in the United States and the largest of 21 Lutheran bodies in the country, with over 4.9 million baptized members. There are 10,585 congregations in 65 synods, which are grouped into nine regions and who are served by 17,694 clergy (3,140 of the clergy are women). Synod assemblies elect bishops. The Church membership is overwhelmingly white, its largest group of people of color being a bit over 54,000 African Americans. The ELCA has 8 seminaries, 28 colleges and universities (4 each in Minnesota and Iowa), 16 high schools, and 210 elementary schools. Its social ministries serve 3,000 communities. Annual giving per conformed member averages about $550.

The ELCA officially began on the first day of January 1988 with the merger of the American Lutheran Church, the Association of Evangelical Lutheran Churches, and the Lutheran Church in America. German, Dutch, and Scandinavian immigrants to America brought Lutheranism to America as early as the 1620s. Mergers or unions of Lutheran synods became the norm as originally immigrant churches gradually abandoned use of their mother tongues for English. The American Lutheran Church had been created in 1960 out of the merger of German, Danish, and Norwegian groups. The Lutheran Church in America had been formed by the merger of German, Slovak, Icelandic, Swedish, Finnish, and Danish synods in 1962.

The ELCA takes a wide view of what *church* means: it is the fellowship of all those who have returned to God through Jesus Christ, no matter the denomination. The Church has retained the use of the Apostles' Creed, the Nicene Creed, and the Athanasian (Trinitarian) Creed. The ELCA recognizes baptism in other Christian churches. Those who are already baptized may join the Church merely by going to a membership meeting at a local church. As its history of unions intimates, the ELCA is open to and active in ecumenical discussions, but it retains its Lutheran heritage. The Church believes in Martin Luther's three *solas:* salvation by the grace of God alone, salvation through faith alone, and the Bible as the sole norm of doctrine and living. However, the ELCA recognizes differing biblical interpretation. Thus, while the Bible is the authority in faith and practice, it is not necessarily accurate in historical or scientific matters.

The ELCA is active in social advocacy and encourages its members to be engaged in these issues. The Church has spoken out, among other things, for peace, arms control, human rights, corporate responsibility, proper care of creation, access to health care and decent and affordable housing, and the banning of assault weapons. It has opposed capital punishment, repeal of the federal tax on estates (the so-called death tax), and expressed the need to address hunger, poverty, racism, and immigration issues humanely. The ELCA has also recognized that government has a legitimate role in regulating abortion, but it has opposed laws that would deny access to safe and affordable justified abortions. While contraception is the best way to prevent unwanted pregnancies, the Church has taken the position that abortion can be justified and morally responsible if the mother's life is in danger, in cases of rape or incest, if conception takes place in dehumanizing circumstances, or if there is a fetal abnormality. Abortion can never be justified, however, if the fetus can survive separated from the mother.[46]

### The Lutheran Church—Missouri Synod

The Missouri Synod originated with German Lutherans who immigrated to Missouri in 1839 and formed a synod that first met in 1847. It is the second largest Lutheran body in the United States, with over 2.5 million members, but its numbers have been in decline for 30 years. In 2003, the Synod counted 6,160 congregations with 5,281 pastors among them. Congregation members gave $1.25 billion to their congregations.[47] Of the congregations, 2,526 operate schools or early childhood centers, and associations of congregations operate another 183. For the 2004–2005 year, 143,322 children were enrolled in 1,028 elementary schools and 19,638 in 101 high schools.[48] The Synod, divided into 35 districts and some 600 circuits, also has 10 colleges and 2 seminaries. Synodal Conventions, the Synod's highest governing body, are held every three years. Convention members, one lay person and one pastor, are elected from all the electoral circuits to vote on proposals before the body.

The Missouri Synod sets itself apart from the ELCA in a number of respects, although both retain basic Lutheran theology and the faith of the three creeds. Perhaps most significantly, the Missouri Synod has not been transformed by large mergers. In fact, the Synod has taken the position that ecumenical or merger discussions are without value and even contrary to God's will, unless all parties share the same interpretation of the Bible. (In 1932, the Synod found that the Pope was the fulfillment of the Antichrist of biblical prophesy.)[49] The Missouri Synod holds that the Bible is inerrant in all cases, including science and history, unlike the ELCA. Neither does the Missouri Synod ordain women to the clergy for scriptural reasons.[50]

The Missouri Synod has found no biblical prohibition of capital punishment, contraception, or alcohol, but it has condemned abortion as a sin, except in rare circumstances that the mother's life is in danger, and euthanasia. Likewise, the Synod has opposed human cloning that may destroy embryos. It has also declared racism sinful and homosexuality as "intrinsically sinful," but the Synod has reached out to minister to lesbians and gays.[51]

### Assemblies of God

The Assemblies of God (USA), with headquarters in Springfield, Missouri, is the 10th largest denomination in the United States, with over 12,200 churches and around 2.7 million constituents. Of the churches, 8,640 are characterized as white; 2,092 as Hispanic; 471 as Asian/Pacific Islander; and 269 as African American. Both men and women may be ordained into the ministry, but males outnumber females almost five to one.[52] The Assemblies of God is the largest group to believe in speaking in tongues, a phenomenon that occurs, its adherents claim, when people are baptized in the Holy Spirit. This Pentecostal church traces its origin to the revivalism that swept the United States at the end of the nineteenth and beginning of the twentieth centuries, and more specifically to a prayer meeting in Topeka, Kansas, on January 1, 1901. The Pentecostal movement spread to California from Kansas, Missouri, and Texas. At the Azusa Street Mission in Los Angeles, a three-year revival meeting helped to put Pentecostalism on the map, and in 1914, a group of preachers and lay people met in Arkansas to discuss forming a fellowship of spirit-baptized believers. Enthusiastic religion characterized by speaking in tongues was anathema to mainline Protestant churches as well as Fundamentalists and most evangelical churches. The General Council of the Assemblies of God was formed to unite the individual churches, which would remain self-governing, and further their beliefs. In 1916, the council approved a Statement of Fundamental Truths.

Recognizing the Trinity and the scriptures as divinely inspired, the Fundamental Truths declare belief in the humanity and divinity of Jesus Christ and mankind's willing sin, which ushered in evil and physical and spiritual death. There are four cardinal doctrines: that salvation will restore fellowship with God to all who accept Christ's offer for forgiveness; that baptism, which follows salvation, empowers people for witnessing and service; that divine healing of the sick is a privilege made available to Christians by Christ's death; and that Jesus Christ will rapture his church before he comes again to rule the earth for 1,000 years. The unrepentant will spend eternity in a lake of fire. In addition, the members of the Assemblies of God, who, like the members of many other Protestant denominations, recognize the ordinances of water baptism and Holy Communion, believe that speaking in tongues is the initial physical evidence of baptism in the Holy Spirit and that their salvation requires them to evangelize the world.

Today, the Assemblies of God church operates 19 Bible and liberal arts colleges and a seminary in the United States. The Assemblies' emphasis on world evangelization, however, has created a denomination, originally American, that has more adherents outside the United States than inside it. The church counts 236,022 churches in 191 countries, with 1,891 international Bible schools and 48 million overseas members. The Assemblies of God has taken positions on a number of issues. True believers cannot be possessed by demons because the devil is to them an external force that must be fought. Abortion and euthanasia violate the sanctity of human life. Alcohol, even in moderation, is "providing Satan an opening." Because the Bible identifies God as the creator, evolution is not possible.[53]

### The Episcopal Church

What was originally the Church of England, the Episcopal Church came to America with English colonists and became established as the church of high society. With the end of the American Revolution, it adopted the name Protestant Episcopal Church in 1783 and, in 1967, the Episcopal Church. During the last half of the nineteenth century, the Church expanded beyond its colonial roots on the Atlantic coast and spread through the country. Since the 1950s, however, membership has dwindled to 2.46 million.[54] The Episcopal Church, a member of the Anglican Union, has 7,200 parishes and missions and 17,209 clergy. There are nine Episcopalian colleges in the United States.[55] A presiding bishop is elected every nine years and presides over the House of Bishops. A General Convention is held every three years, in which deputations from dioceses and the House of Bishops make policy and worship decisions.[56]

Some 72 million Anglicans around the world are united in the use of the *Book of Common Prayer,* which blends the twin traditions of Anglicanism in the Reformation and Roman Catholicism. Styles of worship may differ significantly from one church to another, but liturgies through the *Book of Common Prayer* share a common feel. Baptism and the Holy Eucharist are recognized as sacraments. The other sacraments recognized by Roman Catholics—confirmation, ordination, matrimony, reconciliation, and unction—are considered means of grace, but not necessary. Episcopalians have insisted that worship be held in native languages, and they believe that the Bible should be interpreted in light of tradition and reason. In order words, historical criticism of the Bible may lead to new understandings; the Bible is not inerrant in all respects.

The Episcopal Church has long been active in promoting social justice and peace through direct action and advocacy. Through its ministries, the Church has worked against racism, for the protection of the environment, for peace in the Middle East, and for criminal justice. It has reached out to victims of AIDS. The Episcopal Church has passed official resolutions opposing the preemptive use of nuclear weapons, the infringement of the rights of minorities and immigrants, and the unilateral invasion of Iraq. It has supported nuclear disarmament, international debt relief, poverty programs, respect for religious diversity, and the millennium development goals of the United Nations.[57]

The openness of the Episcopal Church to ecumenism—any baptized person may receive communion (the Eucharist) in an Episcopal Church—and to new biblical interpretations can lead the Church in new directions. In 1976, the Church's General Convention approved the ordination of women into the priesthood, which meant that women could become bishops. By 2005, there were 2,033 active and employed ordained women priests and 1,329 deacons. Since 1989, 12 women have been ordained as bishops. Ordaining women was one thing, but the ordination of homosexuals would prove another. In 1979, the General Convention disapproved of ordaining homosexuals, yet a bishop went on and did so in 1989 with no final consequence. In 2003, an overtly practicing gay man was ordained bishop of the diocese of New Hampshire and affirmed by the General Convention. This would have consequences that are still to be played out in full.

Even before the ordination of the gay bishop, schism was fomenting. In 1996, dissidents formed the American Anglican Council with the goal of "proclaiming the Biblical and orthodox faith" by advocating for and providing assistance to those who want to remain Anglicans but disagree with the progressive religion that, they aver, is being preached by the Episcopal Church. The council claims that the real issue is not homosexuality, blessing homosexual unions, or even the ordaining of homosexuals, although its literature repeatedly returns to those subjects, but rather an understanding of Jesus Christ and revisionist interpretations of the Bible. The acceptance of pluralism by these revisionists has made every religion the same, thereby denying biblical truth and giving birth to an "anything is OK" theology and lifestyle. This has all led, of course, to a dissolute Episcopalian youth. The council points to a study that found that only 70 percent of young Episcopalians believe in God; 40 percent find faith important in their daily lives; 60 percent think morality is relative; and 45 percent think adults are hypocrites. Early in 2004, a movement called the Anglican Communion Network was created. Its plan is to become the new biblically based American Anglican church recognized by the Anglican Union, thus leaving the Episcopal Church in schism. In fact, 22 of the 38 provinces in the Anglican Union have declared the Episcopal Church in broken union.[58] Local Episcopal churches around the country have been divided. Some have left the Episcopal Church and, calling themselves Anglicans, rather than Episcopalians, allied themselves with conservative African bishops who welcome their orthodoxy and their intention to remain in the Anglican Union.

### Churches of Christ

The Churches of Christ, with 1.5 million members in the United States, emerged out of America's Second Great Awakening, which commenced at the beginning of the nineteenth century, and the so-called Restoration movement that resulted. While its greatest numbers of American members are in the South, particularly in Texas, Tennessee, Alabama, and Arkansas, there are

Churches of Christ in all 50 states and in 109 other nations. Worldwide, the Churches of Christ claims 2.5–3 million adherents in 20,000 congregations.

The message of the Restoration movement was that Christ's true church needed to be restored to its original foundation: a church based not on denominational doctrine, but on simple Christianity; a church based squarely on the Bible and only the Bible; a church that promoted the practices of simple New Testament Christianity. Thus the Churches of Christ is not a denomination, but a group of independent, self-governing churches that may coordinate some social works but has no trappings of denomination such as governing boards, annual conventions, or publications. The congregations of the Churches of Christ believe their church is Christ's church.

Becoming a Christian through hearing the Gospel, repenting, accepting Christ, and baptism by immersion makes a person a member of the church. The Churches of Christ believe that faith can come to anyone through listening to the word of the Lord; there is no such thing as God's having predestined people to heaven or hell. The task of the church is to teach the New Testament "without modification" to lead people to Christ. The creed of the Churches of Christ is the New Testament. The individual churches elect elders from their male membership to govern themselves. They also select deacons. Worship is centered on the practices of the first-century church: "singing, praying, preaching, giving, and eating the Lord's Supper." Some congregations, the so-called noninstrumental churches, employ no musical instruments in the singing because the New Testament makes no mention of instruments in liturgical worship. The Lord's Supper is observed each Sunday.[59]

### Jehovah's Witnesses

Jehovah's Witnesses grew out of a Bible study group in Allegheny, Pennsylvania, led by Charles Taze Russell. In 1879, the first issue of *Zion's Watch Tower and Herald of Christ's Presence* was published, and two years later, the Zion's Watch Tower Tract Society was formed, which later took its current name, the Watch Tower Bible and Tract Society. The members of the society adopted the name Jehovah's Witnesses in 1931.

Most American households have been visited at least once by the Witnesses' home missionaries, dressed in plain black pants and white shirts. They go door to door through neighborhoods to distribute the society's tracts and publications with the hope of interesting people in Bible study with them. This particular technique brought the Witnesses to the U.S. Supreme Court, which ruled in their favor. The Witnesses have no clergy class or special titles. Their magazines *The Watch Tower* and *Awake!* continue to be primary communication tools, but the Witnesses have also made extensive use of newspaper, radio, and television to evangelize. While they now claim some 90,000 congregations worldwide, it is estimated there are about 1.8 million Jehovah's Witnesses in the United States.

Jehovah, the Witnesses' name for God, had a purpose in all created things. God's creation reflects God's glory, and God created the earth so it could be inhabited, the sin of Adam and Eve notwithstanding. The act of creation precludes any belief in human evolution. Witnesses believe that souls die with physical death, but through the sacrifice of Jesus Christ, they will be resurrected. (Contrary to popular thinking, Jehovah's Witnesses are Christians, who believe Christ is the son of God, but inferior to him.) Witnesses believe further that the end of the world as we know it is near, and Christ, who rose from the dead "as an immortal spirit person," will rule the earth in an ideal, peaceful, and righteous kingdom. Because God created the earth with a purpose, the earth will not be destroyed or depopulated, but the "wicked will be eternally destroyed," and those who God approves will live forever. Death, the punishment for original sin, will be no longer. However, only 144,000, a number biblically wrought, who are born again will "go to heaven and rule with Christ."

Clearly Witnesses believe that the Bible is "God's Word and is truth." Good Witnesses are expected to pray only to Jehovah through Christ, use no images in worship, keep separate from the world and avoid ecumenical movements, and obey laws that do not conflict with God's laws. They are also expected to act in a biblically moral way, serve God through the example set by Christ, and publicly testify to biblical truth. Baptism by complete immersion is considered a symbol of dedication. Perhaps the Witnesses' most controversial belief, rendered from scripture, is that "taking blood into body through mouth or veins violates God's laws." A good Jehovah's Witness would not receive a transfusion of another person's blood.[60]

### Judaism

Eighty-five percent of the 5.2 million Jews in the U.S. population were born in the United States. Of those born outside the United States, 44 percent migrated from the former Soviet Union. The Jewish population is not uniformly located around the country. Some 43 percent live in the Northeast, 22 percent in the South, 22 percent in the West, and only 13 percent in the Midwest. Jewish adults are generally better educated (55% have at least bachelor's degrees vs. 28% in the total population) and have a higher median annual household income ($50,000 vs. $42,000 in the total population) than the general population. Still, 19 percent of Jewish households classify as low income ($25,000 a year or less). Thirty-five percent of American Jews identify themselves as Reform; 26 percent as Conservative; 20 percent secular (not attending temple or synagogue); 10% orthodox (containing many sects); and 9 percent all other.[61]

As non-Christians in a Christian country, Jews in the United States have been subjected to discrimination and prejudice. Anti-Semitism has long been a feature of right-wing American nativism and has reared its head in the White House (President Richard Nixon and evangelist Billy Graham on tape in 1972 agreeing that Jews have a stranglehold on media), among business leaders (Henry Ford was openly anti-Semitic), in the media (Father Charles Coughlin, Catholic priest and radio personality of the 1930s and 1940s, was finally suppressed for his rabid anti-Jewish views), and in presidential and state elections (David Duke, former Grand Wizard of the Ku Klux Klan, ran for various offices). The truth is that these cultural representatives gave voice to a common and persistent American prejudice against Jews based on the old Shylock stereotype.

Just as religious freedom in America opened Christianity, particularly Protestantism, to a tremendous diversity of theological and religious beliefs and practices, Judaism, too, was transformed by the American experience. In 1885, a group of rabbis meeting in Pittsburgh, Pennsylvania, declared the principles that would govern Reform Judaism, the movement they were undertaking. Recognizing the so-called God-idea as a central truth, the Bible as "the most potent instrument of religious and moral instruction," the rabbis went on to discard Mosaic Law other than moral law because it did not speak to modern times. Likewise, they discarded orthodox dietary laws, priestly purity, and traditional dress. Reform Judaism would be "no longer a nation, but a religious community." They wanted Judaism to be "a "progressive religion" that made every attempt to be in accord with reason as it strove for truth, justice, and peace. Reform Jews would be duty bound to involvement in social issues and reach out beyond Judaism to welcome converts.[62] Reform Judaism, which affirmed its commitment to the equality of men and women by ordaining women as rabbis and investing women cantors and welcoming gays and homosexuals into Jewish life, is now the largest Jewish movement in the United States, with 1.5 million members and over 900 congregations. The Central Conference of American Rabbis has been active since its inception in 1889 in adopting hundreds of resolutions on social issues, including civil and minority rights, discrimination, and world peace. The Conference stands for a woman's right to choose abortion but is against abortion on demand as well as any legal restrictions on abortion. It has supported gay and lesbian civil marriage and the rights of homosexual rabbis to fulfill their vocations.

In reaction to the modernizing tendencies of Reform Judaism, the United Synagogue of Conservative Judaism was founded in 1913. Now with 760 affiliated synagogues in North America, the Conservative movement has tried

A boy reading the Torah during his bar mitzvah. Corbis.

to steer a midway between Reform and orthodoxy by maintaining historical continuity with Jewish tradition. This includes, among other things, observing biblical dietary restrictions, loyalty to the Torah, and using Hebrew as the language of worship.[63]

## Islam

The number of Muslims in the United States is the subject of some debate. Estimates vary from around 1 million to 6.5 million. The best guess is that there are a bit fewer than 2 million, more than half of whom were born in the United States to immigrant families, some as long as three generations ago.[64] Turmoil at home brought Muslim immigrants to America: the breakup of the Ottoman Empire, the aftermath of World Wars I and II, civil war in Lebanon, and revolution in Iran. Changes in U.S. immigration policy brought new waves of Muslims to America from Africa and Asia. What is known is that there are 1,209 mosques in the United States, and 62 percent of them were founded after 1980. California has 227 mosques, New York has 140, and New Jersey has 86, but there are mosques spread across the country. America's oldest mosque is located in Cedar Rapids, Iowa. While only 7 percent of mosques are attended by a single ethnic group, many began as ethnic places of worship. A third of them were South Asian in origin; 30 percent, African American; and 25 percent, Arab. Only 1.6 percent were white American. Over 20 percent of the mosques operate full-time schools. Some 71 percent of American Muslims believe that the Koran should be interpreted in light of modern experience, and 70 percent believe strongly that they should be involved participants in American institutions and democracy.[65]

Muslims, like Jews, have been misunderstood and ostracized as non-Christians in the United States. There is a strange confusion in American culture that all Muslims, save for indigenous African American Muslims, are Arabs, which, of course, is not true. In part because of a lack of knowledge about Islam, Americans tend to make Muslims victims of stereotyping, and some conflate the radical Islam of terrorists with mainline Islam. The stereotype is an Arab Muslim, derisively referred to as a rag head. This stereotype melds the Sunnis, Shi'ites, and all other varieties and nationalities of Muslims in America into the mistaken single category of "Arabs." Hate crimes against Arabs, whether Muslims or not, rose after the September 11, 2001, terrorist attacks on New York and Washington, D.C. Yet American Muslims, like American Jews, have assimilated well into American life and adopted American lifestyles. The have found that Islam is in no way at odds with American culture and democracy.

### The Nation of Islam

The Nation of Islam (NOI), sometimes referred to as the black Muslims, publishes no membership numbers, but is believed to have between 50,000 and 100,000 members. While its numbers may be small, its influence is not. Minister Louis Farrakhan, leader of the NOI, has quite remarkably been the force behind the Million Man March on Washington, D.C., in 1995 and the Million Family March in 2000, also in Washington. With these marches, Farrakhan wanted to establish positive public images of African Americans and demonstrate the principles of atonement, reconciliation, and responsibility in the search for black empowerment and family stability.

Farrakhan, a fiery speaker given to controversy, resurrected the teachings of Wallace D. Fard (Wallace Fard Muhammad). Fard disdained white men's religion—Christianity—started a mosque in 1930 in Detroit, Michigan; and claimed his mission in life was to lead the original members of the tribe of Shabazz from the lost nation of Asia, who had been captured and placed into slavery in America, down the road of independence into a higher civilization. Elijah Muhammad, to whom Fard revealed himself as the Mahdi, or messiah of Islam, ruled the NOI from 1935 until his death in 1975. During his rule, civil rights figure Malcolm X joined the NOI but left to form his own group. Elijah Muhammad's son took over NOI leadership in 1975, abandoned the

Minister Louis Farrakhan of the Nation of Islam religion is known for his charisma and passionate speeches. © AP Photo/Carlos Osorio.

doctrine that Fard was the long-expected Mahdi, and eventually took his movement back into traditional Islam. In 1978, Farrakhan reestablished the NOI and the traditions of Fard and Elijah Muhammad.

The NOI claims to have mosques and study groups in 120 cities in the United States, Europe, and the Caribbean. It also has missions in South Africa and Ghana. The members of NOI believe in one God, Allah; in the Koran; in the writings of all God's prophets; and in the truth of the Bible. The Bible, however, has been tampered with and filled with untruths. It is thus in need of new interpretation. They believe that judgment will come, but not in the resurrection of the dead; rather, it will come in mental resurrection, and Allah's chosen people will be resurrected first. NOI members believe in justice for all and in equality, but equality is not possible between slave masters and freed slaves. Integration is a deception. Thus African Americans and whites need to be separated, and African Americans need to identify themselves with names that do not recall their former masters' names. The NOI stands firmly against its members' participation in war as good Muslims, noting that Muslims should not be forced to fight in America's wars because they have nothing for which to fight.

The NOI has a concerted social program based on its religious beliefs. The Muslim Program calls for freedom, equal justice, and equality of opportunity.

Descendants of former slaves should be allowed to establish their own separate state or territory in North America or elsewhere, and the former masters should underwrite that state or territory for up to 25 years or until self-sufficiency can be established. African Americans should be able to vote on whether they want to go to the separated state or remain where they are. Muslims in federal prisons and African American men and women sentenced to death should be freed from prison. Police brutality and mob attacks against African Americans must end, and African Americans need the protection of courts. African Americans should not have to live in poor housing conditions or be dependent on charity. African Americans should be exempt from all taxation. Muslims want an educational system that is equal, with boys and girls separated, and African American pupils should have African American teachers. Finally, the NOI calls for the prohibition of race mixing through intermarriage.

The Nation of Islam also calls itself the Nation of Peace and the fulfillment of the Old Testament promise to free the enslaved. NOI members do not carry firearms; the Brotherhood of Islam precludes aggression. Black Muslims acknowledge their respect for the laws of the United States. They believe in respect for others, good manners, and clean living. They forsake alcohol, smoking, or the abuse of any substance that would prohibit a healthy lifestyle. They dress modestly. Farrakhan's incendiary rhetoric, replete with the bombastic delivery of occasionally outrageous opinion, however, does not lend the NOI the image of peacefulness. Indeed, its message of hope for the descendants of black slaves—a separate state made up exclusively of blacks—runs against the prevailing American efforts toward total integration of all peoples into the fabric of American society. Progressive Americans want to be color-blind, and the laws passed during and after the civil rights movement of the 1960s guarantee, as much as laws can, that at least before the law, race may never be the basis of any kind of discrimination.[66]

### Itinerant Preachers, Televangelists, and Nondenominational Churches

There is no accurate count of how many local churches or houses of worship there are in the United States. Anyone can start a church anywhere, and there is no need for it to be allied with a religious denomination. Freedom of religion and free speech provide a superior foundation for a variety of religious expression.

Itinerant preachers have been important players in American history and culture. They are responsible for the waves of evangelical awakenings that have periodically ripped through America since the 1730s and continue until today. They are the ones who once pitched their revival tents and preached the Bible to all who would listen. They converted slaves to Christianity in the South and spread an enthusiastic religion of the heart throughout the land. Some were charlatans who found personal uses for the collection offerings. Most were God-fearing men on a mission.

Revivals remain part of American life, but they now are more likely to take place in sports stadiums than in tents. The Reverend Billy Graham has been America's most admired itinerant preacher since he emerged out of the Youth for Christ movement in the 1940s. He set up the Billy Graham Evangelistic Association to keep him free of any hint of financial scandal. He used media effectively, first through a weekly radio show, "The Hour of Decision," which was also televised in the early 1950s, and then through tapes, magazines, books, and films. Most Americans know him, however, as the preacher who set up so-called crusades in cities all over the world, many of which were televised, to evangelize the globe with the simple biblical message that repentance and acceptance of Christ into your heart will bring eternal salvation. Graham ingratiated himself with U.S. presidents after his first attempt with Harry Truman failed. Whenever a president after Truman was in some kind of crisis, Graham seemed to be invited to the White House. Presidents knew that in the public mind, association with Graham gave a kind of blessing and assurance that everything was right with God.

Although Graham was very much a feature of the Cold War, as he patriotically stood up for American, Christian values against the godlessness of Communism, he favored reconciliation, rather than confrontation. He rejected the agenda of the Religious Right for active political involvement, but Graham remains a recognized leader of evangelical Protestant Christianity.[67]

Itinerant preachers do not have to pitch tents to preach anymore; they can buy a television station. That is what Pat Robertson did in 1960 when he purchased a little station in Virginia and called his operation the Christian Broadcasting Network (CBN). This was the birth of Christian television broadcasting in the United States. In 1977, Robertson founded CBN University, now called Regents University. CBN now claims to provide Christian programming by cable and satellite to around 200 countries. A prayer line is open all day and night. *The 700 Club,* a show featuring Robertson's Christian commentary on news issues, has been on the air since 1966.[68] Never far from controversy, in 2002, he called Islam an unpeaceful religion bent on domination and destruction. In 2003, he suggested that a nuclear device should be used to obliterate the U.S. Department of State. He made apologies in 2005 for saying that Hugo Chavez, the president of Venezuela, should be assassinated and for his prophecy of death and destruction for the town of Dover, Pennsylvania, where creationist members of a school board were thrown out and replaced with proevolution advocates. In 2006, Robertson again made an apology, this time to Ariel Sharon's son, for saying that the former Israeli premier's cerebral hemorrhage was God's retribution for his division of Israel.

Evangelists Paul and Jan Crouch founded the Trinity Broadcasting Network (TBN) in 1973. TBN advertises itself as "the world's largest Christian television network," reaching every major continent through 47 satellites and 12,460 television and cable affiliates. In the United States, TBN is also the largest religious network, with 6,459 cable affiliates, 67.7 million cable and satellite subscribers, and 420 affiliated broadcast stations. TBN reaches over 92 million American households. According to TBN, its viewers tune in because they possess the core values of "faith in God," "love of family," and "patriotic pride." These are the values "that have been attacked and ridiculed by our pop culture and news and entertainment media." TBN produces original Christian programming and even live coverage of Christian events. There are channels for children ("completely free of the violence and crude humor" found elsewhere and containing the "best moral and Biblical teachings"), youths, and TBN Enlace USA for the Hispanic community. The Crouches have a Christian chat show, *Praise the Lord,* on which guests share their faith.[69]

TBN viewers can also watch church services on the Church Channel and experience God's healing powers on the Healing Channel. Some evangelists appear regularly on their own shows. Dr. Jack Van Impe, convinced by Bible prophecy that the Second Coming of Christ is immanent, has charted out the future in a prophecy chart and even produced a Middle East invasion map so believers can follow what the Bible says will happen soon. Charismatics Kenneth and Gloria Copeland offer Bible-based financial advice. Even better, evangelists Marilyn Hickey and her daughter Sarah Bowling have a Miracle Provision afghan with all the various names of God, which, for an offering of $149 or more, they have anointed so that it will bring the recipient a miraculous cure of financial problems. Benny Hinn heals the sick by his anointings and may speak in tongues. Dr. Kreflo A. Dollar preaches and lives the gospel of prosperity. Charismatic author and televangelist Joyce Meyer wants to pray and take action against all the ungodliness that has crept into American life.[70] Televangelism helps keeps religion in the public domain at all times. Channel surfers cannot click their remote controls fast enough to miss a religion program with an evangelical message. Religious television programming is part of most cable and satellite packages.

Most itinerant preachers are not concerned with religious denomination; they are concerned with personal salvation. No nondenominational church could be more emblematic of the growth of all-American Evangelical Protestantism than the Saddleback Church in Lake Forest, California, which is located in suburban, Republican south Orange County. Pastor Rick Warren and his wife arrived there in 1979 knowing no one and determined to start a church. From humble beginnings, Saddleback is now a megachurch with more than 20,000 members. Warren claims that 80,000 names are on the rolls. Warren is a pastoral Horatio Alger, pull yourself up by your own bootstraps story. His 1995 book *The Purpose Driven Church* focused on five biblical purposes that led to his church's success: worship, fellowship, discipleship, ministry, and evangelism. His later best-selling book *The Purpose-Driven Life* took this message to a personal level and is used as a devotional, self-improvement text for the small worship and study groups that propel the church's mission forward. Perhaps Warren's greatest insight into American evangelicalism is that conversion must remain an intensely personal phenomenon. Going to church on the weekend is not conversion—worship and fellowship follow conversion.[71]

The beliefs espoused at the nondenominational Saddleback Church are straightforward. There is one triune God. Sin is an attitude that separates God from mankind. Heaven and hell are eternally real. Jesus Christ suffered and died for the sins of mankind and arose from the dead. No amount of self-improvement or good works can save a person because salvation is a gift from

Pastor Rick Warren, author of *The Purpose-Driven Life,* sits in his mega-church in Saddleback, California. © AP Photo/Chris Carlson.

God that comes with faith in Jesus Christ, and salvation is maintained by grace, not by any special human effort. The Holy Spirit guides good Christians through life, just as the Holy Spirit inspired the Bible, the supreme source of unerring truth.[72]

This kind of unvarnished theology—God, sin, personal salvation, heaven—appeals to many Americans' sense of individual power and supremacy, whether before the law, before God, or within society. It is in stark contrast to religions like Roman Catholicism, Judaism, and Islam, which emphasize the good of the faith community over any one individual and have layers of complicated theological traditions. Yet the middle-of-the-road evangelicalism of the Saddleback Church is not simply that old-time religion. Contrary to evangelical tradition, the members of Saddleback give generously to and become involved in social causes, from AIDS to assistance for tsunami victims. The church has some 200 ministries.

The old stereotype of an evangelical worship service as dull Bible-thumping fire and brimstone sermonizing, as depicted in Hollywood films, does not exist at the Saddleback megachurch. In fact, the church has developed venues for various tastes in worship. The main service has a full band. The Praise venue features a gospel choir. The OverDrive venue has rock 'n' roll. El Encuentro features music in Spanish. The Traditions venue has favorite old songs and hymns, along with a videocast on a large screen. The Ohana venue presents island music with "hospitality and hugs," and members can learn worship "through signing or hula." The Elevation venue is for singles and has live music. The Country venue is "country music, boots, and buckles" with a message—line dancing follows the service.[73]

## OTHER RELIGIOUS THOUGHT IN AMERICA

Two religious groups not native to America have maintained a strong and constant voice for peace. Mennonites, who came out of the Anabaptist tradition in Europe and were persecuted there for their beliefs, found a safe home in America in the late seventeenth century. Although Mennonite groups, whose core population remains in Pennsylvania and spread westward to Missouri, differ on various doctrinal issues, they strive to be Christ-centered in every aspect of their lives, accept the Bible as inspired by God, and baptize only adults who have declared their faith in Jesus Christ. Most significantly from a cultural viewpoint, many of the 320,000 Mennonites in America have been active in protesting military objectives, objecting to defense budgets, and supporting conscientious objectors to military service.[74] The Religious Society of Friends (Quakers), who number only about 93,000 in the United States, has likewise been influential in protesting war and furthering peace movements.

An Amish farmer working on his farm with his horse-drawn plow. Corbis.

The Amish, who number around 128,000, share the Anabaptist traditions and beliefs in baptism and peace. Amish do not serve in the military. The Amish, however, choose to have no voice in national affairs, preferring to separate themselves from the modern world. The Amish have spread out from Pennsylvania to Ohio, to Indiana, and to some small degree westward from there. The Old Order Amish continue to speak a dialect of Swiss-intonated German found nowhere else because their language has developed in a closed community. Agrarian communities, the Amish elect their own religious leaders. They have no churches; they meet in homes. Local congregations make determinations on how they will relate to the modern world. Some congregations, for example, may permit an outer layer of rubber on a buggy wheel; others may not. The strictest of them dress plainly, use no electricity, do not own automobiles, and forego the frills of curtains on windows of their homes. It is a strange irony that tourists beg Amish for photographs of them standing next to their horses and buggies, not understanding that the Amish consider photographs graven images.

Old traditions of Christianity could be protected in America, but American creativity could also take Christianity into new territory. In the first part of the twentieth century, snake handling began showing up in Appalachia at the Church of God with Signs Following. There are at most about 2,000 members of this Pentecostal, literally interpreted Bible-based church, who believe that once filled with the Holy Spirit after repentance, salvation, and leading a Christian life, they can follow the signs. The signs may include serpent handling as well as drinking poison and casting out demons.[75]

The Unitarian Universalist Association, which claims about 158,000 members, has taken a different tack. Formed in 1961, Unitarians and Universalists believe that a modern understanding of human nature and Jesus Christ combined with the knowledge that a good God wants salvation for everyone means that anyone, believers of any faith and atheists alike, should be welcomed into the church. Unitarian universalism is fundamentally based on humanism. Proud of its historically liberal views, the association has worked to operationalize the feminist agenda in the church; stood for rights for gays, lesbians, and bisexuals; and ordained gay and lesbian clergy.[76]

The Church of Christ, Scientist, was the creation of Mary Baker Eddy in 1879. In her 1875 book *Science and Health with Key to the Scripture,* she claimed to have discovered the predictable and reproducible science of Jesus Christ's healing power. The Bible and Eddy's book are the twin foundations of the Church's beliefs. Christian Science reading rooms dot the country and the world, where people can go to understand this science of religion. With no ordained clergy, Baker hoped to restore the primitive Christian church and a better world based on a fuller understanding of God.[77]

## RELIGION AND POLITICS

While it may have been true at one time that religious beliefs could be equated with certain political beliefs, this certainly is no longer the case. A broad spectrum of sociopolitical and moral opinion has developed even within individual denominations. On the hot-button issues of abortion and gay rights, for example, there is clear division. Where there is some coalition of values, however, is across denominational lines. Those who consider themselves religious conservatives no matter the denomination might agree that abortion should be outlawed and gay rights should not be recognized, whereas those who consider themselves moderates or liberals may not.[78]

Fifty-one percent of Americans believe that churches should speak out on social and political issues against 44 percent who think they should not. Among white evangelicals and African American Protestants, however, 67 percent favor churches taking such positions. Forty-five percent of the population finds that conservative Christians have exceeded an acceptable boundary in attempting to impose their beliefs on the country, but an equal percentage say they have not. Thirty-nine percent of Americans think political leaders do not speak enough about their religious convictions, but 26 percent think they express them too much. A solid 66 percent of all Americans support govern-ment funding to churches for social services. Only 33 percent oppose it.[79] Clearly Americans are divided on the role of religion in public society and politics, even though they appreciate the good works performed by churches through their charitable activities. Indeed, many Americans hold their per-sonal religious views closely and would not consider imposing their beliefs on anyone else. To some Americans, however, the kingdom of God is at hand, and America is not prepared.

The so-called new Religious Right is a multidenominational (and nonde-nominational) group of like-minded traditionalists. They have banded to-gether to push a political agenda of so-called old-fashioned American values and overturn what they see as a secular, Godless social movement that is ruining American culture. The Religious Right is overtly political, allied with and energized by the Republican Party, and has sought to interpret Ameri-can history as well as foresee America's future in terms of biblical prophecy. Patriotism (called *nationalism* when applied to other nations) must, there-fore, be part and parcel of the believers' arsenal. These traditionalists have, then, both the patriotic and the moral duty to act against perceived transgres-sions against traditional American values and beliefs. These efforts take many turns. When a large corporation was found to have advertised its products in a gay magazine, an instant boycott of all the corporation's products was announced. The corporation's first reaction was to pull the ads, but it finally went ahead with them. When President George W. Bush's Christmas card favored the inclusive phrase *Happy Holidays,* rather than *Merry Christmas,* he was accused of taking God out of Christmas.

Through the efforts of the Religious Right, America is the only Western na-tion where the teaching of evolution is contested. Right-wing religious groups have, in some cases, taken over public school boards to press for the con-comitant teaching of the theory of intelligent design. Scientists contend that this is no theory at all, for it has no scientific basis; rather, it is another way for conservative religious people to teach the biblical creation story in public schools. The frustration of the Religious Right is understandable. Series of lawsuits have taken God out of the schools in the effort to maintain religious freedom defined as church-state separation. Religion may not be taught in the schools, and even the daily recitation of the Pledge of Allegiance to the flag, which declares "one nation, under God," is considered a violation of the sepa-ration principle. To the Religious Right, whose universe of truth is the Bible, religion and public life cannot be separated. How can they be asked to violate their beliefs by sending their children to a Godless public school? The more important question, however, is how a pluralistic American society will deal with a crusading religious movement with a political agenda.

There may be a clue in the debate over evolution. Seventy-eight percent of Americans believe life on earth to be God's creation. Forty-eight percent believe life has evolved, but 42 percent think God created it as now found from the beginning of time. Curiously, however, 64 percent of Americans believe intelligent design (creationism) should be taught alongside with evolution. Even 32 percent of creationists agreed.[80] This would seem to indicate the desire of a majority of Americans to avoid conflict and end the debate with a good business-type negotiation that is inclusive, rather than divisive. This is the pragmatic way Americans solve problems.

Fundamentalists are frequently portrayed as hotheaded lunatics spurting out Bible verses while banging on the Good Book. In real everyday life, this is not so. There is a certain innocence and honesty to all of this. When a good Christian teacher at a small public school in a tiny Tennessee mountain town asked a Jewish woman if her daughter could play Mary in the Christmas pageant since Mary was Jewish, too, she clearly betrayed a complete lack of understanding of the pluralistic society America has become. She did not and could not understand what it meant to be Jewish or why it might be difficult for a little Jewish girl to go to temple as the mother of Jesus Christ. Americans like this well-intended teacher are not unusual in this predominantly Christian nation.

## THE SOCIAL ROLE OF CHURCHES

Churches play a vital role in American society. They are woven into the fabric of service organizations that tend to special social needs. Frequently referred to as faith-based communities, perhaps in an attempt to discharge the use of more obvious religious language that would openly test the church-state relationship, churches are very much involved in medical care through hospitals, education from the youngest age through graduate school, and the promotion of social justice through charitable activities.

Catholic Charities, for example, traces its beginnings to New Orleans in 1727, when an order of nuns opened an orphanage. Today, it serves over 7 million people with annual resources of nearly $3 billion, 60 percent of which is derived from government. Catholic Charities employs around 50,000 staff members and coordinates the work of nearly 200,000 volunteers through 137 agencies and their 1,341 branches and affiliates. More than 4.5 million people benefit from its food service operations, which include food banks, soup kitchens, and home-delivered meals. More than 3 million people, including many at-risk persons, receive social support and neighborhood services as well as health-related and educational enrichment services. Thousands more receive services designed to strengthen families, including counseling, mental health, addiction, refugee, pregnancy, and adoption services. Catholic Charities also provides housing services, from temporary shelters and supervised living to permanent housing, and basic needs services to the poorest of the poor such as assistance with clothing, utility bills, finances, and medication.[81]

One of President George W. Bush's first acts as president was to sign Executive Order no. 13199, which established the White House Office of Faith-based and Community Initiatives. The office was created to identify and eliminate any barriers that might impede faith-based and community organizations (FBCOs) from participating in federal grants and to pursue legislation to prevent discrimination against FBCOs by extending charitable choice provisions, to protect the religious freedom of the FBCOs, and to maintain the religious hiring rights of the FBCOS.[82] President Bush was named America's most influential Christian in a list of 50 owing in great part to setting up this office in 2001.[83]

There are now Centers for Faith-based and Community Initiatives in 11 federal agencies, including Homeland Security. The White House has claimed success in this venture by reporting that in the federal government's 2005 fiscal year, faith-based organizations (FBOs) received more than $2.1 billion in grants from seven government agencies and that FBOs are successfully winning more grant money in the competition for funding. From the administration's point of view, this initiative has expanded the choices of people in need. There were also legislative and judicial triumphs for the program. The Deficit Reduction Act of 2005 extended the charitable choice provision (FBOs providing social services do not have to change their religious identities or hiring policies) another five years and added to new grant programs to be covered under the provision: a healthy marriages program and a responsible fatherhood program. During 2005, federal courts held that Americorps (a federally sponsored youth volunteer program) grant winners could teach religious as well as secular subjects in religiously affiliated schools and that funding for social services does not make an FBO a quasi-governmental organization, thus leaving them completely autonomous in their hiring decisions.[84]

It appears that as America experiences this new awakening of evangelical fervor, the definition of the separation of church and state is being revised. Neither the churches, which find their social works as well as some of their beliefs furthered by government funding (FBOs have received federal funds to fight HIV/AIDS through abstinence programs), nor the American people as a whole want to return to the notion of a strict separation. Americans agree that religious organizations make society a better place by aiding the less fortunate. The Religious Right had long argued that separation did not have to make the state godless—the protector of secularism. Thus the state can advocate for putting God (churches) back into American life. What the state simply may not do, however, is regulate what anyone believes.

## NOTES

1. Philip Hamburger, *Separation of Church and State* (Cambridge, MA: Harvard University Press, 2002), 3, 491–92.

2. "Largest Religious Groups in the United States of America," http://www.adherents.com.

3. National Council of Churches, *2006 Yearbook of American and Canadian Churches* (Nashville: Abingdon Press, 2007).

4. William Martin, *With God on Our Side: The Rise of the Religious Right in America* (New York: Broadway Books, 1996), 10–11.

5. United States Conference of Catholic Bishops, Office of Media Relations, "Catholic Information Project: The Catholic Church in America—Meeting Real Needs in Your Neighborhood," http://www.usccb.org.

6. Ibid.

7. Ibid.

8. Mary L. Gautier, "Lay Catholics Firmly Committed to Parish Life," *National Catholic Reporter,* September 30, 2005.

9. Ibid.

10. CBS News Polls, "U.S. Catholics Want Change," CBS News, Special Report, http://www.cbsnews.com.

11. Gautier, "Lay Catholics."

12. United States Conference of Catholic Bishops, Priestly Life and Ministry, "The Study of the Impact of Fewer Priests on the Pastoral Ministry," Executive Summary, June 2000, http://www.usccb.org.

13. CBS News, "Poll: U.S. Catholics Angry at Church," May 2, 2002, http://www.cbsnews.com.

14. United States Conference of Catholic Bishops, "A Catholic Response to Sexual Abuse: Confession, Contrition, Resolve," Presidential Address, Bishop Wilton D. Gregory, Dallas, Texas, June 13, 2002, http://www.usccb.org.

15. United States Conference of Catholic Bishops, National Review Board for the Protection of Children and Young People, "A Report on the Crisis in the Catholic Church in the United States," February 27, 2004, http://www.usccb.org.

16. PBS Online NewsHour, "Church Studies Show More Than 10,000 Reported Abuse Cases," February 27, 2004, http://www.pbs.org.

17. United States Conference of Catholic Bishops, "Catholic Information Project," http://www.usccb.org.

18. Ibid.

19. United States Conference of Catholic Bishops, "Catholics in Political Life," http://www.usccb.org.

20. United States Conference of Catholic Bishops, "Faithful Citizenship: A Catholic Call to Political Responsibility, 2003," http://www.usccb.org.

21. United States Conference of Catholic Bishops, Office of Media Relations, "Bishops' Administrative Committee Reaffirms Support for Federal Marriage Amendment," March 15, 2006, http://www.usccb.org.

22. William M. Newman and Peter L. Halvorson, *Atlas of American Religion: The Denominational Era, 1776–1990* (New York: Altamira Press of Rowman and Littlefield, 2000), 75.

23. International Mission Board, "About Us: Historical Reflection: God at Work from 1845–2005," http://www.imb.org.

24. International Mission Board, "About Us: Fast Facts," http://www.imb.org.

25. Southern Baptist Convention, "The Baptist Faith and Message," http://www.sbc.net.

26. Ibid.

27. Ibid.

28. The National Council of Churches *2006 Yearbook* reports membership of 5 million, but the Convention's Web site claims 7.5 million members. See National Baptist Convention, USA Inc., "Overview," http://www.nationalbaptist.com.

29. The National Baptist Convention, USA Inc., "History of the National Convention, USA, Inc.," http://www.nationalbaptist.com; see also "Articles of Faith," http://nationalbaptist.com.

30. National Baptist Convention of America Inc., "Who We Are"; see also "Ministry Objectives," and "History," http://www.nbcamerica.net.

31. National Council of Churches, *2006 Yearbook.*

32. Progressive National Baptist Convention Inc., "History," http://www.pnbc.org; see also "Civil Rights," http://www.pnbc.org; "Progressive Concept," http://www.pnbc.org

33. American Baptist Churches USA, "American Baptists: A Brief History," http://www.abc-usa.org.

34. Randall, Mike, "A Brief History of the BBFI," Baptist Bible Fellowship International, http://www.bbfi.org.

35. United Methodist Church, Archives, "Statistics," http://archives.umc.org.

36. Newman and Halvorson, *Atlas,* 76–77.

37. United Methodist Church, "Distinctive Wesleyan Emphasis," http://archives.umc.org.

38. United Methodist Church, "Our Social Creed," http://archives.umc.org.

39. Ibid.

40. African Methodist Episcopal Church, "About Us—Our History," http://www.ame-church.com.

41. African Methodist Episcopal Zion Church, Bureau of Evangelism, "About Evangelism: Our Denomination," http://beamezion.org.

42. See the Church of Jesus Christ of Latter-day Saints official Web site at http://www.lds.org.

43. Church of God in Christ Inc., "The Story of Our Church," http://www.cogic.org.

44. Church of God in Christ Inc., "The Doctrine of the Church of God in Christ," http://www.cogic.org.

45. Presbyterian Church (USA), "Presbyterian 101," http://www.pcusa.org; Presbyterian Church (USA), Research Services, "FAQ/Interesting Facts," http://www.pcusa.org.

46. Evangelical Lutheran Church in America, "ELCA Quick Facts," http://www.elca.org; see also "Roots of the Evangelical Lutheran Church in America," http://elca.org; "Essential Questions—Christianity and Lutheranism," http://elca.org; "Social Advocacy," http://www.elca.org.

47. The Lutheran Church—Missouri Synod, "LCMS Congregations Report Membership of 2,488,936," http://www.lcms.org.

48. The Lutheran Church—Missouri Synod, "Cochran: LCMS School Effective in Outreach," http://www.lcms.org.

49. The Lutheran Church—Missouri Synod, "Of the Antichrist," http://www.lcms.org.

50. Samuel Nafger, "An Introduction to the Lutheran Church—Missouri Synod," http://old.lcms.org.

51. The Lutheran Church—Missouri Synod, "FAQs: Moral and Ethical Issues," http://www.lcms.org.

52. General Council of the Assemblies of God (USA), "Statistics of the Assemblies of God (USA)," http://ag.org.

53. General Council of the Assemblies of God (USA), "History of the Assemblies of God," http://ag.org; "16 Fundamental Truths of the Assemblies of God," http://ag.org; "Mission and Vision," http://ag.org.

54. National Council of Churches, 2006 Yearbook.

55. The Episcopal Church, "Summary of Statistics," http://www.ecusa.anglican.org.

56. The Episcopal Church, "Governance of the Episcopal Church," http://www.ecusa.anglican.org.

57. The Episcopal Church, "Church Policies Related to Peace and Justice," http://www.ecuse.anglican.org.

58. American Anglican Council, Equipping the Saints: A Crisis Resource for Anglican Laity (n.p., n.d.).

59. Churches of Christ Online, "The Churches of Christ . . . Who Are These People?," http://cconline.faithsite.com.

60. See Jehovah's Witnesses official Web site at http://www.watchtower.org.

61. Jewish Virtual Library, "National Jewish Population Survey, 2000–01," http://www.jewishvirtuallibrary.org.

62. Central Conference of American Rabbis, "Declaration of Principles: 1885 Pittsburgh Conference," http://ccarnet.org.

63. The United Synagogue of Conservative Judaism, "About the United Synagogue of Conservative Judaism: Frequently Asked Questions (FAQ)," http://www.uscj.org.

64. See "Largest Religious Groups in the United States of America," http://www.adherents.com.

65. Hartford Institute for Religious Research, "Mosque in America: A National Portrait, April 2001," in *Muslim Life in America: Demographic Facts* (Washington, DC: U.S. Department of State, Office of International Information Programs).

66. Nation of Islam, "History," http://noi.org; "Muslim Program," http://www.noi.org.

67. See Wheaton College, Billy Graham Center Archives, "Billy Graham and the Billy Graham Evangelistic Association—Historical Background," http://www.wheaton.edu/bgc/archives/bio.html; see also "The Time 100: Heroes and Icons," http://www.time.com.

68. CBN, "About CBN: Mission and History of CBN," http://www.cbn.com.

69. TBN Networks, "TBN Overview," http://www.tbn.org.

70. TBN Networks, "Watch Us," http://www.tbn.org.

71. The Purpose Driven Life, "The Book," http://www.purposedrivenlife.com.

72. Saddleback Church, "What We Believe," http://www.saddleback.com.

73. Saddleback Church, "The Venues," http://www.saddleback.com.

74. Mennonite Church USA, "Who Are the Mennonites," http://www.mennonitesusa.org.

75. Religious Movements, "Serpent Handlers," http://religiousmovements.liblvirginia.edu.

76. Unitarian Universalist Association, "Unitarian Universalist Association Statistical Summary," http://uua.org; "Unitarian Universalist Origins: Our Historic Faith," http://www.uua.org.

77. The Church of Christ, Scientist, "About the Church of Christ, Scientist," http://www.tfccs.com.

78. The Pew Forum on Religion and Public Life, *The American Religious Landscape and Politics, 2004,* http://pewforum.org.

79. The Pew Forum on Religion and Public Life, "Public Divided on Origins of Life," August 30, 2005, http://pewforum.org.

80. Ibid.

81. Catholic Charities, "News & Facts: The Catholic Charities Network at a Glance," http://www.catholiccharitiesinfo.org.

82. White House Office of Faith-based and Community Initiatives, "White House Faith-based & Community Initiative," http://www.whitehouse.gov.

83. "The Fifty Most Influential Christians in America," *The Church Report,* January 2005, http://www.thechurchreport.com.

84. The White House, "Fact Sheet: Compassion in Action: Producing Real Results for Americans Most in Need," http://www.whitehouse.gov.

## BIBLIOGRAPHY

Capps, Walter H. *The New Religious Right: Piety, Patriotism, and Politics.* Columbia: University of South Carolina Press, 1990.

Carpenter, Joel A. *Revive Us Again: The Reawakening of American Fundamentalism.* New York: Oxford University Press, 1997.

Corrigan, John, and Winthorp S. Hudson. *Religion in America.* 7th ed. Upper Saddle River, NJ: Pearson Education, 2004.

Durham, Martin. *The Christian Right, the Far Right and the Boundaries of American Conservatism.* New York: University of Manchester Press, 2000.

Martin, William. *With God on Our Side: The Rise of the Religious Right in America.* New York: Broadway Books, 1998.

Wilson, John F. *Public Religion in American Culture.* Philadelphia: Temple University Press, 1979.

# 3

# Gender, Marriage, Family, and Education

## *Ellen Baier*

Feminism is the radical notion that women are human beings.

—Cheris Kramerae

[Feminism] encourages women to leave their husbands, kill their children, practice witchcraft, destroy capitalism and become lesbians.

—Rev. Pat Robertson

WHAT COULD BE more illustrative of American culture than how Americans live in private, love and marry, and raise their children? American life is an odd melding of liberal freedoms and social conservatism, and different regions hold entirely different viewpoints on the role of the family, of marriage, and of schools. These differences might be based on religious views, political ideologies, or personal opinions, but one thing is constant: Americans pride themselves on their independence. Anyone trying to tell an American how to live his or her life, or what to do in his or her private life, is in for quite a struggle.

Indeed, struggle is an apt word for the history of the United States, whether in public life or private, between races and genders and classes. Since the United States won its independence, and before, there were differing ideas about the best ways to pursue work, divide housework between spouses, and raise and educate children. Though there are a number of other religious traditions throughout America, the United States' history is full of Christian ideology, which informs one major side of the struggle, though not a monolithic, all-encompassing force by any means. The other side is multifaceted, full of secular humanists, liberals, feminists, and activists of all shades, occasionally with internal divisions and opposing goals. Recently, Americans have been preoccupied with family values, which is a concept that is difficult to argue with—who is going to oppose families, after all? But defining the family, and the values, is key in understanding any American's position in the struggle for meaning within well-established economic and social systems that he or she may agree with to a greater or lesser extent.

## GENDER

In pre-Revolutionary America, the roles of men and women were clearly defined. Men were leaders, politically and personally, and women had a single career path—that of wife and mother. However, as the men marched away to war against the British, women were left at home to run stores and maintain businesses. Though they still lacked many legal rights, this was a taste of freedom, and they enjoyed it. Men returned from war and regained control over their households, but many women kept an eye turned outward, awaiting their chance. Prior to the Civil War, the abolition movement for the rights of slaves rallied women into the public sphere, from where they began to organize for their own rights. At a well-known convention in Seneca Falls, New York, in 1848, the first women's rights convention in the United States, Elizabeth Cady Stanton, Susan B. Anthony, and many other prominent feminists of the time created the Declaration of Sentiments, a shocking document that denounced men's tyranny and demanded equal rights, including the right to vote. This first wave of feminism sparked protests and demonstrations, often heated, until women in America earned the right to vote in 1920 through the ratification of the 19th Amendment.

As the Great Depression racked the country, most women were too preoccupied with working alongside their husbands to keep their families from the brink of disaster, but it was a time that saw many legal changes that would turn out to have great effect on gender equity—the New Deal, the Social Security Act, minimum wage laws, and many others. World War II saw the first great entrance of women into the paid workforce. Just as their great grandmothers before them in the American Revolution had held down the home front as men went away to war, women in the 1940s took over—though this time, more than 350,000 women went to war as well, in auxiliary and nursing units. However, in the post–Industrial Revolution era, that looked much different than in the Revolutionary period. Women took jobs in factories, creating munitions, tanks, and planes. Rosie the Riveter, a familiar and popular symbol of women's strength and determination, fueled ambitious fires, and though at the end of the war, many women were fired to allow men to return to their old jobs, women had gained a foothold in the working world.

The postwar boom in population and economic growth kept women at home for a time, but in the 1960s, the second wave of feminism began to peak, along with other civil rights battles that were being fought. The first introduction of the birth control pill in 1960, and the improvement of the IUD soon after, granted women control over their reproductive rights. This control, in combination with the financial independence that many women had as a result of their greater participation in the workforce, led to a period of greater sexual expression than ever before. Men and women began to discuss sexuality openly—laws governing censorship of pornography were overturned, and studies of sexual behaviors and frank educational manuals were published. Abortion was legalized in 1973 with the Supreme Court decision of *Roe v. Wade,* though many states have restrictions on it in practice, and it is still hotly contested.

This increase in control by women over their own bodies led to campaigns against marital rape and domestic battering, and laws against them gained in strength as women began to feel more confident in their right to speak out about abuse. Gay and lesbian activists also began protesting during this time, a period of openness and revolution against the status quo. Activists of color—African Americans, Latinos, Asian Americans, Native Americans— who are enjoined in these struggles also fight a racial bias in the feminist movement, arguing that many of the disadvantages suffered by women are exacerbated by questions of racism. Thus the protests that took place in the 1960s and later were merely the beginning of a struggle for civil rights for all that is currently ongoing.

It is interesting, though perhaps disheartening, to note the fact that, geography aside, the United States would not be welcome to join the European Union because the United States lacks an equal rights amendment for women (or for gays and lesbians). In 1923, an Equal Rights Amendment (ERA) was proposed that would grant women equality of rights under the law. It was not passed by Congress until 1972, and states were given 10 years to ratify or repudiate it, though this deadline was later extended. There was a strong push to get the ERA ratified, but it fell 3 votes short of the required 38, and though it is reintroduced frequently, it has not yet succeeded. There is also debate on the ratification process, some feeling that the process must begin anew since the time period has expired, and some feeling that as long as it is passed in a "sufficiently contemporaneous" time frame—which, for the 27th Amendment, was 200 years between introduction and ratification—the earlier votes should still be current. A new version of the amendment, known as the Women's Equality Amendment, was proposed in March 2007 and does not contain any time limit.

Opponents of the ERA have a number of politically and emotionally persuasive arguments against the measure. They argue that it could be used to force women to participate in the draft process and fight in combat, in the event of war, or to undermine laws in place to protect women. States with their own equal rights provisions have had challenges to restrictive abortion laws on the basis of the policy of sex discrimination, and though those challenges had mixed results, it has become a rallying point for pro-life activists. Same-sex marriages, too, have been the subject of lawsuits to a few state courts, arguing in part that the state's policy of nondiscrimination required restrictions on marriage to be dropped. Both abortion and gay marriage, anathema to social conservatives and the Religious Right, would be enough to provide fervent opposition.

Sexual rights and freedoms are a recurring target of social conservative groups, and the debates receive quite a bit of attention in the media and press. The most charged arguments stem from issues of reproductive rights and family planning. The morality of legal abortions is a frequent subject of political wrangling, and many states, particularly where there are large numbers of conservative, evangelical Christians, have passed laws restricting abortion and access to birth control. The right of the woman to prevent or terminate her pregnancy is in opposition to the doctrine of many churches that an unborn fetus has an equal right to protection. Though there are those who support the woman's unconditional right to choose, there are also those who would uphold the fetus's rights as paramount. In South Dakota, the state legislature passed a ban in early 2006 on all abortions, except those that were necessary to save the life of the woman, but voters overturned the ban by referendum in the midterm elections later that year.

There are laws in place that allow health care providers to decline to provide certain medicines or procedures without fear of reprisal. There are nearly 20 states that have these laws, known as refusal clauses, and some corporations allow their employees this right of refusal nationwide. These laws are most commonly called on when the medical service relates, even tangentially, to abortion or contraception. This means that women in more conservative areas have reduced access to prescribed birth control, emergency contraception, and legal abortions. When reproductive rights are abridged due to lack of access, access to treatment for sexually transmitted infections may also be restricted, putting both women and men at risk. Typically, women's rate of infection for many sexually transmitted infections (STIs) is somewhat higher than men's, but this is not the case for the major incurable STI in the United States: AIDS.

HIV and AIDS existed as small, isolated cases in the United States prior to 1981, but the Centers for Disease Control classified the spread of AIDS as an epidemic in mid-1981, primarily among gay men, but also among intravenous drug users and prostitutes, among many others. About 1 million people in the United States are living with HIV right now, with nearly 40,000 new cases reported each year, mostly in the East and South, plus California. A disproportionate number of African American men are infected, related to that group's disproportionate incarceration rate and the high levels of risky behavior, such as unprotected anal sex, that occur in prisons. African American women who partner these men after their release from prison are also at increased risk. Unfortunately, the high cost of the drug cocktail that treats the disease places it largely out of the reach of the at-risk population. Young men and women, particularly younger gay men, who grew up never *not* knowing about AIDS, are also at a higher risk, a few studies suggest, because they do not take the disease as seriously as it deserves and may be less likely to take precautions. Young people under 25 account for nearly 50 percent of new cases each year.[1] On the other hand, other STIs, like herpes and syphilis, are becoming more and more treatable with advances in medical science.

An example of this advance in medical treatments is the treatment of human papillomavirus (HPV), a common STI that is linked to certain reproductive cancers. Merck received approval from the Food and Drug Administration for distribution of their HPV vaccine, Gardasil, in June 2006. The vaccine, which is given only to young women aged 9–23, protects women from four of the most common strains of the virus, which may lower their risk of cervical cancer. In Texas, Governor Rick Perry issued an executive order that girls must receive the vaccine by sixth grade to attend public school, as of the 2008–2009 school year. Two other governors, in New Mexico and Virginia, have indicated an intention of following suit. However, the Texas State House and Senate overturned the order overwhelmingly. The vaccine is considered controversial because HPV is a STI, and the vaccine can be given to girls as young as nine. Its opponents argue that the vaccination will encourage girls to engage in more risky behavior, considering themselves universally protected.

Oddly, these same opponents who fear for the ignorance of teenagers and young adults are frequently the same folks who support teaching abstinence-only curricula in the place of full sex education and delaying any discussion until high school, when the programs may be too late to reach all students appropriately. The abstinence-only programs, based in conservative religious beliefs, simply tell students of the importance of remaining chaste until marriage, withholding information on STIs or birth control and, on occasion, providing false information about the failure rates of birth control in an attempt to scare teens into chastity. They also ignore the students who are currently unable to marry their partners, even if they would like to—gay and lesbian students. Proponents of comprehensive sex education, on the other hand, favor arming students with knowledge about the actual risks of premarital sexual behavior and allowing them to come to their own moral conclusions. There is some evidence that in schools with abstinence-only education, levels of teen pregnancy are higher than in schools with comprehensive sex education. While it is true that when teenagers undergo abstinence-only education, they engage in sexual behaviors at a later age, they also tend to do so in less safe ways than their more educated peers—and teen pregnancy is not the only danger of unprotected sex.[2]

Though they might be at risk, for various reasons, of getting in metaphorical *trouble,* girls in general seem to get in less trouble than boys. In school, girls are less likely to repeat grades or be diagnosed with a learning disability or attention-deficit (hyperactivity) disorder and are punished less severely for misbehavior. Despite this attentiveness on the part of girls, boys tend to receive more attention in class than girls, both positive and negative. There are differentials in test scores, but not always to the benefit of boys. Girls tend to do better than boys in reading and writing, but less well in science and math. In high school, girls are equally likely to be enrolled in upper-level math and science classes, but they report feeling as though they are bad at, or that they dislike, math and science. A social stigma still exists for young women who excel in these areas, and though many girls falsely proclaim their mathematical incompetence, it seems that this becomes a self-fulfilling prophecy in their later test scores. This pattern persists throughout both secondary and higher education. Girls are more likely to get advanced credit in humanities classes, while boys are more likely to get credits in math and science classes. Women, especially younger women, are slightly more likely to have a bachelor's degree than are men, but their majors are more likely to be in health, education, or psychology. Men's majors, on the other hand, are more likely to be in computer science or engineering, and the same pattern holds true for advanced degrees.

Overall, fewer women are in the paid workforce than men, but as their level of educational attainment goes up, proportionately higher numbers of women work. However, just as their patterns of degree choice are skewed toward less technical fields, so are women more strongly represented in teaching and caring professions, and less represented in business, computer, and technical occupations. Even when they are in these fields, though, women tend to earn much less than their male peers. In 1970, workingwomen earned an average of 57 cents to every man's dollar. According to recent census figures, in 2005, the median annual salary for a woman, working at least 35 hours per week, year-round, was $32,168, while the median salary for a man was $41,965, making the pay gap 76.7 cents paid to woman to every man's dollar. For a woman working in the relatively well-paying fields of finance or law, however, the gap sinks to 55 percent or less, while social service occupations are the only field where women earn even 90 percent of their male peers—though salaries for either gender are below the national median income. The pay gap also varies by age: it is 88 percent for women aged 25–34 but between 74 and 76 percent for women workers older than 35.[3]

There are many possible reasons for this pay gap, both historically and ongoing. Women are more likely than men to take several months—or years—off for bearing and rearing children, just when their male peers are working toward promotions and gaining experience for taking a step upward on their career ladder. Even if a woman has no intention of becoming a mother, employers may be hesitant to hire young women at the same rates as young men, for fear that they will shortly be forced to hire a replacement. Though it is illegal to decide explicitly not to hire a woman for this reason, it is difficult to prove outright discrimination. Women may be barred from higher-level positions in this subtle way, or they may choose less demanding, more flexible careers, in which they can take time without losing as much ground because there is less ground to fight over in the first place. There is also a perception that women are not as assertive as men in requesting raises and benefits in hiring negotiations and throughout their careers, leading to a higher pay gap. Because of these perceptions, women face challenges in entering higher levels of business, a highly lucrative and powerful—and male-dominated—field. Women are much less likely to be promoted into upper management, still confronting a glass ceiling, though the term has fallen out of popularity. Conversely, in traditionally female-dominated fields, such as nursing or elementary teaching, men are subject to much swifter promotion than their female peers—they are placed on a glass escalator, to use a comparable term.

Another form of discrimination that women, and some men, face on the job, which negatively affects their job performance, is sexual harassment. Though illegal under Title VII of the Civil Rights Act of 1964, sexual harassment was not systematically confronted until the early 1990s. More women started reporting sexual harassment after the Clarence Thomas Supreme Court confirmation hearings, in which a subordinate, Anita Hill, testified that he had harassed her, creating a hostile work environment. Though her claim was not corroborated, it shed light on a major problem in American workplaces. Each year, nearly 15,000 claims are filed with the U.S. Equal Employment Opportunity Commission, including about 15 percent of men with a claim. Students of both genders also report being sexually harassed at school, girls more so than boys. This harassment commonly comes from peers but may be directed at students from teachers, though harassment in the workplace may come from a coworker but is more likely to come from a supervisor or manager. Retaliation is common when the victim complains, and male victims are likely to be ridiculed. The impact on the worker, and the workplace, can be disastrous, and employers are becoming more and more motivated to minimize the risk of incurring claims of harassment. The care that is being taken will help to create more equitable working environments.

At another level, a fairly good indicator of gender equality is the election of women to the highest levels of government. As of 2007, one of the nine justices serving on the Supreme Court was a woman. Sandra Day O'Connor, who had been on the Court since 1981, retired in 2006, leaving only Ruth Bader Ginsburg, who had joined her in 1993. Another woman, Harriet Miers, was proposed by President George W. Bush as a replacement for O'Connor, but she declined the nomination amid protests that her qualifications were inappropriate for the position. The position was filled by Samuel Alito instead, leaving only one woman on the bench. Until 1994, there were at most two women in the Senate at any time, and no more than 20 in the House. Those numbers have risen, and currently, there are 16 female senators and 67 female representatives—a bare 15 percent of Congress. Despite this, the most powerful position in the House of Representatives, speaker of the House, was held by a woman, Rep. Nancy Pelosi, as of January 2007. Additionally, a front-running candidate in the 2008 Democratic presidential campaign was a woman, Hillary Rodham Clinton, and more than 78 percent of voters have indicated that they would be willing to vote for a woman for president.[4]

The struggle for equality between the sexes seesaws back and forth. Currently, the term *feminist* is out of vogue; young women enjoy their rights and try to fight back when they see gender discrimination, but to be a feminist is somehow supposed to represent a militant attitude or a hatred of men. The conservative men's rights movement exaggerates this antifeminist perception, while more liberal, antisexism activists try to avoid alienating potential allies. Male privilege in America has been pervasive, particularly in the economic and public sphere, yet gender-based inequalities are not limited to women. For instance, women in the United States have a life expectancy nearly six years longer than that of men. Both suicide and homicide rates are higher for men than for women, and the most dangerous jobs, with the highest levels of workplace deaths, are held primarily by men. In many physical careers, such as the military or law enforcement, the entrance requirements are gender-normed, meaning that men must pass more stringent requirements than women, and men's rights advocates argue that this differential leaves men with a heavier burden than their female peers. Additionally, only men must register with the Selective Service System so that they may be drafted into military service, and only men may serve in infantry combat roles, on submarines, or in special programs such as the Navy SEALs.

Furthermore, there is a differential treatment of statutory rapists by gender. Women who have sex with young men aged 13–16, if they are prosecuted at all, are likely to receive probation, community service, or a token prison sentence, while men who have sex with young women of the same age are likely to receive sentences of 20 years in prison and are forced to register on sex-offender lists, with nary a smile to be found. The sexuality of young men is treated with indulgence, while the sexuality of young women is protected, despite the fact that both boys and girls can be harmed by these relationships, particularly with teachers and others in a position of authority above them. Men are cast as sexual aggressors in both cases, and women as victims or, at best, coconspirators, and this perception does no one justice.

The view of men as aggressors is pervasive and, in cases where men are victimized, harmful. Though the vast majority of reported intimate partner violence cases are instances of men abusing their female partners, it is unclear how many men are silent victims of violence from partners of either gender. The stigma that attaches to domestic violence makes it difficult to gauge levels of abuse that occur behind closed doors. Most of the support systems for intimate partner violence, such as shelters, are in place for women who have been abused by their male partners and ignore the needs of women fleeing abusive female partners or men fleeing their intimate partners. Shelters for battered men exist, but at a much smaller proportion to shelters for battered women.

Not all gender identification is based in this sort of male-female duality. There are a number of people, though it is difficult to know how many, who do not feel as though they fit into traditional male-female categories. Some were born with ambiguous sexual characteristics, and some come to feel that their physical and social gender categories are in opposition. Many cultures have a category for male-identified people who were born as women, or female-identified people who were born as men, as well as those who were born in ambiguity, and America is no different, although this gender fluidity is still technically defined in the fourth edition of the American Psychiatric Association's *Diagnostic and Statistical Manual of Mental Disorders* as *gender identity disorder,* a mental illness. Nonetheless, many people in the United States live contrary to their original gender assignment, whether or not they choose to take hormones or undergo surgery to complete the change. There are also those who prefer androgyny, but this is even more difficult than changing one's gender—in the United States, gender is important, however it is decided on.

## MARRIAGE

The institution of marriage in the United States is constantly being redefined. When British settlers first began to arrive in the seventeenth century, a wife's status and legal position was closer to property than partnership. Divorce was nearly impossible. However, as the American Revolution began to bring more republican values, even marriage was changed. The conception of marriage began to shift toward ideals of love and partnership. Those ideals were not translated into legal equality until quite recently, but modern conceptions of marriage include relative egalitarianism, in legal, if not always practical, terms.

What exactly is marriage? There are four components, some or all of which may be present: a civil bond, a personal bond, community recognition, and religious recognition.[5] The civil bond represents recognition by the state, such as in the issuance of a marriage license, that the couple intends to wed, and the religious recognition of the bond is the affirmation of that bond within the couple's house of worship. The personal bond is the private agreement between two people to share their lives, and the community recognition is the public declaration of that agreement. Couples who elope are no less married than couples who wed in front of 200 of their friends and family members; couples who are legally prohibited from obtaining a civil marriage can commit to each other privately and feel just as married. For instance, before the Civil War, slaves were prohibited from marrying. They nonetheless developed ceremonies of their own within their community that celebrated the personal commitments of devoted couples. To be considered wed, the couple merely needed to jump over a broomstick in the presence of witnesses, a practice adapted from a West African marriage tradition. Some African Americans incorporate it into modern ceremonies as a reminder of their ethnic heritage. In addition, after the Civil War, many states had antimiscegenation laws, which prohibited African Americans and whites from marrying. The Supreme Court decision in *Loving v. Virginia* overturned those laws in 1976, despite widespread popular disapproval for interracial marriage. Today, few would bat an eye at an interracial relationship.

The patterns for American marriages have been changing. More and more, young people of both genders are leaving their parents' houses after finishing school (either high school or college) and establishing single homes on their own before deciding to wed. This can be shown by rising age at first marriage. In 1980, the average ages at first marriage were just over 23 years for men and just under 21 years for women; in 2005, that had become 27 and nearly 26 years, respectively. Most Americans do marry eventually, though. By the age of 35, 72 percent of Americans have been married, and by the age of 65, that number rises to 96 percent, except for African American men and women, only 90 percent of whom have ever been married by age 65, and for Asian American women, 99 percent of whom have been married at least once by age 65.[6]

Couples do not necessarily stay married, however. In recent years, there have been approximately 7.5–8 new marriages for every 1,000 Americans, and 3.7 divorces per 1,000 each year.[7] At first glance, that seems to point to a 50 percent divorce rate since the legalization of no-fault divorces around 1960. This conventional wisdom that half of all marriages end in divorce, which is a statistic frequently cited by social conservatives fearing for the disappearance of the so-called traditional family arrangement, is often seized on to monger fear. However, this number is a bit misleading, as any statistician could explain. Very few of those 3.7 divorces are from the marriages formed that year; couples divorce anywhere from 60 days into a marriage to 60 years into it. However, many failed marriages tend to end within the first decade, and most (80%) marriages that fail do so within 20 years.[8]

Additionally, this number of 3.7 divorces per 1,000 people in 2004 shows a decline in gross numbers of divorces per year over the last 25 years: in 1980, there were approximately 5.3 divorces per 1,000 people. The actual longitudinal divorce rate is that approximately 31–35 percent of all marriages will end in divorce, down from the 41 percent of 25 years ago.[9] That statistic shows a growing split by educational attainment as well: college graduates are about half as likely to end up divorced than non–college grads.[10] Perhaps it is the later age at first marriage that contributes to the growing stability of the relationships. Perhaps the greater economic stability of college graduates contributes to stability at home as well. Whatever the reason, American marriages are becoming more stable, not less.

Despite the fact that most people marry at some point in their lives, there are other types of relationships and living arrangements, in addition to legal marriages. In actuality, married couples are in the minority these days. According to 2005 census data, out of 111.1 million households, only 49.7 percent of them were composed of married couples—with or without children. There are a number of factors that contribute to this decline. Because of the rising age at first marriage, many young men and women live alone, or with roommates, after finishing their education but before they get married, accounting for over one-fourth of the remaining households. Additionally, couples increasingly feel free to cohabit without stigma, and that number is rising. These unmarried couples made up 5 percent of the households. There are also households headed only by women or by men as a result of divorce. A fourth factor, the gap in life expectancy between men and women, means that women may live for several years as widows.[11]

There are other unmarried couples, who, unlike the above families, might prefer to get married. But just as African slaves could not wed before the Civil War, or African American and white couples for a century after it, they are legally barred from obtaining a civil marriage. Currently, the rights and privileges of marriage are restricted only to heterosexual couples. Indeed, it has only been in the last few decades that other types of couples have been recognized as existing at all. Until as recently as 2003, homosexuality has actually been against the law. Many states had laws in place that prohibited certain sexual acts that could be used to prosecute the behavior of consenting adults within the privacy of their own homes. Though heterosexual privacy had been protected since 1972, it was not until June 2003 that the Supreme Court struck down the sodomy laws of Texas, and all others like it, as unconstitutional in *Lawrence v. Texas.*

American gays and lesbians had fought for civil rights for many years, with increasing success, as social norms expanded to accept a wider range of sexual expression. Though there were some moderate and tentative attempts at social activism prior to 1969, the Stonewall riots are generally credited with beginning the modern fight for civil rights. For a week in late June 1969, a group of gay and transgender club-goers in Greenwich Village rioted against the police raids and persecution that they could no longer tolerate. Soon after, the Gay Liberation Front was founded, as well as a number of other activist groups, and many legal and social battles were launched. For the next several decades, gay rights groups fought for antidiscrimination laws in employment, housing, parenting and adoption, medical treatment, and other civil rights. Religious and conservative groups opposed these laws, and only 17 states (and the District of Columbia) prohibit discrimination on the basis of sexual orientation. Additionally, gays may not serve openly in the U.S. military, though they may do so if they are celibate and silent about their orientation—a law passed by President Bill Clinton in 1992 and better known as don't ask, don't tell.

There is another civil right for which gay and lesbian groups are currently fighting. In 1996, President Clinton signed into law another piece of legislation, the Defense of Marriage Act, which defined marriage as "a legal union of one man and one woman as husband and wife" and *spouse* as "refer[ing] only to a person of the opposite sex who is a husband or a wife" for the purposes of federal law. It also allowed states to decide individually whether or not to allow for same-sex marriage, but it provided that no state is forced to recognize the marriages that may be legal in another.[12] There are over 1,000 federal laws that apply only to married couples, relating to taxation, property rights, immigration, inheritance, and benefits. For example, heterosexual married couples can file taxes jointly, inherit property with no estate tax, receive survivorship benefits, and obtain visas for non-American partners. Gay couples are thus at a significant economic disadvantage compared to their straight neighbors.

Some states and regions are taking steps to minimize that disadvantage, even though the federal government does not recognize their decisions.

Limited rights, in the form of a reciprocal beneficiary registration, have been available in Hawaii since 1997. In 2000, Vermont governor Howard Dean signed into law a provision for civil unions for gay and lesbian couples that would guarantee their rights in the eyes of the law, introducing the idea of a parallel civil institution into the common debate. New Jersey and Connecticut followed suit. A few other states—California, Maine, and the District of Columbia—have passed protections for domestic partnerships for couples regardless of gender, and a number of large cities have done so as well. For a brief period of time in February 2004, marriage licenses were issued to over 4,000 same-sex couples in San Francisco, before the mayor was forced by the state government to cease, and these marriages were voided by the state supreme court a few months later. Del Martin and Phyllis Lyon, who had been a couple for 51 years, became the first gay couple to marry in the United States. In May 2004, Massachusetts legalized marriage for gay and lesbian couples, and there are seven other states, mostly those with civil unions, that are considering that legislative step. There are a number of

Phyllis Lyon, left, 79, and Del Martin, right, 82, both of San Francisco and a couple for 51 years, hold up their marriage certificate outside city hall after they were married in a civil ceremony in San Francisco. © AP Photo/Eric Risberg.

companies that are friendly to their gay employees as well and offer partner benefits, though those benefits are classified as taxable compensation, where comparable benefits to straight partners are not. Despite these benefits, the Defense of Marriage Act prohibits the federal government from recognizing any of these types of unions as legal.

The idea of gay marriage was a hot-button issue for every election since 1996, and in 2004 and 2006, many states passed amendments to their state constitutions ruling that marriage must remain an exclusively heterosexual right. Paradoxically, some states that have protections for gay couples also have laws or constitutional amendments defining marriage as a strictly heterosexual right. Opponents of gay marriage protest that allowing marriage between two men or two women is one step closer to condoning polygamy, incestuous marriages, or human-animal marriage. They argue that the sanctity of marriage must be preserved, and if even a portion of the definition of marriage is relaxed, the institution would be meaningless. This emotional argument appealed to voters, and most amendments passed with high percentages of the vote in states where they were proposed. At an extreme level, President George W. Bush put forward a Federal Marriage Amendment during his 2004 campaign, which would modify the Constitution to define marriage as belonging only between a man and a woman and would eliminate the already established benefits in any city or state that has previously allowed them.

Some states are battlegrounds over gay marriage and civil unions. In May 2006, the Nebraska ban on gay marriage, civil unions, domestic partnerships, and all other forms of gay partnerships was struck down by a district court on the grounds that it violated the rights of gay couples to assemble for advocacy, protected both by the 1st Amendment and the due process clause of the 14th Amendment. Only a month later, a similar ban, on both gay marriages and civil unions, was struck down in Georgia, based on a ruling that the ban violated the state's rule that all amendments be limited to a single subject. However, the ban was almost immediately reinstated by a superior court. The struggle over the real definition of marriage is ongoing.

## FAMILY

Just as marriage changed in Revolutionary America, the ideals of motherhood and family changed as well. Out of the ashes of the Revolution was born the cult of true womanhood, a set of ideals that mirrored the Victorian idealization—even fetishization—of the mother as a virtuous, perfect, almost goddess-like ruler of the domestic sphere. As the Industrial Revolution and the changing economic patterns drew families from farms into cities, and workers into factories, men became the driving force for economic support, and women were established as the backbone of the home. Though some social conservatives have enjoyed invoking this nostalgic picture, with everyone in an appointed role and content to stay there, the traditional picture of a family—mother, father, and 2.5 children—has been steadily changing over the last half decade in the United States. Not only do mothers work outside the home at increasing rates, but families themselves are structurally changing, and the numbers of heterosexual nuclear families have been shrinking. In 2005, just over 67 percent of children lived with two parents, down from the nearly 90 percent who did so in 1960. The majority of the remaining third of children lived with just their mother, though 5 percent lived with just their father and 7 percent did not live with either parent, living either with a grandparent or in foster care. The average family size has also been shrinking over the years, from an average of 2.3 children per family in 1960 to 1.18 in 2005.[13]

Because of these changes in family structure, many in the United States who feel an emotional or religious connection to the nuclear family are eager to hear politicians speak of family values. Over the past 15 years, family values have been coded by conservative groups to refer to an overtly Christian viewpoint that opposes abortion, homosexuality, pornography, sex education in schools, and other such morally questionable activities. They rhetorically look back on an easier, more morally sound time in history. However, liberals have begun to co-opt the term, pointing out that supporting universal health insurance, equality in education, regular raises in the minimum wage, and worker's rights may contribute more concretely to the well-being of families, speaking to an economic sensibility, rather than a moral one.

As women began to enter the workplace in large numbers, the goddess of the household ideal held, at the same time that her economic impact on the family was greatly increased. Mothers were effectively turned into superwomen, capable of having a rewarding career and lovely family at the same time, with seeming effortlessness. This effortlessness was only in evidence in magazine articles and advertisements, however. Women were able to permeate the working world with much more ease than they were able to share responsibilities for the work that still needed doing at home, a second shift of labor that they were expected to perform when they got home from work. The women's liberation movement that gained force in the 1980s emphasized a change in women's roles, without a corresponding emphasis on change in men's roles, with the result that housework became an odd sort of minefield. A prominent sociologist in California, Arlie Hochschild, performed a study in the late 1980s on gender equality in housework. She found that in her sampled study of heterosexual, dual-income, middle- and working-class families with young children, women performed the vast majority of the housework (child care, cooking, cleaning), despite their own expectation of an equal partnership in their family life. This disparity remains largely unchanged: in a 2005 time use study, 84 percent of women performed some household tasks on an average day, while 65 percent of men did so. Of the respondents, women reported doing 2.7 hours of housework on an average day, while men reported only 2.1. Care of young children was similarly skewed along gender lines, with women averaging 3.6 hours of care to men's 1.8.[14]

There are many possible explanations for the negotiation to result in this differential. The first, and most often cited, is that women choose to do the work, willingly or no. Either she or her husband believes in traditional male and female roles around the house, and thus the woman does the housework that needs doing. The second explanation is that women do not have as much bargaining power in the household relative to men because of women's weaker position in the workforce. Because women cannot afford to push the issue and risk the marriage, particularly when children are involved, they must accept a less than equitable negotiation. The average income of women after divorce declines sharply, while men's income actually rises modestly. Because the past economic system has created a situation in which most women are the primary caregivers for children after a divorce, they are more likely than men to be awarded custody of their children. Maintaining two households is more expensive than one, and the one with children is more likely to experience a dip in its standard of living. Perhaps implicitly, it is understood by women that accepting a larger portion of the household work will avert this crisis.

A third explanation for the differential in sharing household work is that because women typically work in lower-paying jobs, at a rate of about 75 cents to every man's dollar, they can afford to take time and energy away from the job, but men tend to be more well paid and thus have to devote more energy into maintaining the career. The second and third explanations are related, obviously, because women cannot strengthen their position in the workplace until they can devote their full energy into their careers, but they cannot afford to do so at the risk of their partners' positions.[15] Most of these explanations apply more broadly than at the level of the individual family—few, if any, couples have this blunt conversation explicitly. Many couples even describe their housework arrangement as equal, even when it is clear that it is not, and some happily embrace the disparity. However, women wishing for a lighter share of the second shift must weigh their unhappiness more carefully than men when deciding to dissolve a marriage.

Many women avoid this struggle before tensions can escalate and devote themselves to full-time housewifery and motherhood. There is a small but growing number of men who make this choice as well, leaving their partners in the workforce while they choose to remain at home. Only 52 percent of married couples with children under 18 are both employed full-time, though that number is much higher in the upper Midwest and Northeast and much lower in the South and West, particularly in rural areas. While this choice may contribute to familial harmony, there are significant economic costs, even the obvious loss of a second salary aside. The family is dependent on the main earner for health insurance and retirement savings. There is also a risk the at-home parents take because by leaving the paid workforce, they are allowing their résumés and skills for paid work to deteriorate. If divorce or death of their spouse forces them back into the workplace, they are thus at a significant disadvantage. Nonetheless, many stay-at-home parents are happy to be deeply invested in their home life and are aware of the difficulties of the path they have chosen.

There are difficulties in any family life, especially at the very beginning. Most countries guarantee a few weeks of paid maternal leave, and a few guarantee a few days to a few weeks of paid paternal leave. The United States does not guarantee so much as a single day of paid leave, either maternal or paternal, though as long as an employee has worked for at least a year for a certain type of large employer or the government, they are allowed up to 12 weeks of unpaid leave within each year. This leave is protected by the Family Medical Leave Act of 1993, which also guarantees leave to take care of any family member or oneself, not just a new infant. Some states have more generous policies, such as California's recently guaranteed six weeks of paid family leave, but family-friendly policies are generally left to the uncertain goodwill of individual companies. Smaller companies are more likely to be flexible in helping employees, while larger companies have more resources to be generous with benefits, leave, and programs like on-site day care.

When this last benefit is not provided by the employer, parents must make other arrangements for the care of their children. There are a number of options for those who can afford to pay: in-home care, such as a nanny, can be quite expensive, and places in good day care centers can be hard to find. The cost and availability of quality care is a significant factor, especially when the mother of a young child wants or needs to work. Finding and paying for day care is a problem, especially for single parents, and may be involved in keeping one partner at home, if his or her job does not pay enough to cover the expenses involved in taking it.

A few working-class or single parents, for whom working is not a matter of choice, are lucky enough to have family nearby who can pool resources to care for children. If they can find a small provider, likely a woman who cares for several children in her own home, this is likely to be the next most cost-effective option. Some low-income families also qualify to send their children to federally funded preschools known as Head Start, although funding has been steadily decreasing for these programs. Just as the U.S. government does not provide for mandatory parental leave, it also does not provide for adequate day care for those same working parents. Day cares can range significantly in quality, and the effects are frequently reflected in the behavior of the children that they help to raise. Children who were in day care at young ages for longer periods of time were more likely to be considered aggressive, assertive, and disobedient when starting kindergarten, though better-quality care was less likely to encourage those behaviors. However, parental sensitivity, income level, and educational attainment were significant mitigating factors in decreasing undesirable behavior. Nonetheless, there are public figures that consistently express disapproval at parents—mostly at mothers, in fact—who send their children to day care, as if by working, they have somehow failed their children through participation in paid employment.

For a significant amount of time in the history of the United States, children were expected to contribute to the household economy, especially children of lower and working classes. When born to a farming family, they would perform chores from a young age; when born to a city family, they might help at a family business, be apprenticed out, or be expected to take factory work. After 1938, however, the minimum age for child workers was set at 16, with possible exceptions for 14- and 15-year-olds, if their work did not interfere with their schooling. In modern households, children are generally expected to perform light chores, for which they may or may not receive an allowance, until they turn 16. There are a number of younger teens with lawn-mowing or babysitting gigs, but after age 16, unless the casual work is lucrative, most teenagers take a part-time job in retail or food service—low-paying but flexible positions. Most dangerous jobs are restricted from teenagers, but it has become an expected norm that high school students will either hold a part-time position or pursue a particularly rigorous academic schedule—idleness is seen as laziness or sloth, and working even low-status positions can confer adult respect to teenagers. The jobs can also provide some adult freedoms, allowing the teenager to purchase an inexpensive car and pay for dates and other social activities away from the parental home. This independence is encouraged, within limits. There are limits on how many hours teenagers may work, and some areas still have curfews that restrict their free movements.

There are other laws that are designed to help protect children such as laws restricting certain behaviors until a set age, such as drinking or sexual activity. The drinking age in the United States is set at 21, though adulthood, in the form of voting rights or participation in military services, is usually conferred at the age of 18. This leaves young adults between 18 and 21 in a somewhat awkward position, uniquely among their global peers. It is only in the United States that a 20-year-old, who may be legally married with a child or two, cannot be served a glass of wine with dinner—for his or her own protection. There are also laws governing the age that a young adult can consent to sex or marriage, generally from 16 to 18 in most states.

There are also mandated protections for children's safety and welfare at a younger age. There is a program known as WIC, the Special Supplemental Nutrition Program for Women, Infants, and Children, run by the federal government, that provides low-income women and their under-five children with health care screening, nutrition education, and some subsidized foods, mainly dairy products, juices, and cheap proteins such as beans, tuna, and peanut butter. Beyond the most basic needs, the state also carefully monitors children's physical safety with their parents, with mandatory reporting laws making nearly every public employee a required reporter of suspected abuse. When a parent cannot adequately or safely care for a child, there is a system for foster care in place. Though there are federal laws governing the general requirements, each state has its own guidelines in place for investigating claims and making care plans for at-risk children.

If a child has been abused, a report is made to Child Protective Services (in some states, this department is known as the Department of Children and Family Services, in an attempt to create a less contentious atmosphere). If the claim is judged as valid after investigation, the child is removed from the parents' home and placed in foster care, either with foster parents or in a group home. Foster parents generally receive a small stipend for the care of the children they take in, and states may require that they be licensed or otherwise credentialed to provide care. There have been several well-publicized cases of foster parents taking in more children than they can handle for the stipend that they would bring, but those cases are vastly outnumbered by the people who choose to bring abused, needy, and time- and emotionally demanding children into their homes, for a sum that is laughably inadequate for the costs of the care required. Additionally, some foster parents later adopt foster children they have cared for, once parental rights have been terminated.

Adoption, however, would be an exceptionally good outcome; most children remain in foster care for several years and have multiple placements, bouncing from home to home. There are over half a million children in foster care nationwide, a number that has more than doubled in the last 40 years due to tightening of reporting laws for child abuse. A disproportionate number of these children are children of color, particularly African American children, largely owing to racial inequality in treatment by the system—white children receive more services and are more likely to be reunited with parents, and are thus removed more quickly from the system. Though the stated goal of foster care is to find children families, whether through reconciliation or adoption, many more children are placed into foster care each year than leave the system. The Adoption and Safe Families Act of 1997 was passed in an attempt to limit the amount of time children spend in the system by shortening the amount of time between their entry into foster care and the termination of parental rights to 15 months and demanded that a care plan be made for children so that they and their caseworkers have a stated goal. However, most children in foster care are emotionally and psychologically fragile, and many have special physical needs as well; finding adoptive parents is a bit more easily said than done. A few hundred African American children are finding homes outside of the United States, reversing a popular trend for foreign adoption, but this is still an infinitesimal portion of the children needing permanent homes.

If the reason for a familial upheaval is not abuse, but the parents are still unable to care for their children, a social worker may help the family place the child with relatives such as grandparents. As single parenthood has increased, the role of the grandparent has increased in many families. A significant number of children live with a grandparent, some with parents present and many without. These types of households are more likely than any other to be in poverty for a number of reasons. Multigenerational homes of this sort are likely to be composed of African American or Latino families, who are more likely to be in poverty in general compared to white families. Also, the sort of familial upheaval that produces the social conditions under which this is an option—teen parenthood, drug abuse, un- or underemployment of a parent—is not one that lends itself to economic success. Additionally, the grandparents may likely be retired from the workforce and on a limited pension or Social Security benefit and less capable of finding supplemental income than a younger caretaker. There are many households headed by grandparents that receive public assistance.

There are a number of couples, or single people, who wish to have children but cannot. For them, adoption can be a good option. There are several different types of adoption in the United States. Children can be adopted publicly, from foster care. As discussed previously, this can be a troubling process, but foster children benefit greatly from receiving a permanent, caring home. Prospective parents can also choose to go to a private agency, especially if they particularly wish to adopt an infant or a child without the risk of the social problems that affect the abandoned and neglected. This can be an expensive option, and the wait for an appropriate child may be several years long. If the parents wish to ensure that they adopt an infant with particular characteristics—his curly hair, or her blue eyes, for instance—they can pursue an adoption independently, with a pregnant young woman with whom they reach an agreement. This is not legal in all areas of the United States, however, and can be just as expensive as private agency adoption.

Another option for prospective parents is international adoption. About 13 percent of adopted kids are from overseas, nearly 21,000 of the 65,000 that took place in 2006. This can be a highly expensive option for would-be parents: there are agency fees, at least two trips overseas to visit the child's country, and there is a high risk of expensive health care being needed. Despite this financial barrier, the number of international adoptions has been steadily rising for over a decade, and the option has been seen as an increasingly popular one, particularly because of some highly publicized cases of celebrities adopting foreign orphans. However, the increasing demand for orphaned foreign children also increases the risk of child trafficking, either by desperately poor parents willing to sell their children to orphanages for mutual profit, or by private brokers stealing children to sell to American parents. The International Criminal Court (ICC) at the Hague has attempted to prevent this sort of exploitation, but it remains a concern for adoptive parents, and enforcement is difficult within the United States as it is not a member of the ICC as of 2007. Countries that provide the largest numbers of adopted children have been taking steps to slow international adoptions themselves, at least in some cases. In 2006, there were tightening restrictions on parents wishing to pursue foreign adoptions from China, South Korea, and Romania, and those new barriers have led to decreasing numbers of adoptees. Prospective parents have new requirements for age, weight, mental health history, and sexual orientation—single people adopting from China must affirm that they are heterosexual, for instance—and fewer parents can pass the more stringent tests.

Adoption is not open to all in the United States, either. There are several states, in the South and Midwest, that explicitly ban gay couples from adopting, and Utah even bars cohabiting straight couples from adopting children together. Every state but Florida allows gay and lesbian people to adopt individually, though the parental rights cannot be legally shared. Some states, mostly those that have more liberal gay union laws, allow for second-parent adoption, but most areas have inconsistent court records on the matter. In many cases, one partner loses all visitation rights over children that they may have raised from infancy should the partnership dissolve, and they would be considered legal strangers.

When all is said and done, the real definition of family is created by the participants; however, much legal definition might restrict or allow some rights. In the United States, there are as many definitions of family as there are members of families. Extended kinship ties can be strong, creating a small-town

A family consisting of seven adopted children hold hands in prayer before eating dinner. © AP Photo/The Daily News, Bill Wagner.

feeling with a large and close-knit group of members, or weak, with great distance among its members, who might see each other rarely. A family can be composed of mother, father, and seven children, or a cohabiting couple, or a grandmother with a clutch of grandbabies—and any possible permutation thereof. The only necessity for a family is ties of love.

## EDUCATION

Education in the United States is seen as a great equalizer; 72,075,000 Americans, from prekindergarten children to graduate students and adults of all ages, were enrolled in educational institutions in the fall of 2005. Prekindergarten, kindergarten, elementary, and secondary enrollment totaled 54.7 million, and postsecondary enrollment, 17.3 million. Of all these students, over 61 million, or a bit more than 85 percent, were enrolled in public schools where opportunities are thought to be equal. There are some problems with this idea, but in general, a motivated student of any race or class can indeed succeed throughout the public school system. The more than 10 million students in private educational institutions have not only equal opportunity, but also receive a deliberately value-based education: 7.6 million of the private school enrollment is in Roman Catholic schools, colleges, and universities, dwarfing the enrollment of other religiously based schools and colleges. The literacy rate in the United States is estimated by the United Nations to be 99.9 percent, tied for the top spot with 20 other nations.[16]

Schooling in the United States can begin for children as young as three or as old as six, depending on the region. Six out of every 10 children attended some form of prekindergarten school in 2005.[17] Some larger cities have Head Start preschool programs for poor or at-risk children; parents can also choose private or church-run preschools to begin teaching their children. Among more exclusive circles, such as the Upper West Side of Manhattan in New York City, entrance into the correct preschool is seen as crucial to getting into a highly ranked prep school, and from there into a top-tier university. Waiting lists for those schools are often longer than the prospective student is old.

The next step for most children is kindergarten, begun at age five. Ninety-eight percent of American children attend at least four hours of kindergarten per day before beginning primary school. The first American kindergarten was begun in 1856 in Watertown, Wisconsin, by a German immigrant, and it was conducted entirely in German. The first English-speaking kindergarten was begun four years later in Boston, Massachusetts. The program, originally a nurturing environment for young children to transition into schooling, gradually became more of a practical learning environment: many or most programs have reading and math instruction every day. Kindergarten, which can be either a half- or a full-day program, is more common in large cities and small towns, where it is offered in 64 percent of public schools, than it is in suburban areas or smaller cities, where only 46 percent of public schools offer it. Additionally, students in the South are more likely to benefit from kindergarten programs as 84 percent of public schools offer full-day programs.[18] In the Midwest, 57 percent of public schools have full-day programs, and only 38 percent in the West and 37 percent in the Northeast offer full-day programs. Children who take full-day kindergarten classes begin first grade with a distinct learning advantage over their half-day or no-day peers. Despite this, there is no national requirement for kindergarten. Kindergarten is required in only 14 states and is generally available, but not required, in the other 36.[19]

After kindergarten comes primary school, or elementary school; grade levels in the United States are counted with ordinal numbers, not cardinal numbers. Thus, while one might find a Canadian child in grade one, the corresponding American child would be in first grade. Elementary school lasts for six years, and the 12- and 13-year-old children leave in seventh grade to attend junior high school for two years. Some areas add sixth grade to their junior high, and others add ninth grade—this is commonly called a middle school, rather than a junior high school.

Secondary education includes 9th through 12th grades. In most states, students are required to remain in high school until they are 18, while in others, they are permitted to leave school at age 16 if they choose. Nearly 90 percent of American students complete high school, although dropout rates tend to be higher in urban than in suburban and rural areas. Boys are more likely to leave school earlier than girls, and African American and Hispanic students are more likely to leave earlier than non-Hispanic white students. Those who leave high school without a diploma find themselves at a significant disadvantage in the job market, and many—up to two-thirds—of those who leave school early choose to pursue a diploma or General Educational Development certificate within eight years.[20]

Public high schools are open to all students who wish to attend, though several different vocational tracks are available. For students who plan to continue in their education, and who score well on tests conducted in the eighth grade, a college preparatory track, consisting of upper-level mathematics, science, and literature courses, will provide a thorough grounding in basics that the students can draw on. Some of these courses, Advanced Placement and International Baccalaureate, can even be given college credit if a high score is achieved on an examination. For those students who do not plan to continue their education or who tested below the benchmark for college preparatory classes, less rigorous courses are available as well as some vocational training. In many cities and towns, all-vocational high schools are becoming more frequent for increasing numbers of students.

Arguments have been made that this tracking system is unfair to the students who might be planning to attend college but do not test well enough in junior high to enter the most elite math and science courses. Even if they improve midway through high school or change their minds about their college plans, it is difficult, if not impossible, to catch up and move upward in the track. The tracking system benefits the top 20 percent of students, but the students who perform well in the average classes are inadequately prepared for college coursework, even if they express a desire to continue to college. The debate over tracking is further charged by the fact that many students who tend to be systematically misdirected toward lower tracks are poor or belong to ethnic and racial minority groups.

There are other systematic forms of racial discrimination that still persist in the schools. Following World War II, massive expansion of suburbs combined with high levels of race-based housing discrimination left urban and suburban areas racially segregated. As a result, neighborhood schools were largely racially segregated, and in 1971, the Supreme Court found that the separate schools perpetuated and exacerbated a system of inequality between white students and African American students, and the Court mandated the bussing of students of color from their local schools to mainly white, suburban schools, and white students to mainly African American, urban schools.

This was not a popular order in many cities, and in south Boston, several antibussing protests turned violent throughout the 1970s. As of the 1990s, bussing programs have been phased out, although some school districts have voluntarily retained the practice.

Despite attempts at correcting the inequalities, it cannot be denied that some schools are better funded than others. Schools are primarily funded by local property taxes, with major funding coming from the state and a small proportion of the funds coming from federal money. Because of this emphasis on the local, schools tend to reflect the socioeconomic status of the neighborhood that supports them. In wealthy suburbs, public schools can be lavish, with well-maintained athletic facilities and pools and high levels of per-student spending. At the other extreme are schools in poor, urban districts; while poor parents may pay a higher proportion of their income into property taxes, the schools struggle to provide an adequate environment, let alone sufficient books or desks for the large number of students in each class.

Another attempt at correcting this differential is through establishing magnet schools in urban areas, which have a broad area of potential recruitment. Rather than accepting only students from a limited neighborhood, magnet schools have an entrance process—either aptitude or lottery based—for all students within bussing distance. To make these schools appealing to potential students, magnet schools will offer specialized or particularly innovative programs such as in the arts or sciences. These schools tend to be more racially and ethnically diverse and to have a better academic reputation than many nearby schools. The downside, of course, is that there are limited spots for students eager to attend. These types of schools account for only 3 percent of public schools nationwide, with predominance in California, Illinois, and Virginia.

Other types of educational reforms in public schools are frequent, in an attempt to improve performance and accountability of schools and teachers. Usually, those reforms have been enacted at the state and local level, not at the national level. A national initiative was, however, signed into law on January 8, 2002—the No Child Left Behind Act—was intended to increase the quality of education by increasing the accountability of schools. The act (commonly known as NCLB) requires states to outline guidelines for improvement, which are to be assessed yearly, and schools that do not improve are subject to increasing administrative sanctions as well as provisions that require the district to offer parents the option to transfer their children to another school. NCLB also requires that all teachers be rated as "highly qualified" by the end of the 2005–2006 school year. Under these guidelines, many students have tested higher in reading and math than ever before, and the gaps in achievement between African American and white nine-year-olds as well as a few others in some areas have lessened. Additionally, NCLB provides more detailed data on the achievement of marginalized groups of students than has been previously available such as poor students, students with disabilities, and students of color. Although it is true that if even one such group fails to improve over a year, the entire school is rated as needing improvement, tracking the economic or racial achievement gaps that exist in schools is the first step to closing them. Each school must also provide a detailed report to parents on the progress of the school as a whole every year.

NCLB has a few major shortcomings, however, that limit its helpfulness in total educational reform. Though the stringent requirements that even the poorest school district is expected to complete are thoroughly outlined, the funding for those requirements has not been attached. Many school districts are already stretched to their limits, and though they would like to hire only highly qualified teachers and afford them all possible professional development, that is simply not feasible without increasing funds. There has also been increased pressure over test scores, leading to claims that some administrators are either encouraging teachers to coach students directly to the tests or are outright manipulating their schools' statistics. Many schools have had to cut time from other subjects to provide more time for teaching reading and math, the only two subjects currently tested. For poor, urban schools that experience high student turnover each year, including a large influx of new immigrants who are not fluent in English, the annual testing and sanctioning procedure seems extraordinarily harsh. Some school districts in California have restricted access of children of illegal immigrants to public education, at least partly because of the effects of NCLB. In Utah, a law has been passed that rejects several of the provisions of NCLB, and at least eight other states are on the verge of following Utah's lead. The act is up for reauthorization in 2007, and all signs point to significant revisions that may leave more leeway for states' use of federal funds.

At a more local level, district school boards have a great deal of leeway over what is and is not taught in schools. School boards may have control over controversial points of curricula, but the publicly elected boards can be forced from office, as happened in Dover, Pennsylvania, over the required teaching of creationism, newly renamed and reframed as intelligent design. Intelligent design is a biblically based origin theory that presupposes the existence of a creator. Some conservative Christian groups are trying to lobby public schools to "teach the controversy," or present the religious explanation as an alternative to the scientific theory of evolution, despite the fact that in the scientific community, no such controversy exists. Intelligent design is not testable and not provable and thus cannot be considered to be a science.

The teaching of origin theories in science classes has been controversial since 1925, when a teacher, John Scopes, was arrested and fined over the teaching of evolution in a Tennessee public school. Eighty years later, a Pennsylvania court found that mentioning creationism as a disclaimer to a discussion of evolution violated the establishment clause of the First Amendment, and the members of the school board who supported intelligent design were voted out of office in late 2005.

The division between church and state in schools is a flexible one that in more religious areas of the United States may be nonexistent. In Texas, one would be hard-pressed to find a high school football game that did not begin with a prayer, for example, and most courts have ruled that the students may express themselves in prayer, unless they cause a substantial disruption thereby. Following these rulings, there have been attempts to reintroduce a formal prayer at the beginning of the school day in many areas, but the most that seems to be allowed is a silent moment for prayer or reflection, rather than allowing outright prayer in schools. In addition to a level of support for religious expression in schools, there are also voucher systems in some states that allow parents to pull their children from public school to attend religious private schools and help pay the students' tuition, thereby providing some level of public funding to parochial schools.

There are steps short of private schooling, however. If traditional public schools cannot serve a student sufficiently, in 40 states, there are alternative forms of publicly funded schools: charter schools, which were created in 1988. These generally urban schools have relatively more autonomy from procedures and requirements than traditional public schools and serve students who may not do as well in public schools. Their purpose is innovation and inspiration to best serve their students, most of whom had bad experiences in other schools. In Michigan and California, the only states where it is allowed, many of these schools operate on a for-profit basis, which gives rise to concerns that the funding that might otherwise benefit students is instead reserved for profits. Even in nonprofit charter schools, though, per-pupil funding tends to be lower than traditional schools, even with donations from businesses and foundations, and it is common for newly chartered schools to flounder. Recent studies have suggested that students in charter schools do not perform as well as students in traditional schools, but charter proponents argue that more accurate demographic correlation of the data would disprove that claim.

One of the reasons students might have for choosing to attend charter schools might be in relation to violence and bullying in public schools. Fighting and bullying are serious problems for nearly one-third of students, and about 6 percent of high school students felt so unsafe that they did not attend class at all. Yet from a statistical view, students are far safer at school than nearly anywhere else, but schools, especially high schools, are perceived as particularly dangerous. Less than 1 percent of homicides among teenagers occurred at school, but those homicides received an extremely high level of media attention. The shooting at Columbine High School in Littleton, Colorado, on April 20, 1999, in particular, in which 12 students and a teacher were killed, and another 24 injured, served to frighten the entire nation. In the wake of the Columbine shootings, there seemed to be a rash of disaffected, bullied young men bringing guns to school and taking aim at their tormentors. Columbine and the other shootings spurred drug searches, often with dogs, and the installation of metal detectors. Zero tolerance policies became popular for punishing minor infractions. However, these policies are falling out of favor, nearly a decade later, as they limit discretion on the part of the school, and there is little evidence that they are effective.

Another tactic taken by school boards in an attempt to increase levels of discipline is mandating a dress code or uniform policy. Most schools have dress codes, which restrict students from wearing obscene or inappropriate clothing, but some public schools, about one-fifth nationwide, with that number much higher in urban areas, require a uniform. A few uniform programs are voluntary, but in most cases, any students who wish to attend that school must purchase and wear the uniform. There are frequently programs in place to help provide low-cost or free uniforms to needy students, and at $35–40 each, depending on region, many uniforms cost less than street clothing. The benefits of uniform policies include reductions of school violence, reductions of gang-related activity, reductions of obvious economic differences among students, and increased focus on studies. However, there have been few studies that track long-term effects of uniforms, and most of the reports of increases in discipline have been anecdotal. Additionally, some students have brought suits against school districts, arguing that uniform policies violate their freedom of speech. Courts have tended to uphold the right of the school district to impose uniforms to improve learning conditions, and the lawsuits have been largely unsuccessful.

With all the controversy and fear surrounding public schooling, it is unsurprising that some parents would wish to send their students to private or parochial schools or choose to teach them at home. As of October 2005, approximately 12 percent of students were enrolled in private schools.[21] Parents with means have always had the opportunity to decide on private schooling, and there are several thousand day schools and a few hundred boarding schools, many of which are quite expensive. These private schools can, and do, offer a number of high-level college preparatory courses, but they can also offer help to struggling or troubled students, preparation for a military career, education in the arts, or religious education. The student-to-teacher ratio is usually much lower than in public school, which allows students much more individual attention.

These positives come with a hefty price tag, however, and many lower-income parents—or even middle-class parents—want the option to withdraw their children from public schools and apply the funds that would otherwise be provided to the public schools to the private school tuition. This presents the obvious problem that only a few parents would have this option open to them, and removing funding from the public schools only worsens conditions and the quality of education for the students who are forced to remain in the absence of other options. Additionally, many private schools have a religious affiliation, and channeling government funds to the private schools instead of the public schools could be seen as a violation of the separation of church and state. The constitutionality of a voucher system was upheld in Wisconsin but struck down in Florida, and several other cases are currently ongoing in other states.

There are several other options for parents who feel that neither traditional public nor private schools can provide the right education for their children. There are about 5,000 schools that follow the Montessori method, some 300 of which are publicly funded, and 157 Waldorf schools, both of which espouse particular holistic teaching philosophies that are not considered mainstream by current educational theory. The Montessori schools are based on the philosophy that children want to learn and will teach themselves if guided properly in a collaborative environment. Students are not strictly age segregated, most school assignments are not graded, and positive social skills are emphasized. Success is met with increasing academic challenge, and much of the learning is self-paced. The Waldorf schools similarly emphasize community—students stay with the same teacher from first through eighth grade. However, the Waldorf method involves more structure and a slower introduction to task-based work. Reading is taught later than is traditional, and the education is mapped onto preestablished developmental stages. Both of the methods include preparation for college as a stated goal for the students.

Parents who decline these options, or who live in an area where they are not available, may choose to homeschool their children. In many nations, homeschooling is not a legal option, but as long as students pass compulsory testing, parents are afforded much leeway in the United States. Traditionally, homeschooling has been perceived as highly religiously oriented, but it is gaining in popularity among less conservative families. Nearly 1.1 million students were being taught at home in 2003, which is about 2.2 percent of the student population.[22] The majority of these students were in rural areas, in the South, and with one parent in the labor force and one parent who was not. There are many reasons for choosing to homeschool such as the parents' feeling that they can do a better job of educating their child, their objection to things that are taught in public school, a lack of challenges or resources provided by the local schools, or even transportation issues for rural families, among many others. There are several curricular choices for the parent who homeschools, from Montessori and Waldorf to a variety of private home-schooling organizations. Churches and religious institutions also provide some materials, as do some public schools. Homeschooled students tend to do vastly better than their traditionally schooled peers on achievement tests and self-esteem measures. Opponents to homeschooling argue that students' socialization is limited by not attending school, but most homeschooling families are careful to foster civic engagement in their children.

After high school, students can continue on to postsecondary studies if they so choose. In 2005, nearly half of young adults—over 17 million of them—were enrolled in some form of higher education, though the majority of students in higher education are women—56 percent of those who are enrolled. College attendance has risen sharply in the last few decades, and nearly one-third of Americans have a bachelor's degree, though the propor-tion who have degrees is higher in the Northeast and lower in the South. This is likely due to population density and the number of urban centers, which employ more degreed professionals, rather than any real geographical characteristic. There is also a racial gap in educational attainment, with pro-portionately low numbers of African Americans and Hispanics achieving an advanced degree, though these numbers have risen every year.[23]

Access to higher education is open to all students, in theory, though some options may be limited by a student's means. The U.S. military pays for the higher education of its veterans through a program called the G.I. Bill, first introduced after World War II. Many young men and women who would not otherwise have the resources to attend college join the military for three or four years to take advantage of this benefit. Additionally, there are federal grants and loans for which needy students may apply as well as loans and grants awarded by private institutions and foundations. Students in private colleges, even religiously based ones, are eligible for federal financial aid if they qualify on a standard needs basis. Some states also subsidize the higher costs of private college expenses with fixed grants that go directly to its student citi-zens. Church-state separation is not violated, it is argued, because grants and loans go through the schools directly to the students. Private schools are also eligible for federal research and other special funds with the proviso that no federal money may be used for religious purposes. Colleges and universities also have their own need- and merit-based financial aid awards for poor or particularly talented—academically or athletically—students. Despite these attempts at financial aid, tuition rises every year, and many students graduate with a heavy student loan burden.

There is no national system of colleges in the United States, with the exception of the military academies; instead, the existing public universities have been established by individual states. These schools can be quite affordable for low-income and working students, and though some have better reputations than others, millions of students matriculate in state universities and colleges each year. There are several options other than state college. For students with even more constrained budgets, community colleges and technical institutes offer certifications and practical degree options at a lower level. There are also colleges that serve particular groups, such as women's colleges, historically African American colleges, or tribal institutions. For students with greater loan or scholarship opportunities, or simply wealthier parents, private colleges abound, from the small and local schools to the large and prestigious Ivy League universities. These prestigious schools also attract nearly a half million foreign students, from all regions of the globe.

Entrance to these prestigious schools can be highly competitive. As in many other countries, there is a strong market for tutoring and test preparation tools. In trying to gain entrance to the college of their choice, students and their parents may spend thousands of dollars on professional preparation. High school students pay a fee to take standardized tests, either $41 for the SAT Reasoning Test for students on either coast, or $29 for the ACT Assessment for students in the Midwest and South, or both, if they plan to apply to colleges in a diverse geographical area, though these fees may sometimes be waived if a student can demonstrate hardship. There are a number of companies that offer tutoring directed toward raising scores on these tests, and there is a large market in manuals and preparatory books. Because this intensive training is usually quite effective in raising test scores, teenagers with greater access to economic resources are advantaged in this aspect of university admission. They also have an advantage in the academic black market; there are a growing number of services from which a struggling student can purchase a prewritten essay. Though the specter of expulsion hangs over this market, desperate students with means have been known to go to desperate lengths for better grades.

There are other transgressions, besides the possibility of cheating their way in, for determined troublemakers to find at college. Students at residential colleges are less likely to be victims of violent crime than their nonstudent peers.[24] However, the popular perception of a college experience includes a great deal of *Animal House*–esque drunken revels, resulting in the sort of crimes that generally result from heightened levels of alcohol consumption such as sexual assaults, hazing, and assaults. Though many residential campuses are quite pretty—a haven of green grass and shady trees in the midst of a city—they are often not nearly as much as an uncorrupted sanctum as they appear. Increasingly, crime on campus is attracting attention. A horrifying incident at Virginia Tech on April 16, 2007, in which a 23-year-old male student opened fire in two different locations, killing 32 students and faculty and wounding many more, brought awareness to campus violence, just as the shooting in Littleton, Colorado, brought awareness of high school violence in 1999. However, such violence at university campuses is rarer than at high schools; the last such incident occurred in 1966. Despite these well-publicized horror stories, the fact remains that crime is much lower on campus than in the United States overall: the murder rate in the United States was 5.7 per 100,000, and the murder rate on campus was 0.13 per 100,000.[25]

After safely obtaining an undergraduate degree, many students opt for further schooling, continuing to graduate, medical, law, and business colleges for advanced degrees. Fifty-nine percent of the students who choose to do so are women. Many of the students who continue their education work full-time, in addition to attending school. Though some fields pay stipends to graduate students, full funding is rare for all but the most highly sought after students. Graduate school is traditionally a time of poverty for students, even while working or with family support. There is not necessarily an expectation of a large payoff, as there might be at professional schools, such as medical school, if the graduate student expects to remain in academia as a professor, though a master's degree or doctorate may pay dividends in the private sector. The salaries for those with advanced degrees are considerably higher than for those with bachelor's degrees, of course. Training for the higher-paying professions of business, medicine, and law also causes students to incur high levels of debt, in most cases. Doctors, in particular, must train for many years before seeing any benefit of the high expected salary and must pay down student loans for many years after graduating. This risk of debt is not enough to discourage prospective doctors, it must be noted.

Other types of education come at a bit of a premium. There has recently been a rise in the field of universities operating for profit. There are dozens of schools offering degree options, typically to older students who are already in the workforce and want to return to school to maximize their earnings potential but have trouble attending traditional college. Some of these schools offer distance learning, so students anywhere can take courses from the University of Phoenix, for instance. Unlike traditional models of colleges, which require students to take general education courses and expect professors to be leaders in academic research, these for-profit schools offer directed courses in fields with high demand—nursing, computer science, and accounting, for example—and hire teachers only to teach. Anyone with the money for tuition is accepted into the program, and the course schedules are quite flexible.

Detractors of for-profit education raise some legitimate concerns over these programs. Privatizing education seems contrary to American ideals, and the prospect of public knowledge becoming the property of a corporation seems antithetical to traditional academic systems. In this model, the students become customers, and the quality of their education may suffer in deference to the company's profit margin. There have been some scandals and lawsuits involving some of these schools, and students must be careful to research their schools of choice. Many of these schools, however, are careful to emphasize their commitment to their students' success and boast high rates of postgraduate career placement.

There is yet another mode of adult education; in particular, new immigrants who wish to become naturalized citizens of the United States must pass an examination—in English—on the U.S. government and swear an oath of loyalty to the United States. To pass this test, many immigrants enroll in English as a second language courses and civic education courses, available in most communities free or at a low cost. There are currently about

Immigrants from Bosnia-Herzegovina become American citizens as they listen to the Pledge of Allegiance during a naturalization ceremony. © AP Photo/East Valley Tribune, Jennifer Grimes.

35 million foreign-born Americans, 13 million of whom have undergone the process to become naturalized citizens. They go to great lengths to learn about their adopted country and how to succeed as Americans—and what, really, could be as American as that?

## NOTES

1. Centers for Disease Control and Prevention, "CDC Fact Sheet: Young People at Risk—HIV/AIDS Among America's Youth," January 31, 2001, http://www.the body.com.

2. A. Di Censo, Gordon Guyatt, A. Willan, and L. Griffith, "Interventions to Reduce Unintended Pregnancies among Adolescents: Systematic Review of Randomized Controlled Trials," *British Medical Journal* 324 (2002), www.bmj.com.

3. U.S. Census Bureau, "Income, Earnings, and Poverty Data from the 2005 Community Survey," http://www.census.gov.

4. Rasmussen Reports, "Willingness to Vote for Woman President," April 8, 2005, http://www.rasmussenreports.com.

5. R. Claire Snyder, *Gay Marriage and Democracy* (New York: Rowman and Littlefield, 2006), 15.

6. U.S. Census Bureau, "Families and Living Arrangements: 2005," http://www.census.gov.

7. Centers for Disease Control and Prevention, "Births, Marriages, Divorces, and Deaths: Provisional Data for 2004," Table A, http://www.cdc.gov.

8. Dan Hurley, "Divorce Rate: It's Not as High as You Think," *New York Times,* April 19, 2005.

9. Rose M. Kreider, "Number, Timing, and Duration of Marriages and Divorces: 2001," in *Current Population Reports* (Washington, DC: U.S. Census Bureau, 2005), 70–97.

10. Steven P. Martin, "Education and Marital Dissolution Rates in the U.S. Since the 1970s" (working paper, University of Maryland, College Park, n.d.), http://www.russellsage.org.

11. U.S. Census Bureau, "American Community Survey, 2005," http://www.census.gov.

12. *Defense of Marriage Act,* Public Law 104–199, *U.S. Statutes at Large* 100 (1996), 2419, codified at *U.S. Code* 1 (2000), §7 and *U.S. Code* 28 (2000), §1738C.

13. U.S. Census Bureau, Population Division, Fertility and Research Branch, "Living Arrangements of Children under 18 Years Old: 1960 to Present: Household Families," http://www.census.gov.

14. U.S. Department of Labor, Bureau of Labor Statistics, "American Time Use Survey, 2005," http://www.bls.gov.us.

15. Shelly Lundberg, "Gender and Household Decision-Making" (lecture notes, University of Siena International School of Economic Research, Certosa di Pontignano, Italy, 2005).

16. National Center for Education Statistics, *Digest of Education Statistics, 2005,* Table 1, http://nces.ed.gov; National Catholic Education Association, "Catholic Education Questions," http://www.ncea.org.

17. U.S. Census Bureau, Population Division, Education and Social Stratification Branch, "School Enrollment—Social and Economic Characteristics of Students: October 2005," http://www.census.gov.

18. National Center for Education Statistics, "Trends in Full- and Half-Day Kindergarten," 2004, http://nces.ed.gov.

19. National Center for Education Statistics, "Regional Differences in Kindergartners' Early Education Experiences," 2005, http://nces.ed.gov.

20. Child Trends Databank, "High School Dropout Rates," Summer 2006, http://www.childrensdatabank.org.

21. U.S. Census Bureau, "Social and Economic Characteristics of Students: October 2005," http://www.census.gov.

22. National Center for Education Statistics, "Homeschooling in the United States: 2003 Statistical Analysis Report," http://nces.ed.gov.

23. U.S. Census Bureau, *Statistical Abstract of the United States 2007,* Tables 215–218: Educational Attainment by Race, Sex, and State, http://www.census.gov.

24. U.S. Department of Justice, Bureau of Justice Statistics, "Violent Victimization of College Students," December 7, 2003, http://www.ojp.gov.bjs.

25. Federal Bureau of Investigation, *Crime in the U.S. 2004,* September 2005, http://www.fbi.gov; U.S. Department of Education, "Summary of Campus Crime and Security Statistics, 2002–2004," October 6, 2006, http://www.ed.gov.

## BIBLIOGRAPHY

Amato, Paul R., et al. *Alone Together: How Marriage in America Is Changing.* Cambridge, MA: Harvard University Press, 2007.

Baker, David. *National Differences, Global Similarities: World Culture and the Future of Schooling.* Stanford, CA: Stanford Social Sciences, 2005.

Carlson, Allan C. *Conjugal America: On the Public Purposes of Marriage.* New Brunswick, NJ: Transaction, 2007.

Hochschild, Arlie. *The Second Shift.* New York: Avon, 1989.

Lyons, William. *Punishing Schools: Fear and Citizenship in American Public Education.* Ann Arbor: University of Michigan Press, 2006.

National Center for Education Statistics. The Condition of Education, 2000–2006. http://nces.ed.gov/programs/coe.

Newton, Judith Lowder. *From Panthers to Promise Keepers: Rethinking the Men's Movement.* Latham, MD: Rowman and Littlefield, 2005.

Popenoe, David. *War over the Family.* New Brunswick, NJ: Transaction, 2005.

Rosenfield, Michael J. *The Age of Independence: Interracial Unions, Same-Sex Unions, and the Changing American Family.* Cambridge, MA: Harvard University Press, 2007.

Sacks, Peter. *Tearing Down the Gates: Confronting the Class Divide in American Education.* Berkeley: University of California Press, 2007.

Snyder, R. Claire. *Gay Marriage and Democracy: Equality for All.* New York: Rowman and Littlefield, 2006.

Thistle, Susan. *From Marriage to the Market: The Transformation of Women's Lives and Work.* Berkeley: University of California Press, 2006.

Wolfson, Evan. *Why Marriage Matters.* New York: Simon and Schuster, 2004.

# 4

## Holidays and Leisure

### Wende Vyborney Feller

All work and no play makes Jack a dull boy.

—Stephen King, *The Shining*

AMERICANS ARE NOTORIOUS for their reluctance to make time for play. On average, they work five more weeks each year than Brazilians or the British and two and a half weeks more than Canadians, Mexicans, Australians, or the Japanese. While the French average 39 vacation days each year—and use them—Americans accrue only 14 vacation days and typically leave four of those unused. And when Americans do go on vacation, 41 percent of office workers bring their laptops and plan to work.[1]

This appetite for work must be a surprise to the sociologists who predicted, back in the 1950s, that Americans would soon be burdened by an excess of leisure. At the same time, the American standard of 14 vacation days and half a dozen paid holidays represents a significant increase in leisure time from 150 years ago, when 12-hour workdays and six- or even seven-day workweeks were common—and even Christmas was not necessarily a day of rest. Although fairs, celebrations, sports contests, and hobbies appear in the first records of American history, not until 1870 were there official holidays that guaranteed many workers a day without labor. Today, as Americans come to expect around-the-clock shopping and entertainment, holidays are again becoming unstuck from the idea of rest and play.

## HOLIDAYS

Holidays in American culture encompass a wide range of events. The closest approach to a list of national holidays is the 10 federal holidays, which represent vacation days given to employees of the federal government and which are often also given as paid holidays by state and private employers: New Year's Day, the birthday of Martin Luther King Jr., Washington's birthday, Memorial Day, Independence Day, Labor Day, Columbus Day, Veterans Day, Thanksgiving, and Christmas. This federal holiday list scarcely defines what Americans see as events worth celebrating since it omits three of the holidays that Americans celebrate most enthusiastically: Valentine's Day, Mother's Day, and Halloween.

Broadening the definition to include official observances makes almost every day a holiday. There are enough federal observances to average one per week, year-round. Add state observances, and it is possible to pack a dozen holidays into a single day: May 1 is Loyalty Day, Bird Day, Family Day, Law Day, Lei Day, and a national Day of Prayer as well as the first day of month-long commemorations of Asian Americans, families, keeping Massachusetts beautiful, kindness, law enforcement workers, children, composers, senior citizens, the steel industry, and women veterans.

Given that Thanksgiving was a traditional event before it became a federal holiday, perhaps a holiday may be defined as a community festival that gains nationwide popularity. Certainly there are plenty of festivals vying for consumers' leisure and dollars. Popular festival themes include local history, local industry or agriculture, music, ethnic heritage, gay pride, food, and flowers. A typical festival includes a parade, a craft or art show, food vendors, face painting, musical performances, and possibly a competition to crown a queen or princess from among local young women.

Although it is easy to assume that a festival honoring a community's Swedish heritage or plethora of rattlesnakes has roots in the distant past, few festivals predate World War II. One researcher found that in Minnesota, about one-third of community festivals started in the 1980s, and fully 12 percent were part of a Bicentennial-era surge of interest in local history. Festivals do not necessarily grow organically from local tradition, either. When organizers of the Whigham Rattlesnake Roundup were asked why they chose rattlesnakes, they responded that it was their first idea other than a fish fry.[2]

Even when a festival commemorates an historic event, the festival itself may not be historic. In Apache Junction, Arizona, the Lost Dutchman Days festival celebrates the legend of a mysterious vanishing mine supposedly discovered in the 1880s. The festival dates only to 1965, about 15 years after the community was established.[3]

The Lost Dutchman may be a myth, but being fictitious does not stop events from inspiring a festival. Impersonators of characters from *Gomer Pyle*'s fictitious town of Mayberry appear at festivals throughout the rural South, culminating in Mayberry Days in Airy, North Carolina. Mena, Arkansas, celebrates Lum 'n' Abner Days, based on a radio show that was popular in the 1930s.[4]

Not all community festivals are recent inventions, of course, nor are they all in small towns. In Rochester, New York, the Lilac Festival has been celebrated continuously since 1902 (organizers claim 1892), drawing about 250,000 people each year.[5] San Francisco's Chinese New Year was celebrated as early as the 1860s; New Orleans's Mardi Gras is older yet. One researcher argues that the appeal of festivals is how they allow participants to belong to a community with minimal effort or commitment.[6]

Certainly there are plenty of communities vying for membership. In a single weekend in late February, people who list cooking and eating as their favorite leisure activities can choose from seven events. At the top of the food chain is the South Beach Wine and Food Festival, a Florida weekend that includes the Food Network Awards and is expected to draw 20,000 gourmets who can afford to spend upward of $1,000 on tickets. While this festival dates only to 2002, the Twin Cities Food and Wine Experience and the Newport Seafood and Wine Festival are somewhat older (13 years and 30 years, respectively) and offer more modest ticket prices.

More accessible, owing to free admission, are the Annual Clam Chowder Cook-off in Santa Cruz, California; the Grant Seafood Festival, which draws 50,000 visitors to Oregon and dates to 1996; the Parke County, Indiana, Maple Syrup Fair; and the Annual Florida Gourd Festival. This last event offers not only classes in gourding, but also free parking for recreational vehicles.[7]

Perhaps the most familiar festivals are the county fair and the state fair. The traditional county fair, with livestock exhibitions, parades, performances, and baking competitions, evolved from agricultural and employment fairs around 1811 and was widely popular before the Civil War. Although only about 20 percent of Americans live in rural areas, county fairs have staying power. Though fewer than 1 percent of the residents of San Mateo County, California, work in farming, fishing, or forestry, the county still holds its fair. Even a completely urbanized county like San Francisco sees periodic efforts to start a county fair.[8]

County fairs are held during the summer, as a precursor to the big event: the state fair, traditionally held near Labor Day weekend. As county fairs became popular, the state fair was a natural way to pit county winners against one another and to showcase the state's agricultural bounty—a powerful means of attracting immigrants to settle the frontier states. These larger fairs require a permanent exhibition ground that is also used for other events throughout the year. The State Fair of Texas can gross $2.3 million in a single day.[9]

Most communities put more fervor into their county fair than into celebrating a federal holiday like Washington's birthday. Yet it is unlikely that anyone has ever sent a greeting card to commemorate the San Mateo County Fair. Sending holiday cards is such a thoroughly entrenched American tradition that the term *Hallmark holidays* is used to describe occasions that were reputedly invented by—or at least promoted by—major card company Hallmark to boost sales. Suspected Hallmark holidays range from Valentine's Day and Mother's Day to more obscure Sweetest Day, Secretary's Day, and Grandparents' Day.

Greeting cards and true holidays from work both became popular at about the same time, the mid-nineteenth century. Until the federal government declared four bank holidays in 1870—Independence Day, Thanksgiving, Christmas, and New Year's Day—there was no connection between a celebration and a day off from work.

While even Christmas was celebrated sporadically for years before becoming a major event, Independence Day has been widely celebrated since 1777, the year after the Declaration of Independence was signed. Bands, fireworks, parades, and picnics have been part of the celebration as far back as records go. Today, commemorating independence from Great Britain requires 150 million hotdogs, or approximately one for every two people. No one records how many sheet cakes decorated like a flag with strawberries, blueberries, and whipped cream are served, though the recipe has been a staple of women's magazines since the 1830s. It is also one of the least controversial holidays. Other than a gay rights protest in Philadelphia in 1965, there is little record of the controversies over inclusion that enliven St. Patrick's Day, the Chinese New Year, and Columbus Day.[10] Enjoying outdoor fun raises no public complaints about forgetting the meaning of the day.

For Thanksgiving, the civic meaning—thankfulness for the harvest—slipped away so gradually that little protest surrounds today's custom of serving a large meal amid a long day of watching television, notably the Macy's Thanksgiving Day parade and various football games. Although the holiday reputedly dates to the Pilgrims' first harvest in 1621, and George Washington established a late November date for a day of thanksgiving in 1789, Thanksgiving was not celebrated consistently until after 1863. In 1941, the date was set as the fourth Thursday in November.

Turkey and pumpkins were considered traditional as early as 1854, but the familiar menu for the largest eating holiday of the year was defined largely by army fare in World War II. The dinner served to soldiers in 1941 started with celery and olives, then included almost all of today's standard fare: roast turkey, sage dressing and giblet gravy, cranberry sauce, candied sweet potatoes and mashed potatoes, hot rolls, a vegetable, salad, and pumpkin pie as well as other desserts. The most crucial missing item was green bean casserole, a recipe invented for Campbell's Soup in 1955. By the early 1990s, cooking mavens were promoting nontraditional menus to spice up the day.[11] Turkey remains the centerpiece, but side dishes are where ethnic communities incorporate their own culinary traditions.

The Thanksgiving feast has become a source of stress. Turkey producer Butterball offers videos on thawing, stuffing, roasting, or barbecuing the turkey; the San Francisco *Chronicle* offers Turkey Training Camp for the worst cooks in the Bay Area. More than half of all cooks incorporate restaurant-prepared take-out items in their feast, usually side dishes or dessert, up from one-third in 2002.[12] No wonder people are ready to collapse in front of a football game.

Rest is vital, as the Friday after Thanksgiving marks the kick-off of the holiday shopping season. Although so-called Black Friday is not the heaviest shopping day of the year, the flood of shoppers into stores, along with the

Shoppers, some of whom have been shopping since 5:00 A.M., bargain hunt to grab specials on everything from toys to flat screen TVs on Black Friday, the beginning of the holiday shopping season. © AP Photo/Jeff Chiu.

popularity of door-buster bargains offered as early as 5:00 A.M., provides sufficient mayhem to justify the day's nickname.

The goal of all the shopping is Christmas: the most sentimentalized holiday of the year. While 77 percent of Americans identify as Christians, 95 percent celebrate Christmas. Americans send 1.9 billion holiday cards, cut 20.8 million trees, spend almost $32 billion in department stores alone in December, and mail 1 million packages.[13] Special holiday programming rules the television. The most famous Christmas classic, *A Charlie Brown Christmas,* mentions the birth of Christ and ends with a loosely Christian message of peace and acceptance, but most of the classic programs from the 1960s are more focused on reminding children that Christmas involves Santa Claus and that Santa brings presents.

Although there is a St. Nicholas in the Catholic pantheon, the legend that he brings presents to good children did not become popular in the United States until the early nineteenth century. Before then, it was New Year's Day, not Christmas, that was associated with presents. The vision of a St. Nick as a jolly bringer of presents who drove a reindeer-drawn sleigh and slid down the chimney to fill stockings first appears in Clement Moore's poem "The Night before Christmas" in 1823. Moore's work was part of a movement to establish a traditional holiday based loosely on customs current in Germany, where Americans believed family life was better appreciated.

The fat, jolly, fur-clad Santa Americans know is largely the creation of illustrator Thomas Nash in the 1860s. Department store Santas became common at about the same time, and now no shopping venue is complete without a jolly old elf. A skilled Santa can make up to $18,000 in the six weeks between Thanksgiving and Christmas. So popular is visiting Santa that the Herald Square Macy's alone gets 1,000 visitors per hour. The magic may be more in the eyes of the parents than the children, though: one business professor observed that 82 percent of the children in one line to see Santa seemed bored. It is estimated that a full 20 percent of the people climbing on Santa's lap are adults.[14]

Believing in Santa Claus is one of the benchmarks of childlike innocence; learning that there are no flying reindeer, and that the presents come from parents, is an important, if not traumatic, rite of passage. Santa is also the sign of the so-called wars over Christmas, in which some Christians worry that greed for gifts, and concern over the sensitivities of the non-Christian minority, has taken the Christ out of Christmas. In 2005, the uproar was over Wal-Mart's decision that clerks should say *happy holidays!* instead of *merry Christmas!* By 2006, Wal-Mart was back to *merry Christmas!* Another frequent controversy is whether government agencies can sponsor nativity scenes or other displays of Christian symbols; the answer is usually no.[15]

Christmas is so pervasive that, as one rabbi noted, "This month of December is a rather difficult time for Jews."[16] American Jews have transformed Hanukah, the festival of lights that falls in December, from a minor legend to an eight-day extravaganza of parties and gifts, complete with its own silver-and-blue gift wrap. (In spiritual terms, Hanukah is far less important than Yom Kippur, the day of atonement, and Rosh Hashanah, the Jewish new year, both of which fall between Labor Day and Halloween.)

This shift in the importance of Hanukah brings its own controversies about how much Jews should assimilate with the Christian majority. It will be interesting to see what happens if the Hindu population of the United States continues to double each decade since the major Hindu festivals also cluster in the spring and autumn. Will some lesser Hindu legend gain prominence at midwinter? Even more complicated is the situation with Muslims, the second largest non-Christian religion in the United States, as the monthlong daytime fast of Ramadan falls during the holiday season at least every 12 years.

Attaching a holiday to Christmas has worked for Kwanzaa, the African American celebration invented by Ron Karenga in 1966. Celebrated the week after Christmas, Kwanzaa devotes one day to each of the values of unity, self-determination, collective responsibility, cooperative economics, purpose,

Santa Claus prepares before making an appearance in December. © AP Photo/ Nevada Appeal, Brad Horn.

A member of Sistahs Supporting Sistahs lights the candle
of Ujima, meaning "collective
work and responsibility," during a Kwanzaa celebration. ©
AP Photo/The Holland Senti-
nel, J. R. Valderas.

creativity, and faith. As the festival grows in popularity, some leaders worry
that commercialism is watering down its original meaning of ethnic pride
and self-respect.[17]

Perhaps the most potent rebellion against Christmas, surpassing even Ad-
buster's Buy Nothing Day on Black Friday, is Festivus, "the festival for the
rest of us," invented by the hit television comedy *Seinfeld.* The hallmarks of
Festivus are erecting a bare Festivus pole instead of a Christmas tree, airing
grievances, and performing feats of strength. As quickly as it caught on, the
holiday became commercialized: Ben and Jerry's launched a Festivus-themed
ice cream flavor in 2000, and by 2006, manufacturers were warring over who
produced the authentic Festivus pole.[18]

The last of the original four holidays is New Year's Day, or the morning
after a New Year's Eve party that is supposed to include toasting the strike of
midnight with champagne, kissing, and singing "Auld Lang Syne." Once day
breaks, about 40 percent of Americans make New Year's resolutions, most
often to stop smoking, lose weight, and "be a better person." A WTVU/
Marist College poll found that at the end of 2005, 63 percent of those
surveyed had kept their resolutions, though men were more likely than
women to claim success.[19]

Additional federal holidays were added to the calendar gradually, then generally moved to Mondays with the Uniform Monday Holiday Act of 1968 (actually implemented in 1972). These lengthened weekends were supposed to benefit retailers, but it is doubtful that anyone predicted how thoroughly bargain shopping and minivacations would distract attention from the people being honored.

Many of these holidays were somewhat controversial in their origins. For instance, Memorial Day (originally Decoration Day) started in 1866 as a way to honor Union soldiers in the recent Civil War. The South had its own Confederate Memorial Day, most often celebrated on April 26. It has been noted that African Americans observed federal Memorial Day celebrations, while whites in the South still preferred Confederate Memorial Day.[20] Now settled on the last Monday in May, Memorial Day may be more recognized as an excellent weekend for weddings than as a day of remembrance.

Memorial Day is also often confused with Veterans Day, which honors all who fought, including the living. Like Memorial Day, Veterans Day started with a different name, Armistice Day, and a slightly different purpose: to honor those who fought in World War I, then believed to be the war to end all wars. After World War II, the day became a more general celebration for veterans. Of the approximately 24.5 million living veterans in the United States, about one-third fought in World War II, while 15 percent fought in Vietnam.[21] Although Veterans Day was among the Monday holidays defined in 1968, it has since returned to its original date of November 11. Appropriate activities for both Memorial Day and Veterans Day include decorating the graves of dead soldiers.

Labor Day, assigned to the first Monday in September, developed in the 1880s as a symbolic day of rest for the workingman. At the time, rest was controversial: even Sundays were commonly workdays. As late as 1910, labor leaders and ministers were lobbying for an eight-hour workday and a six-day workweek. Within the next decade, labor leaders adopted Labor Day as an occasion for speeches promoting unionization. Workers must have achieved some rest; by the 1930s, Labor Day had become a big day for trips to the beach.[22]

While Memorial Day has the Indy 500 race, Labor Day has the Muscular Dystrophy Association telethon, hosted by Jerry Lewis since 1966. Perhaps the temptation to stay parked in front of the television on a beautiful fall day has something to do with the reality that school traditionally starts on the day after Labor Day. The start of the school year assumes some of the character of a holiday in its own right, with the average family spending over $500 in 2006, mostly on clothing and electronics.[23]

Also born in the 1880s was the far less controversial holiday honoring the birthday of George Washington. Now celebrated on the third Monday of January and popularly believed to be a Presidents' Day that also honors Abraham Lincoln, the holiday remains officially dedicated to Washington alone. However, enthusiasm for celebrating Washington's leadership has waned substantially since 1855, when New Yorkers turned out for a parade with military bands and floats, plus speeches, songs, and fireworks. By the 1980s, the Manhattan parade had been reduced to a parochial school fife-and-drum corps and the Knights of Columbus, and most celebrating was done at Herald Square department stores.[24]

Martin Luther King Day, the newest of federal holidays, demonstrates how a holiday is pulled two ways. Celebrated on the third Monday in January, the day was added to the federal calendar in 1986 to include an African American in the official pantheon of American heroes. The day was not observed in all 50 states until 2000, when New Hampshire renamed its nine-year-old Civil Rights Day. More predictably, the last serious hold out had been South Carolina, which balanced honors for the civil rights leader by adding Confederate Memorial Day to its official state calendar.[25]

Other than public readings of King's famous "I Have a Dream" speech, there is not yet consensus on how to celebrate the holiday. Some advocate a national day of community service, described as "a day on, not a day off." It

People march in honor of Martin Luther King Jr. © AP Photo/The Fresno Bee, Christian Parley.

is still controversial when a national chain such as Catherine's, a store offering plus-sized women's clothing, holds a Martin Luther King Day sale. Is the chain trivializing the struggle for civil rights, or is it recognizing that African Americans have disposable income and corporate careers? Meanwhile, one small Florida town discovered it could improve turnout for the day's civic events by adding floats, arts and crafts, and food booths—just like other community festivals.[26]

With floats and craft booths, Martin Luther King Day may be doing better than Columbus Day, arguably a failure among federal holidays. From its origins in 1869 in San Francisco, Columbus Day was intended to celebrate Italian heritage along with the European discovery of America. The day was added to the official federal calendar in 1937. Since then, observance has lagged. Workplaces stay open; few traditions are associated with the day; the National Retail Federation does not bother to track spending. Hispanics have redefined the day as Día de la Raza, a celebration of Hispanic heritage, while South Dakota celebrates Native American Day.

This ambiguous status is a comedown from the holiday's heyday near the end of the nineteenth century. In 1892, Columbus Day was one of the holidays deemed appropriate for civic pageants: Bridgeport, Connecticut's, pageant included a reenactment of the landing of the Santa Maria, in which locals dressed as sailors and priests, and Indians dedicated the New England coast to Spain. When Columbus Day first became a state holiday in New York in 1909, celebrations included an 80,000-watcher parade up Fifth Avenue, with 300 Italian American societies participating. With Día de la Raza celebrations having taken over the Fifth Avenue parade route and Native American communities reinventing the pageant, Columbus Day seems to be mutating into a new ethnic holiday.[27]

Día de la Raza raises the question of how an ethnic celebration becomes a popular holiday. Representing the heritage of a large number of Americans helps: St. Patrick's Day, celebrated on March 17 since 1762, has a natural constituency among the 34.7 million Americans who claim Irish ancestry—more than quadruple the population of Ireland. The day calls for eating corned beef and cabbage (an American variant of a traditional Irish dish), visiting Irish pubs, and (in recent years) drinking green beer; parades are also popular. In the mid-1990s, participation in New York City's St. Patrick's Day parade was a matter of dispute as the controversial Irish nationalist organization Sinn Fein was allowed to participate, while gay and lesbian groups were not.[28]

Similarly, Cinco de Mayo can claim support from the fastest growing ethnic group in the United States: Hispanics. The day commemorates the 1862 Battle of Puebla, when an outnumbered Mexican army defeated French

Children from Ballet Folclorico Quetzalcoatl in New York celebrate Cinco de Mayo with a traditional dance. © AP Photo/Tina Fineberg.

forces. An official holiday in Mexico, the celebration of Cinco de Mayo first became popular in states along the Mexican border. Like St. Patrick's Day, Cinco de Mayo has become a bonanza for restaurants and bars; even gringos can appreciate bargain cerveza.[29]

On the other hand, Irish and Mexican are only the fourth and sixth most frequently claimed ancestries among Americans. The others in the top 10 are German, African American, English, just plain American, Italian, Polish, French, and American Indian. While Italian Americans have Columbus Day and African Americans have Martin Luther King Day, celebrations of the other dominant ethnicities remain local: an Oktoberfest here, a Bastille Day there.

Meanwhile, an ethnicity that represents less than 1 percent of the population puts on one of the biggest parties on the West Coast: Chinese New Year in San Francisco. The celebration, dating to the 1860s and held on the lunar New Year in February or early March, rivals New Year events in China and is televised worldwide. The event is so large that Southwest Airlines now sponsors it. And, like the St. Patrick's Day parade in New York, who is in and who is out is a battlefield of identity. In 2006, members of Falun Gong, a movement banned in the People's Republic of China, were barred from participating because they had allegedly broken rules by passing out literature during the 2004 event.[30]

Touching a chord in many lives may be why some festivals grow into holidays. It is hard to oppose honoring mother and father, so there are huge constituencies for celebrating Mother's Day, on the second Sunday in May, and Father's Day, on the third Sunday in June. Both holidays were products of lingering Victorian sentimentality. Anna Jarvis of Grafton, West Virginia, spearheaded Mother's Day in 1908 to honor her late mother. The same year, Grace Golden Clayton of Fairmont, West Virginia, introduced a day to honor fathers killed in a mining accident; two years later, Sonora Smart Dodd of Spokane, Washington, held an event to honor her father's devotion as a single parent. Dodd aggressively promoted the event, which was recognized by Congress in 1956 and became a permanent holiday in 1972.[31] Mother's Day had been on the calendar since 1914.

Mother's Day elicits slightly more spending than Valentine's Day, at an average of $122 per person. According to the National Retail Federation, 85 percent of buyers send greeting cards, 65 percent send flowers, and 32 percent buy gift cards. The enormous greeting card spending is still just 4 percent of annual sales, but Mother's Day is definitely the year's busiest day for phone calls. The tradition most firmly associated with the day is wearing a carnation: red for a living mother and white for a deceased one. However, this practice is an evolution from the original practice of wearing or displaying white carnations to honor all mothers, living or dead.[32]

Father's Day packs nowhere near the emotional wallop of Mother's Day. Only about 100 million cards are sent for Father's Day, versus 150 million for Mother's Day. Hallmark and American Greetings agree that funny cards outsell sentimental ones. While the National Retail Federation mourns that spending is about 20 percent lower than for Mother's Day, the National Restaurant Federation notes that Father's Day is the fourth biggest day of the year for dining out. (The others, in reverse order, are Valentine's Day, New Year's Eve, and Mother's Day.)[33]

A third holiday devoted to sentiment, St. Valentine's Day on February 14, has a cloudier history. The saint's day was established in 496 as a celebration of his martyrdom more than 200 years earlier. Not until 1493 did the legend of Valentine helping persecuted lovers appear. Why a Roman Catholic saint's day gained popular appeal in 1840s America—a time of widespread prejudice against Roman Catholics—is unclear. However, it is known that mass-produced Valentine cards found a market as early as 1847, when Esther Howland of Worcester, Massachusetts, started selling lacy, sentimental confections.[34]

Valentine's Day remains the second largest holiday for greeting card sales, after Christmas, with 190 million cards sold. About 25 percent of these cards are humorous, though 45 percent of men and 34 percent of women claim to prefer humorous cards. In general, Valentine's Day is the second biggest retail holiday after Christmas, the stars of spending being chocolate, roses, jewelry, and dinners out. The National Confectioners Association rates Valentine's Day as fourth among holidays (Halloween is bigger), with about 36 million heart-shaped boxes of candy sold. One-third of Americans send flowers, amounting to 180 million roses and giving florists a reason to raise prices up to 30 percent in the prior week. Among bargain-seeking Wal-Mart shoppers, at least, romance burns most brightly in Mississippi (third in sales of diamonds, first in chocolates, and fifth in roses) and fizzles in Vermont.[35]

This romantic holiday is also reputedly the best time of year to catch lovers cheating. No wonder one poll found that 1 in 10 adults under age 25 feels "depressed, insecure, inadequate, or unwanted" on the day. The same poll determined that one-third of women feel indifferent toward the holiday and that two-fifths of single people feel indifferent or negative. Retailers are rushing to serve this market of the disaffected. In 2007, Altoids opened Anti-V Day shops in New York, Chicago, and Miami, while greeting card manufacturers introduced anti–Valentine's Day lines.[36]

The death of sentimentality is evident in the sudden rise of Halloween. The National Retail Federation calls it the sixth largest holiday for retail spending, worth about $5 billion in 2006, with $1.8 billion spent on costumes alone. Party City says it is the second largest holiday for decorating, trailing only Christmas, thanks to the popularity of plastic bats and faux gravestones. Two-thirds of all Americans attend Halloween parties, with participation reaching 85 percent among 18- to 24-year-olds.[37]

This is not Halloween's first appearance as a festival primarily for adults. In the 1920s, Halloween became a stylish time for high society galas, including one in 1933 that followed the first known scavenger hunt party among New York's smart set.[38] The custom of trick-or-treating at Halloween did not become commonplace until the 1940s. With widespread trick-or-treating came rumors of Halloween treats contaminated with razors, poison, or LSD. However, the Urban Legends Reference can find no documented instance of tainted food being given to children by non–family members.[39]

The popularity of Halloween has also made it more controversial. Although the Día de los Muertos has a legitimate history as a spiritual precursor to All Saint's Day on November 1, some evangelical Christians call Halloween anti-Christian because it shares the calendar with the pagan festival of Samhain. Pagans, in turn, claim the holiday is theirs and always has been. However, it is unlikely that the familiar American celebration with costumes, jack-o'-lanterns, and trick-or-treating descends from either of these traditions. One of the earliest mentions in the *New York Times* appears in 1879, in an article that acquaints the reader with the quaint fortune-telling customs of All Hallows' Eve in England. Just three years earlier, the *Times* had complained that Halloween traditions were entirely forgotten in the United States.[40] As with Christmas, current traditions are probably inventions, based only loosely on European customs.

The other popular holiday for dressing up and letting down inhibitions is Mardi Gras, the Fat Tuesday that precedes the start of Lent, which in turn leads to Easter. In New Orleans, the center of Mardi Gras fun, multiple parades full of elaborate floats, sponsored by social clubs, or *krewes,* with names like Momus and Comus, have been part of the traditional celebration since before the Civil War; women lifting their shirts for *Girls Gone Wild* videos are a newer twist on the revelry. While New Orleans saw only 350,000 visitors in 2006, the year after Hurricane Katrina devastated the city, organizers in 2007 hope for a return to numbers closer to 2005s 1.4 million.[41]

Lent—a period of prayer, fasting, and alms giving before Easter—would seem to be the last event that could attract retail sales. The major Jewish holiday of Passover, which occurs near Easter and commemorates the Jewish people's flight from slavery in Egypt into the promised land of Israel, at least requires unleavened foods that are kosher for Passover. However, the Roman Catholic requirement to eat no meat on Lenten Fridays makes this the season for restaurants to promote their fish menus. KFC has gone so far as to request that the Pope bless its new fish sandwich.[42]

Unlike Hanukah, Passover has not been transformed by proximity to a major Christian holiday: it remains an important religious festival, but advertising does not show the Easter Bunny showing up for the seder. Kosher grocery stores currently do about 45 percent of their annual business at Passover (like Easter, it is a holiday that brings out less observant believers), though they are facing increased competition from mainstream grocery stores trying to reach a Jewish market. For those who dread cleaning every corner of the house to purify it (or seeing their relatives at the ritual dinner), resorts now offer vacation packages that promise to comply with the complex dietary rules of the season.[43]

Meanwhile, Christians celebrate Easter by buying $2 billion in candy, including 1 billion Peeps marshmallow chicks and bunnies, 16 billion jelly beans, and 90 billion chocolate rabbits (most of which will have their ears eaten first).[44] The candy goes into an Easter basket, the traditional reward to children for finding decorated eggs that their parents have hidden on behalf of the Easter Bunny. Although it is now popular to trace the Easter Bunny to pagan customs, the rabbit and the egg hunt were popularized in America in the mid-nineteenth century as part of a fashion for family-focused German customs. These particular customs first appear in German sources after the Protestant Reformation.

The connection between Jesus and colored eggs remains so unclear that some cities have renamed their annual egg hunts to remove references to Easter, though the juxtaposition of egg hunt, church service, and elaborate luncheon remains customary. Of the major holidays, Easter has the least firmly established menu, though spiral-cut hams outpace candy in dollars spent. It is also a holiday that gains appeal from occurring variously from late March to late in April, so that it becomes an occasion for showing off new spring clothes.[45]

The most clothing-oriented celebration is neither Easter nor even Halloween. On few occasions will a typical woman spend as much on a dress as she does for her wedding gown, with an average price of over $1,000. Post–World War II prosperity started weddings' growth to a personalized festival far larger than Christmas and requiring over a year to plan. Each year, almost 2.3 million American couples plan a formal wedding, at an average cost of $26,800, resulting in an industry worth $7.9 billion.[46] While a white gown and veil for the bride remain standard, the wedding ceremony has become more individualized and complex, with couples writing their own vows, lighting a unity candle to honor their families, asking their attendants to read poems or sing, and offering family medallions to children from earlier marriages. A large wedding can expand to fill the entire weekend, with a bridesmaids' lunch, rehearsal dinner, and bachelor party before the big day, a formal reception and dance following the ceremony, and a present-opening brunch on the day after.

Other rites of passage have exhibited the same expansion. One Boston writer commented that lamenting materialism is as much a Jewish bar mitzvah tradition as holding a lavish party after the religious ceremony. Both the ceremony, in which a boy of about 13 is admitted to manhood and reads from holy scripture in front of the synagogue, and the subsequent party did not become widespread in the United States until the 1970s. Peculiarly, for a ritual that was meant to apply only to males, the popularity of the bar mitzvah may have increased as Jewish feminists promoted a parallel ceremony for their daughters.[47]

The Christian ceremony of confirmation, held by Roman Catholics at about the same age as the bar mitzvah, receives a far less lavish treatment. The closest equivalent is the Hispanic *quinceañera*, or 15th-birthday celebration, which calls for elaborate ball gowns, a mass, and a dance. With a typical cost between $5,000 and $10,000, the "quince" is not quite as grand as a wedding. However, the similarity to weddings is obvious to mass-retailer David's Bridal, which markets *quinceañera* gowns; and just as it is possible to have a combined wedding and honeymoon at an exotic location, it is possible to celebrate the *quinceañera* on a seven-day cruise. There is even a magazine for girls planning their quinces. Although the party has a long history in Latin America, it became widely popular in the United States only with a larger cultural shift to embracing ethnic traditions, rather than attempting to Americanize those rituals away.[48]

The 1990s also saw the growth of the kiddie birthday party from a cake, balloons, and pin the tail on the donkey to extravaganzas with clowns, rented zoo animals, elaborate favors, and guest lists of 50 or more. Parents in the San Francisco Bay area call elaborate birthday parties "a fundamental rite of passage." Meanwhile, in Minnesota, the parents behind Birthdays without Pressure are trying to "launch a local and national conversation" about how children's parties are out of control.[49]

## LEISURE

Self-indulgence may have become the theme of today's leisure activities, compared to past generations' interest in community participation and useful hobbies. In his widely discussed best seller *Bowling Alone,* Harvard political scientist Robert Putnam lamented how Americans give less time to civic activism, church, clubs, and even playing bridge or pinochle. In fairness, card games remain a monthly activity for about 3.9 percent of Americans, though the survey does not disclose whether the game was solitaire. Certainly the two most popular leisure pastimes—dining out and watching television—make no one's list of character-building activities.[50]

Building character has been a justification for play as far back as the seventeenth century. Puritan clerics recommended sports that could refresh the spirit but warned against games that might lead to gambling, drinking, and idleness. Of the activities that at least 1.5 percent of Americans enjoy once a month, few would have won approval in colonial Salem. Along with dining out and playing cards, the top activities include entertaining at home, barbecuing, baking, cooking, going to bars, going to the beach, going to live theater, playing board games, photography, scrapbooking, and reading books. Just over a century ago, a similar propensity for sedentary activities led Theodore Roosevelt to urge Americans to take up football and big game hunting to "develop the rougher, manlier traits of their character."[51]

Americans took up football—from the stands. Football's popularity as a spectator sport is almost unrivaled. From 1990 to 2005, attendance at professional and college football games grew 23 percent, pushing it ahead of its traditional rivals, baseball and basketball. Football is the most watched sport on television, making the average professional team worth $898 million, compared to just $376 million for the average baseball team and $353 million for the average basketball team. Thanks to its popularity and its large squads, football is also the men's college sport that fields the most players. However, tackle football and its gentler variant, touch football, rank only 25 and 24 among the most popular participation sports among Americans as a whole, and more than two-thirds of the players are college-age or younger. By the time Americans get into their fifties, they overwhelmingly prefer walking, fishing, swimming, and golf.[52]

Each of the big three sports represents a distinct aspect of American character. Baseball's hotdogs and hot July nights, with the game played under the sky in an old-style brick stadium and on real grass, summons nostalgia for a simpler, quieter, slower time—appropriate for a sport that evolved from cricket before the Civil War. Basketball, which was invented for play in the ghettos of Chicago in 1891, expresses the lightning-fast pace of urban life and the egalitarian ideals of a nation of immigrants. And football, which rose to dominate homecoming games in the 1920s and became a television phenomenon in the 1960s, epitomizes the United States' movement into being a superpower. By the time Joe Namath led the New York Jets to victory in the third Super Bowl in 1969, President Nixon was talking football in campaign speeches to the silent majority as part of his message that America should be number one.[53]

The drive to be number one has resulted in concerns about brutal play ever since football developed from rugby in Ivy League colleges in the 1870s. Even Theodore Roosevelt called for reforms, a movement that led in 1905 to the founding of the organization that is now the National Collegiate Athletic Association (NCAA). College play has also suffered under criticism that the national title is mythical or arbitrary because the teams with the top records are not pitted against one another in a single championship game, thanks to a system of ranking teams based on votes. Modifications to the bowl system, which has matched highly regarded teams on New Year's Day since the first Rose Bowl in 1902, have resulted in a championship game played on the second weekend in January, but there are still criticisms that top teams are excluded.

In professional football, superiority is more clear-cut. Being number one means winning the Super Bowl, in which the winners of the National Football Conference and American Football Conference face off. Super Bowl Sunday, in late January or early February, has become a de facto national holiday. The only bigger day for food consumption is Thanksgiving; the only program to beat the 2006 Super Bowl for total viewers is the 1983 finale of *M\*A\*S\*H.* *Forbes* calls the Super Bowl the most valuable brand in the United States, possibly because people tune in as much for the innovative commercials as for the play. A 30-second commercial spot cost $2.6 million in 2007.[54] The major advertiser is usually Anheuser-Busch, an appropriate choice for a day when traditional party menus feature beer, chicken wings, pizza, chips, and guacamole.

That water systems break during halftime as everyone flushes simultaneously is an urban legend.[55] Producers of the halftime show do their utmost to hold viewers. Since 1992, marching bands have been supplanted by celebrities such as Gloria Estefan, Diana Ross, Stevie Wonder, Paul McCartney, Britney Spears, the Rolling Stones, Prince, and (most infamously) Justin Timberlake and Janet Jackson. Jackson's so-called wardrobe malfunction, when Timberlake's playful tug on her bustier revealed her entire breast, resonated so strongly in popular culture that it led the Federal Communications Commission to crack down on nudity in soap operas. The incident also resulted in a $550,000 fine for CBS, the network that broadcast the 2004 Super Bowl.[56]

No one worries about excess flushing during Major League Baseball's World Series. A best-of-seven-game series simply does not generate the same passion as an all-or-nothing contest, and the television ratings show it. Since the early 1990s, viewers have slumped from an average of about 20 million households to fewer than 10 million households. The 2004 series between the Boston Red Sox and the St. Louis Cardinals temporarily reversed the trend, but the 2005 and 2006 series set new record lows.[57]

The secret is that watching baseball is less a pastime than a lifestyle. One type of hardcore fan is devoted to sabremetrics, the science of statistical analysis of at-bats, home runs, and pitch count. This interest in numbers means that while hitting a game-winning home run at the bottom of the ninth inning, with the bases loaded and two outs, *will* earn a player momentary glory, the lasting heroes are the ones who post numeric records such as Hank Aaron (most home runs over his entire career, at 755) and Cy Young (most career wins as a pitcher, at 511). The true sabremetrician is equally delighted by more esoteric records, such as the left-handed hitter whose ground balls led to the most double plays in a single season (Ben Grieve of the Oakland A's).[58]

A second type of fan attends minor league games, sometimes with so much enthusiasm that a minor league team like the Durham Bulls can draw over 300,000 fans each year and fill a snazzy new ballpark. A third type of fan turns out, 2.8 million strong, for spring training in Florida and Arizona, where the more intimate setting makes it easier to get autographs from favorite players. Some fans fear that as Cactus league stadiums ramp up concessions and events to attract more spectators, ticket prices will skyrocket, and the sense of a special time outside the professional season will collapse.[59]

A fourth type of fan cherishes the ballparks for their own sake, possibly making a project of seeing a game at every major and minor league ballpark. Even casual fans love ballparks: Americans' 150 favorite buildings include four traditional-style ballparks (Wrigley Field, number 31; the original Yankee Stadium, number 84; retro-style AT&T Park in San Francisco, number 104; and Fenway Park, number 113), but just one multipurpose sports center (the Astrodome, number 134).[60]

While baseball's grass and sunshine give it a suburban feel even in the middle of a city, basketball is relentlessly urban, from its asphalt courts to its origins as a low-cost way to keep working-class youth out of trouble. Playing baseball is part of an idyllic childhood, with 2.6 million kids participating in Little League, but the romance of pick-up basketball appeals more to teenagers and adults.[61] And just as Chicago gave birth to the game, it is also the origin of the Harlem Globetrotters, the African American team that amazed Americans with its stunt-filled exhibition play from 1927 until long after basketball had been integrated, even spawning a Saturday morning cartoon in the early 1970s.

In becoming a big-league industry, basketball remains the most egalitarian of the big three sports, offering more opportunities to African Americans and women than either football or baseball. Professional football banned African American players from 1933 to 1946, integrating only when the managers of the new Los Angeles stadium insisted, and then only with two players. Though 65 percent of NFL players are African American, there is some evidence that African American players are shunted into roles that rely more on athleticism than on strategy.[62]

Baseball confined African Americans to the so-called Negro League until 1947, when Jackie Robinson was assigned to the Brooklyn Dodgers; as late as 1959, there was an unintegrated team, and not one Negro League player appears on the All Century Team of the 100 greatest players. Since 1975, the proportion of African American players in Major League Baseball has dropped from 27 to 9 percent—fewer than the proportion of players from the Dominican Republic.[63] Professional basketball, by contrast, permitted African Americans to play in 1942 and integrated with 10 players.[64]

Both professional football and professional basketball have been good for colleges because National Football League and National Basketball Association (NBA) rules forbid recruiting players straight out of high school. Fielding a team gives alumni a chance to watch the next Joe Namath or Michael Jordan. In turn, football and basketball open doors for young African Americans to attend prestigious universities. This situation encompasses controversies: African American student-athletes graduate at a lower rate than white student-athletes but at a higher rate than African American students as a whole, and there are questions about how standards are applied to male student-athletes.[65] There is no question that basketball seems to incite the strongest loyalties at the college level: while professional basketball has stars, college basketball has decade-long rivalries. Matchups between traditional enemies, such as Duke versus the University of North Carolina, help assure that the men's NCAA championship tournament, nicknamed "March Madness," earns television ratings higher than the NBA championship.[66]

Basketball is also more hospitable to women than football or baseball. Despite the influence of Title IX federal civil rights legislation in directing resources to girls' and women's athletics since 1972, there is no NCAA women's football, and women's professional leagues struggle for recognition. Although there are four serious national women's football leagues, the only women's game that rated a mention during 2007 Super Bowl commentary was the Lingerie Bowl, a novelty event featuring models playing in shorts and sports bras.[67]

Baseball gained a more woman-friendly reputation with the 1992 release of *A League of Their Own,* the movie that raised awareness of the All-American Girls' Baseball League (AAGBL) that was popular during World War II. While the AAGBL drew crowds of over 500,000 in a good season, only in their last years did they play true baseball, rather than a cross between baseball and softball. Women are still encouraged to play softball, which uses a larger ball, a shorter bat, a smaller ballpark, and modified rules. Even so, women are enthusiastic about hitting a ball with a bat: the fourth largest number of female college players is in softball, behind soccer, outdoor track, and indoor track.

While basketball is only the fifth most popular sport among college women, it is the hands-down winner among televised women's college sports and women's professional sports. Basketball is the "exploding revenue generator," driving ESPN's $200 million, 11-year deal to televise women's college sports. The professional league, the Women's National Basketball Association, struggles with declining in-person attendance (though television viewership of championship finals was up 33 percent from 2005 to 2006), but has at least managed to outlast the Women's Professional Softball League and the Women's United Soccer Association.[68]

Outside the big three, favorite spectator sports and favorite college sports diverge. Colleges favor sports that require little expensive equipment, so soccer, track, cross-country running, and swimming all appear in the top 10 NCAA sports for both men and women. Of these sports, only soccer lures more than 1 percent of Americans to games at least once a month. Since two-thirds of soccer players are under age 18, the odds are good that many people at games are the middle-class, suburban soccer moms targeted by Bill Clinton in his 1992 presidential campaign.

Track and field events elicit widespread fan interest mostly in Summer Olympics years, particularly when a telegenic athlete sets new records, as Florence Griffith-Joyner and her sister-in-law Jackie Joyner-Kersee did in the

Detroit Shocker's Cheryl Ford holds up her MVP trophy. Beside her is WNBA president Donna Orenda. © AP Photo/Gerald Herbert.

1980s. Similarly, bringing attention to swimming requires, if not a Mark Spitz with seven gold medals and seven world records in the 1972 Olympics, at least a Gary Hall Jr., with 10 medals in three Olympics, a famous family, and a penchant for strutting and shadowboxing.

The cultural importance of a sport is not, however, necessarily tied to its attendance. More Americans regularly watch horseracing than ice hockey, but hockey joins football, basketball, and baseball as the sports where having a major league team is one mark of being a world-class city. Hockey's narrow audience is the result of geography: at the college level, it is played in only 38 states, and most of the players come from Minnesota or Canada. Since 1990, when San Jose was granted a team, professional hockey has followed job migration into the Sunbelt. Civic pride and displaced midwesterners fill local arenas, but hockey struggles with television ratings; the average hockey team is worth only $180 million, about half the value of a baseball or basketball team.[69]

The sport that people are actually attending—and watching on television—is the races sponsored by the National Association for Stock Car Auto Racing (NASCAR). NASCAR is the second most watched sport on television, after football, and claims one-third of Americans as fans. About 2.5 million Americans go to the races at least once a month, even though auto racing tracks are even less widely accessible than hockey rinks. For corporate sponsorship, NASCAR roars past football, with $1.5 billion in sponsors.[70] With motors alone costing $40,000 each, and a team using two or more motors every weekend, the need for big corporate money is obvious. Happily, NASCAR fans have a reputation for being intensely loyal to brands that sponsor cars and races.

Despite its reputation for beer-swilling, Confederate-flag-waving, redneck antics, NASCAR owes its importance in American sports to its clean-cut, family-friendly, Christian image. More women watch NASCAR on television than football or baseball, and one ESPN survey estimates that 42 percent of total fans are women.[71] NASCAR is unique among the major sports in that women compete alongside men, rather than in separate leagues, though women drivers remain few, and none has ever won a major race nor gained the fame of Indy racer Danica Patrick.

What distinguishes Indy from NASCAR is the cars: Indy racing uses open-wheel, rear-engine cars, while NASCAR racers drive stock Fords and Chevys, modified to handle the demands of 500-mile drives at over 200 miles per hour. The difference in cars parallels the distinct origins of the two sports. The most famous Indy race, the Indianapolis 500, dates back to 1911 and

NASCAR beats out baseball and basketball as one of America's most popular sports. Courtesy of Photofest.

has its origins in owner Carl Fisher's passion for designing cars for speed. NASCAR developed out of a popular pastime in the prosperous years after World War II, when men would turn out at local dirt tracks to race the family car. Thanks to interest in Patrick, the 2006 Indy 500 showed a respectable upswing in television ratings, though it still ate the exhaust of NASCAR's Coca-Cola 600.[72]

In its spectacle of hard-jawed, laconic heroes who harness horsepower to their will, NASCAR resembles an older, but equally rural, sport: rodeo. Focused on demonstrating skills at roping cattle and breaking broncos, rodeo developed from the real chores of ranch hands in the American West, almost died with the closing of the frontier, then was revived in the 1920s by entrepreneurs who sensed a market for nostalgia for a simpler time. Today, rodeo's most popular event is bull riding, billed as the world's most dangerous sport. Women compete only in barrel racing, which involves guiding a horse through tight turns along a preset course. Rodeo is big enough to play Las Vegas, which credits its annual National Finals Rodeo with bringing $50 million to the community, comparing favorably to the $85 million generated by the local NASCAR weekend.[73]

NASCAR and basketball are not the only sports to show upward mobility as events to watch. Professional boxing, a rough-edged bachelor pastime in the late nineteenth century, turned all-American in the 1960s. The figure who looms largest is heavyweight champion Muhammad Ali, whose popularity survived his conversion to Islam and his refusal to be drafted in the Vietnam War. His fight against underdog Chuck Wepner inspired the 1976 movie *Rocky,* which is one of only two films about American sports to win an Oscar for Best Picture. (The other winner is a movie about a female boxer, *Million Dollar Baby.*)

Despite his controversial beliefs and flamboyant lifestyle, Ali became an icon of American sportsmanship, paving the way for bad boy star athletes like boxer Mike Tyson, basketball player Charles Barkley, and skier Bode Miller. In retirement, Ali has been heaped with honors, including Sports Illustrated's Athlete of the Century in 1999, a Presidential Medal of Freedom in 2005, and a Nobel Peace Prize nomination in 2007.[74] In Ali's gloves, boxing became so respectable that for sheer down-market brutality, it is necessary to turn to the professional wrestling mania of the mid-1980s, when matches that were more soap opera than sport made stars of Hulk Hogan and future Minnesota governor Jesse Ventura.

Conversely, tennis and golf have tried to shed their image as sports for the country club set, hoping to increase revenues by broadening their appeal. Among participants, the country club image sticks: half of the players boast household incomes of $75,000 or higher. While wealthier Americans generally participate in sports at a higher rate, the most affluent families represent only about one-third of billiard players, bowlers, or hikers.

Some top players of the past, such as Billie Jean King, who started the first women's professional tennis tour and was the first woman to be *Sports Illustrated*'s Sportsperson of the Year, learned to play on public courts, not at the country club.[75] So did the first African American tennis stars, including activist Arthur Ashe. But the icons of upward mobility through tennis are sisters Serena and Venus Williams, whose parents groomed them to be professional players as a path out of the slums of Compton.

Part of the Williams' magic is how young they burst into the top ranks of professional tennis, winning their first open tournaments in their late teens. Similarly, a part African American child prodigy, Tiger Woods, is credited with broadening interest in golf. Woods started winning amateur matches at age eight and won the Masters by age 22, making him the youngest ever winner as well as the only Masters winner of African American or Asian descent.

However, if Venus Williams's five Grand Slam singles titles, Serena Williams's eight Grand Slam singles titles, or Tiger Woods's 12 major professional golf championships have increased youth interest in tennis or golf, the effect is not dramatic. The National Sporting Goods Association reports that between 1995 and 2005, the number of 12- to 17-year-old tennis players fell just 1.5 percent, compared to 11.5 percent for all ages. The number of golf players in the same age group grew 7.4 percent, notably more than the 3 percent in the general population.[76]

Young people from ages 7 to 17 are losing interest in traditional team sports, with the possible exception of ice hockey and soccer. Even basketball and bicycle riding, which involve more than 7 million teenagers each, attract fewer participants than they once did. The growth sports are skateboarding, snowboarding, and (only among the age 7–11 set) alpine skiing. Participation in skiing may be the result of ski resorts doing more to attract families, but the growing appeal of skateboarding and snowboarding are surely tied to the sports' extreme reputations. Unlike older sports that reward teamwork or sheer speed, skateboarding and snowboarding include competitions that emphasize showmanship in performing complex stunts. The tension between speed and style was bitterly demonstrated at the 2006 Winter Olympics, when Lindsay Jacobellis lost her commanding lead in the snowboard cross event because she inserted a trick into a high-speed run—and wiped out.[77]

The not-so-young prefer gentler sports, with walking, camping, swimming, exercising with equipment, bowling, net fishing, bicycle riding, freshwater fishing, billiards, and aerobic exercise leading the pack. Despite numerous studies showing that Americans are getting fatter, health clubs are a $15.9 billion

U.S. snowboarder Shaun White won several gold medals during the 2006 Winter Olympic games. © AP Photo/Lionel Cironneau.

industry, with over 41 million members. The International Health, Racquet, and Sportsclub Association estimates that about 15 percent of Americans belong to a health club; membership increased 17 percent from 1995 to 2005. The number of members who work out frequently has doubled since the mid-1990s. For affluent professionals, the health club may be replacing the country club, as half of all health club members have a household income greater than $75,000. Clubs keep their revenues up by exploiting trends like Pilates, the yoga-like stretching exercises that burst into popularity in 2002, with participation increasing 96 percent in a single year.[78]

Passion for sports is not limited to traditional athletes. Athletes with physical challenges, such as cerebral palsy, limited vision, or amputations, compete in the Paralympics, which follow the Olympics in the same venue. Attempts to include athletes with intellectual disabilities in the Paralympics have generated controversy; these athletes are more likely to compete in the Special Olympics. First developed in 1968 in Chicago by Eunice Kennedy Shriver, whose sister Rosemary may have been intellectually disabled, the Special Olympics now serves about 550,000 athletes in the United States, competing internationally in 30 sports. Unsurprisingly, given the American belief that sports build character, one of the Special Olympics' official goals is to increase respect for people with intellectual disabilities by displaying their ability to succeed on the playing field.[79]

Among ordinary Americans, the favorite sports that do not take place at the gym tend to take place in parks. Interest in developing parks started around 1838, when the rural cemetery movement remade the outdoors as a place to picnic while musing on eternal values. The first major noncemetery park project, New York's Central Park, developed in 1858, was widely copied in other major cities. By the end of the nineteenth century, Chicago had become the home of a populist drive for play parks, or smaller urban parks where working-class youth could work off their excess energy. Since the 1920s, play parks have been a routine part of new suburban developments, only recently supplemented by hiking trails.

The original impetus for developing state and national parks was less access to recreation than awe of the grandeur of the untamed West. The first national park was founded in 1872 to preserve the area known as Yellowstone and its spectacular geysers; it was designated a national park because the area crossed the boundary of Wyoming into Montana and Idaho. Of the 33 national parks defined before 1916, all but 4 are in the 11 western states.

The popularity of motor travel spurred growth in the number of national parks after World War II, as a camping trip made an affordable and potentially educational family vacation. As of 2007, there are 390 national parks. The system has been extended beyond natural wonders and campgrounds to include historic sites as well as urban areas such as the Golden Gate National Parks in San Francisco. Visitors surpassed 285 million in 1999, the last year for which the National Park Service provides statistics.[80]

State park systems also provide recreational facilities. Although Indian Springs in Georgia has existed since 1825, making it the oldest state park, most state park systems had their growth spurt in the 1930s, with the help of the Civilian Conservation Corps. For sheer size, the winner is Alaska, boasting 3.2 million acres of park system.[81]

The domesticated cousin of the state park is the amusement park, once a raucous and slightly unsavory scene of rickety rides, bathing beauties, and bearded ladies. Today's family-friendly amusement park was invented by Walt Disney in 1955, with the opening of Disneyland amid the orange groves of Anaheim, California. More than 515 million people have visited Disneyland since it opened. The second Disney park, Disneyworld in Florida, is the largest single-site employer in the nation. The Disney vision is so popular that the company was able to populate an experimental new urbanist community in Celebration with people who were eager to live at Disneyworld.[82]

Much of the appeal of Disneyland and Disneyworld is the opportunity to participate in a fantasy, whether of small-town America on Main Street USA or of the future in Tomorrowland. Some people take their fantasies further. Over 2 million Americans participate in more than 180 Renaissance Faires each year, dressing in the garb of the Middle Ages and reenacting jousts, feasts, and revels.[83] Another popular fantasy is reenacting battles, particularly from the Civil War; participants claim that this is one of the fastest-growing pastimes in the United States.[84]

War takes place on the tabletop, too. While simulations of battles have been used as a way to teach strategy all the way back to the invention of chess, recreating battles on a playing board or an elaborate tablescape started a rise in popularity in the 1970s, about the same time that role-playing games like Dungeons and Dragons became widespread.[85]

Perhaps surprisingly, board games and card games are holding their own against video games. Board games sales increased 18 percent in 2005, possibly because these games offer a quiet way for 20-somethings to gather for fun.[86] The most quintessentially American board game must be Monopoly, the real investment game that is played worldwide and includes sanctioned state and national tournaments. While classic games like Clue (solve a murder), Risk (invade Russia), and Trivial Pursuit (answer questions on pop culture) originated outside the United States, Americans can take credit for inventing the crossword-style game of Scrabble and the iconic game for small children, Hungry Hungry Hippos. Scrabble games are found in one-third of all American homes, and its competitiveness has grown to a scale similar to that of chess, complete with international tournaments and books on how to master advanced strategy.[87]

The most American of card games is probably poker, played in numerous variants since it appeared in the 1820s in New Orleans. Movies about the Old West are as incomplete without poker games as they are without horses and shoot-outs, and ability to maintain an expressionless poker face while bluffing about one's hand is a test of a strong, silent man. A championship tournament like the World Series of Poker can pay over $7 million to the winner. Televised tournaments have become quite popular. The importance of silence over interaction also makes poker ideal for online play.[88]

Not all tabletop games are taken seriously. Bingo, once the territory of blue-haired ladies down in the church social room, is enjoying a resurgence as a campy, kitschy game for younger people, particularly at gay bars. There is online bingo, too, a $710 million industry, where only 10 percent of the players are over 55, and 28 percent are under 34.[89]

Gaming is more serious business for Native American tribes, who have been permitted by the U.S. government to run casinos since the 1988 passage of the Indian Gaming Regulatory Act. In 2006, 387 casinos generated over $25 billion in revenue. Foxwoods, operated by the Mashantucket

Pequot Tribal Nation of Connecticut, is the largest casino in the world, boasting 100 poker tables, over 7,000 slot machines, and more than 40,000 guests each year. However, Indian gaming tends to benefit a handful of tribes, some of which applied to be recognized by the government in order to operate casinos: in 2002, just 13 percent of casinos, largely in states with few Native Americans, generated 66 percent of total Indian gaming revenue.

The gaming trail always leads back to the computer because electronic games have been popular since the heyday of arcade video games in the early 1980s, when Americans spent 75,000 man-hours playing. People still play Pong, the ping-pong-like game from 1972 that was the first arcade game to be widely successful; it also was the defining game of the first home gaming units in 1977. This success was followed by Space Invaders, the iconic shoot-the-aliens game, but it was Pac-Man, released in 1980, that truly captured the popular imagination. More than 100,000 machines were sold in the United States, followed by 30 licensed versions of the game and multiple sequels; Pac-Man even appears as a guest character in unrelated games. Pac-Man inspired an eponymous Saturday morning cartoon and a board game, along with a controversy when President Ronald Reagan sent a congratulatory letter to eight-year-old Jeffrey Yee for a Pac-Man score that many players deemed impossible to achieve. Pac-Man is still in play, now on fifth-generation iPods.[90]

Today's home gaming systems, which feature more realistic graphics, can be counted on to be among the year's hot Christmas gifts when a new version is released. In 2006, Sony's Playstation (PS) 3 was so heavily in demand that online auction giant eBay had to restrict sales to established sellers to decrease fraud. Even so, more than 3,000 PS3s were listed two days before the official launch, with bidders offering over $2,000 for a gaming system that would sell for $600. The launch of the competing Nintendo Wii, later in the same week, excited similar passion.[91]

More realistic graphics have led to more realistic violence. The flagship for complaints about promoting bad values is the Grand Theft Auto (GTA) series, in which players roam a major city and earn points for committing crimes. Grand Theft Auto: Vice City, in a setting loosely based on 1980s Miami, has the distinction of inspired complaints from Cuban and Haitian immigrants for racism, two lawsuits claiming the game caused teenagers to commit crimes, and an episode of CSI: Miami. The game is so widely recognizable that Coca-Cola's 2007 Super Bowl campaign featured a GTA-style character spreading sweetness, light, and Coke as he passed through a city.[92]

The next step from realism is an alternate reality, initially defined by the world-building computer game Sim City in 1989, which was followed by a dozen variants, including The Sims, the best-selling game for personal computers. While Sim City was about building and managing a metropolis, The Sims offered players the opportunity to live an alternate life.[93] But a true alternative life requires joining the online Second Life, a virtual world inspired by Neal Stephenson's novel *Snow Crash*. A rush of media attention in late 2006 brought 4 million accounts to Second Life, though economic statistics suggest that the number of active participants is closer to 450,000, with about 230,000 active enough to spend fictional Linden dollars. Because Linden dollars can be converted to normal U.S. currency, it is possible to make a real fortune in the virtual world: Ansche Chung of China was the first person to make $1 million from deals in Second Life.[94]

More hands-on hobbies include collecting, cooking, gardening, handicrafts like knitting or embroidery, and model-building pursuits such as train layouts, rocketry, or dollhouses. Not all building hobbies are miniaturized: the number of experimental home-built full-sized aircraft registered with the Federal Aviation Administration has been increasing by 1,000 a year for 15 years, surpassing 28,000 in 2007.[95]

Many hobbies evolved from handicrafts, such as sewing and building, that were useful on the frontier, but the heyday of hands-on hobbies occurred in the years immediately following World War II, when experts recommended hobbies as a way of coping with excess leisure. Although hands-on hobbies

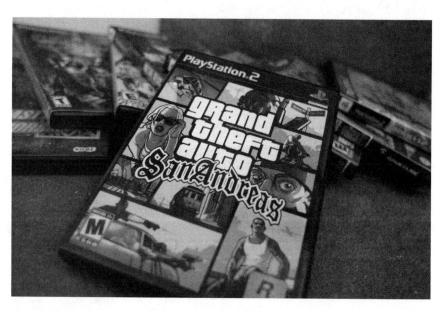

Grand Theft Auto is one of many popular, yet controversial video games. © AP Photo/Paul Sakuma.

struggle to attract a generation accustomed to video games, gracious-living guru Martha Stewart is credited with making pastimes like needlework and cake decorating respectable for middle-class women with professional careers. Easily the most popular of the feminine hobbies is scrapbooking, which transforms a basic photo album into an elaborate production of patterned papers, crops (ways to cut photos), die cuts (paper shapes used as decoration), stickers, ribbon, and colored ink. Since its inception in 1995, scrapbooking has grown into a $2.55 billion industry, with over 32 million participants.[96]

The popularity of scrapbooking may be fueled by the rise of more elaborate celebrations, which may in turn be related to how access to leisure has changed. Trends over the past four decades indicate that the people with the lowest-paid jobs saw the greatest gains in leisure, while the upper middle class are working more hours. So the people who have time do not have money, and the people who have money do not have time.[97] Bigger parties, with more lavish entertainment plus constant photography and videotaping, may be trying to pack a month's worth of fun and a year's worth of memories into a few hours' worth of party. Work hard; play hard. That is the American way.

## Notes

1. Porter Anderson, "Study: U.S. Employees Put in Most Hours," August 31, 2001, http://www.cnn.com; Tory Johnson, "The Death of the American Vacation," July 4, 2006, http://www.abcnews.com; Ellen Wulfhorst, "Laptops in Tow, More Americans Work on Vacation," *PC Magazine,* July 26, 2006.

2. Robert H. Lavenda, *Corn Fests and Water Carnivals: Celebrating Community in Minnesota* (Washington, DC: Smithsonian Institute Press, 1997), 11–12; Rodger Lyle Brown, *Ghost Dancing on the Cracker Circuit: The Culture of Festivals in the American South* (Jackson: University Press of Mississippi, 1997), 20–21.

3. Lars Jacoby, "Find Fun at Lost Dutchman Days," *Arizona Republic,* February 21, 2007, http://www.azcentral.com; Troy Taylor, "The Lost Dutchman Mine," http://www.prairieghosts.com; Apache Junction Chamber of Commerce, "Annual Events," http://www.apachejunctioncoc.com.

4. The Lum n' Abner Site, http://www.lum-abner.com; National Lum n' Abner Society, http://www.inu.net/stemple; Lum and Abner Festival, http://gomenaarkansas.com/lumNabner.asp.

5. "Park History," http://www.lilacfestival.com; Robert W. Brown, "Week of Lilacs at Rochester," *New York Times,* May 11, 1947, X15.

6. Lavenda, *Corn Fests,* 45.

7. See http://www.foodreference.com; South Beach Wine and Food Festival, http://www.sobewineandfoodfest.com; Twin Cities Food and Wine Experience, http://www.foodwineshow.com; Newport Seafood and Wine Festival, http://www.

newportchamber.org/swf; "Special Events," http://www.ci.santa-cruz.ca.us; Grant Seafood Festival, http://www.grantseafoodfestival.com; "Maple Syrup Fair," http://www.parkecounty.com; Florida Gourd Society, http://flgourdsoc.org.

8. U.S. Census Bureau, 2000 Census, http://factfinder.census.gov/; San Francisco County Fair, http://www.sfcountyfair.com.

9. "Top Fifty North American Fairs," *Amusement Business,* December 2004.

10. James R. Heintze, Fourth of July Celebrations Database, http://www.american.edu/heintze/fourth.htm; U.S. Census Bureau, "Facts for Features: The Fourth of July," May 17, 2006, http://www.census.gov; Amy Chozick, "A Slice of America," *Wall Street Journal,* July 2, 2004; Janice Podsada, "Where Is the Cradle of Gay Liberty?," *The Grand Rapids Press,* April 11, 2005, A6.

11. "Make Ready for Thanksgiving," *New York Times,* November 24, 1854, 4; "The Thanksgiving Dinner," *New York Times,* November 19, 1864, 8; "A Day for Giving Thanks," *New York Times,* November 28, 1878, 5; "Thanksgiving Is at Hand," *New York Times,* November 26, 1893, 18; Display ad, *New York Times,* November 28, 1923, 15; "750 Tons of Thanksgiving Turkeys Ordered by Army for 1,500,000 Men, Plus All Fixin's," *New York Times,* November 9, 1941, 44; Richard L. Eldridge, "Spilling the Beans about Holiday Casserole's Origins," *Atlanta Journal-Constitution,* December 17, 2005, A1; Kristin Eddy, "Shaking up the Traditions: Alternative Tastes That Stay True to Thanksgiving," *Washington Post,* November 20, 1991, E1.

12. Butterball, http://www.butterball.com; Stacy Finz, "Thanksgiving 101: Turkey Training Camp," *San Francisco Chronicle,* November 15, 2006; National Restaurant Association, "Nation's Restaurants Ready to Aid Busy Americans with Their Thanksgiving Feasts," November 13, 2006, http://www.restaurant.org; Janet Raloff, "Home Cooking on the Wane," *Science News* 162 (2002), http://www.sciencenews.org.

13. Dana Blanton, "Majority Okay with Public Nativity Scenes," June 18, 2004, http://www.foxnews.com; U.S. Census Bureau, "Facts for Features: The Holiday Season," December 19, 2005, http://www.census.gov.

14. Jack Kenny, "Yes, Virginia, There Is a Santa Employment Agency," *New Hampshire Business Review,* December 14–27, 2001, 15–16; "Bob Rutan: Director of Annual Event Operations at Macys, New York," *T+D,* December 2006, 96; Mary Beckman, "Ho Ho Hum," *Science Now,* December 12, 2003, 2–3; Alex Mindlin, "Santa's Knee Belongs to Everyone," *New York Times,* December 17, 2006.

15. M. Z. Hemingway, "A Lull in the War on Christmas," *Los Angeles Times,* December 24, 2006, M2; Warren Richey, "Nativity Scene Is Too Religious for New York Schools," *Christian Science Monitor,* February 22, 2007, 4.

16. Marianne Bernhard, "Jews and December," *Washington Post,* December 24, 1980, A7.

17. Maulana [Ron] Karenga, The Official Kwanzaa Web Site, http://www.officialkwanzaawebsite.org; Dorothy Rowley, "Kwanzaa: Celebration of Culture or Retail Lure?," *Afro-American Red Star,* December 23–29, 2006, A1.

18. "Buy Nothing Day," http://adbusters.org; Joseph P. Kahn, "Yes, Virginia, There Is a Festivus," *Boston Globe,* December 18, 2006, D12; "Time Line," Ben & Jerry's, http://www.benjerry.com; Brian Cochrane, "Pole Position," *Variety,* December 25, 2006, 4; Philip Recchia, "'Festivus' Flap Tickles the Rest of Us," *New York Post,* December 24, 2006, 11.

19. "National Poll: Americans Resolve to Change," December 28, 2006, http://www.maristpoll.marist.edu; "Americans Make Resolutions, Stick to Them," December 29, 2006, http://www.ktvu.com.

20. "An Incident of Memorial Day," *New York Times,* June 7, 1868, 3; Tony Horwitz, *Confederates in the Attic* (New York: Vintage Books, 1998), 206.

21. U.S. Census Bureau, "Facts for Features: Veterans 2006, November 11," October 12, 2006, http://www.census.gov.

22. "Labor Joins Clergy in Sunday Fight," *New York Times,* March 14, 1910, 4; "Calls Union Labor to Study Its Record," *New York Times,* August 31, 1921, 6; "Record Throng Here on Labor Day Tours," *New York Times,* September 6, 1931, 1.

23. Muscular Dystrophy Association Telethon, http://www.mda.org/telethon; "Electronics and Apparel to Fuel Back-to-School Spending, According to Latest NRF Survey," July 18, 2006, http://www.nrf.com.

24. C. L. Arbelide, "By George, It IS Washington's Birthday!" *Prologue Magazine* 36 (2004), http://www.archives.gov; "Washington's Birthday," *New York Times,* February 23, 1855, 1; James Barron, "Washington's Nonbirthday Pretty Much a Non-Event," *New York Times,* February 19, 1980, B1; Jane Gross, "Shoppers Honor Washington by Flocking to City Stores," *New York Times,* February 18, 1986, B1.

25. "New Hampshire Becomes Last State to Create Martin Luther King Day," *The Gazette* (Montreal), June 8, 1999, B8; "State Holiday in S.C. Remembers Confederacy," *Cincinnati Post,* May 11, 2001, 2A.

26. Natasha Altamirano, "Volunteers Take 'Day On' for King," *Washington Times,* January 16, 2007, A1; Heidi Prescott and YaVanda Smalls, "It Was Only a Matter of Time: Is an MLK Day Sale an Honor or Enethical?," *South Bend (IN) Tribune,* January 13, 2007, 1; Gordon Jackson, "Kingsland Creates Festival; Organizers Put New Twist on Annual Salute to Martin Luther King, Jr.," *Florida Times-Union,* January 20, 2004, B1.

27. "Columbus Day at Bridgeport," *New York Times,* September 24, 1892, 8; "Big Crowd Cheers Columbus Paraders," *New York Times,* October 13, 1909, 7; Robert Dominguez, "Happenings Honor Hispanic Heritage," *New York Daily News,* September 15, 2004, 24; Tasha Villalpando, "NARD Opening Ceremony Kicks Off Native American Activities," *Au-Authm Action News* (Scottsdale, AZ), October 2005, 1.

28. U.S. Census Bureau, "Facts for Features: Irish-American Heritage Month (March) and St. Patrick's Day (March 17) 2007," January 17, 2007, http://www.census.gov; Adam Nossiter, "Sinn Fein President Will March in St. Patrick's Day Parade," *New York Times,* March 15, 1996, B3.

29. U.S. Census Bureau, "Hispanic Population Passes 40 Million, Census Bureau Reports," June 9, 2005, http://www.census.gov; Courtney Kane, "Marketers Extend

Their Holiday Efforts to a Mexican Celebration and Even to Lent," *New York Times,* May 2, 2003, C2.

30. "From California," *New York Times,* February 23, 1860, 2; Southwest Airlines, "History of the San Francisco Chinese New Year Parade," http://www.chineseparade. com; Vanessa Hua, "Chinese New Year Parade Accusations Widen Dispute," *San Francisco Chronicle,* January 21, 2006, B3.

31. Kelly Barth, "First Father's Day Service in 1908," *Morgantown Dominion Post,* June 21, 1987, http://www.wvculture.org; Vicki Smith, "The First Father's Day," *Martinsburg Journal,* June 15, 2003, http://www.wvculture.org.

32. "High Gas Prices No Match for Mom," April 19, 2006, http://www.nrf.com; John Hogan, "Dear Mom," *Grand Rapids Press,* May 10, 2003, D4; James Gallo, "Card Industry in a Slump," *Baltimore Sun,* May 4, 2004, 10C; "Celebrate Mother's Day," *New York Times,* May 10, 1909, 18; "House Honors Mothers," *New York Times,* May 11, 1913, 2; "Keep Mother's Day without Flowers," *New York Times,* May 2, 1920, 12.

33. Barri Bronson, "Dumping on Dad," *Times-Picayune,* June 14, 2004, 01.

34. "St. Valentine," http://www.catholic.org; "Making Valentines: A Tradition in America," http://www.americanantiquarian.org.

35. "Are Men More Romantic Than Women?," February 2007, http://www. greetingcard.org; Julie Jette and Brad Kelly, "Fond of the Season," *The Patriot Ledger* (Quincy, MA), February 14, 2006, 19; Angus Loten, "For Specialty Retailers, Love Is in the Air," *Inc.,* January 22, 2007, http://www.inc.com; Renee DeFranco, "10 Things Your Florist Won't Tell You," January 18, 2007, http://www.smartmoney. com; Rob Lowman, "We Know What You Want for Valentine's Day," *Los Angeles Daily News,* February 14, 2006, N1; "Does Your State 'Show the Love' for Valentine's Day?," *PR Newswire,* February 9, 2007, http://www.prnewswire.com.

36. Rob Lowman, "We Know What You Want for Valentine's Day," *Los Angeles Daily News,* February 14, 2006, N1; "Valentine's Day Broken Hearts," February 14, 2000, http://www.ipsos-mori.com; "Anti-Valentine's Pop-up Shop," February 9, 2007, http://www.springwise.com; "Card Makers Capitalize on 'Anti-V Day,'" *New York Times,* February 11, 2007, http://www.nytimes.com.

37. David Hinkley, "Monster Mash," *New York Daily News,* October 31, 2006, 37; Pia Sarker, "More Treats Than Tricks," *San Francisco Chronicle,* October 31, 2006, D1.

38. "'Scavenger Hunt' Provides Thrills," *New York Times,* November 2, 1933, 24.

39. "Halloween Poisonings," http://www.snopes.com.

40. "Witches' Night," *New York Times,* September 28, 1879, 3; "The Decadence of Halloween," *New York Times,* November 1, 1876, 8.

41. Helen Anders, "New Orleans Rising to the Occasion," *Austin (TX) American-Statesman,* February 11, 2007, J14.

42. "KFC Asks Pope to Bless New Fish Sandwich," February 22, 2007, http:// msnbc.com.

43. June Owen, "Food News: Passover Dishes Reviewed," *New York Times,* March 28, 1952, 29; Janet Forgrieve, "Metro Markets Go Kosher for Passover,"

*Rocky Mountain News,* April 7, 2006, 1B; Debra Morton Gelbart, "Tripping over Passover," *Jewish News of Greater Phoenix,* December 22, 2006, S28.

44. Candy Sagon, "Record Easter Candy Sales Expected," *Tulsa World,* April 12, 2006, D3.

45. C. W. Nevius, "Chocolate Bunny Meltdown," *San Francisco Chronicle,* March 11, 2007, http://www.sfgate.com; Cliff Morman, "Tide of Easter Purchases Rising," *The Sun* (San Bernardino, CA), April 14, 2006.

46. The Wedding Report, http://www.weddingreport.com.

47. Mark Oppenheimer, "My Big Fat American Bar Mitzvah," *Boston Globe,* May 22, 2005, D2.

48. Carolina A. Miranda, "Fifteen Candles," *Time,* July 19, 2004, 83; Lisa Gutierrez, "As Hispanics' Quinceaneras Get More Popular, Many Get More Lavish," Knight Ridder Tribune News Service, June 16, 2006; Rob Walker, "The Princess Buy," *New York Times Magazine,* October 15, 2006, 26.

49. Wendy Tanaka, "Party Profits," *San Francisco Examiner,* January 28, 1996; Ilene Lelchuk, "Are Children's Birthday Parties Getting Out of Control?," January 16, 2007, http://www.sfgate.com; Birthdays without Pressure, http://www.birthday swithoutpressure.org.

50. Television watching is the number one use of leisure hours, according to the U.S. Department of Labor, Bureau of Labor Statistics, Time Use Survey, 2005 (http://www.bls.gov/). According to a study by Mediamark Research, cited in the U.S. Census Bureau's *Statistical Abstract of the United States, 2007* (http://www.cen sus.gov), dining out was the leisure activity most likely to have been performed in the past 12 months, second most likely to take place once a month, and third most likely to take place two or more times per week. Unless otherwise cited, this study is the source of all statistics on participation in leisure activities and attendance at sporting events.

51. "With Theodore Roosevelt," *New York Times,* December 3, 1893, 23.

52. Kurt Badenhausen, Michael K. Ozanian, and Maya Roney, "The Business of Football," August 31, 2006, http://www.forbes.com; Michael K. Ozanian and Kurt Badenhausen, "The Business of Baseball," April 20, 2006, http://www.forbes.com; Kurt Badenhausen, Michael K. Ozanian, and Christina Settimi, "The Business of Basketball," January 25, 2007, http://www.forbes.com; National Collegiate Athletic Association (NCAA), 2004–2005 Participation Survey, quoted in Bureau of Labor Statistics, *Statistical Abstract;* National Sporting Goods Association (NSGA), "Sports Participation," http://www.nsga.org. Unless otherwise cited, throughout this chapter, statistics on college participation come from the NCAA study, and statistics on general participation come from the NSGA survey.

53. Stewart Alsop, "Nixon and the Square Majority," *The Atlantic Monthly,* February 1972, 41–47.

54. Susan Conley and Matt Baun, "USDA Offers Food Safety Advice for Your Super Bowl Party," January 27, 2007, http://www.fsis.usda.gov; "Super Bowl 2nd-Most Watched Show Ever," February 7, 2006, http://www.msnbc.msn.com; Peter J. Schwartz, "Super Bowl Tops Forbes' Most Valuable Brands," January 31, 2007,

http://sports.espn.go.com; Peter Hartlaub, "The 10 Best Super Bowl Ads of All Time," February 1, 2007, http://www.msnbc.msn.com; Seth Sutel, "Super Bowl Winner to Be…Ad Revenue," *Los Angeles Daily News,* February 1, 2007, http://www.dailynews.com; Marc Berman and John Consoli, "CBS' Super Bowl 2nd Most-Watched in History," February 5, 2007, http://www.mediaweek.com.

55. "Super Bowl Legends," http://www.snopes.com.

56. "FCC Says Soaps Need to Be Cleaned Up," April 8, 2004, http://www.soapcentral.com; John Dunbar, "CBS Defends 'Wardrobe Malfunction' in Court," *Washington Post,* November 21, 2006, C07.

57. "World Series: Series' Ratings Drop from '92," *New York Times,* October 25, 1993; Richard Sandomir, "Baseball: Notebook; World Series Ratings," *New York Times,* October 22, 1997; "World Series Ratings Lowest Ever," October 31, 2005, http://www.sportbusiness.com; Rudy Martzke, "Fox Cleans Up in Series Ratings Despite Sweep," *USA Today,* October 28, 2004, http://www.usatoday.com; Michael Hiestand, "World Series Starts Strong, but Ratings Lag," *USA Today,* October 25, 2005, http://www.usatoday.com; Ronald Blum, "World Series Ratings Hit Record Low," *Washington Post,* October 29, 2006, http://www.washingtonpost.com.

58. "Baseball Records," http://www.baseball-almanac.com.

59. Durham Bulls, http://www.durhambulls.com; Charles Passy and Jon Weinbach, "Rating the Parks of Spring Training," *Wall Street Journal,* March 8, 2007, D1.

60. America's Favorite Architecture, American Institute of Architects, http://www.aia150.org.

61. "Participation in Little League Reaches 3-Year High," http://www.littleleague.org; Chris Ballard, *Hoops Nation: A Guide to America's Best Pickup Basketball* (New York: Henry Holt, 1998); Timothy Harper, "The Best Pickup-Basketball Player in America," *The Atlantic Monthly,* April 2000, http://www.theatlantic.com.

62. Tim Wendel, "Global Trend Remakes the Face of Team Sports," http://www.hoopdreams.org; Jason Chung, "Racial Discrimination and African-American Quarterbacks in the National Football League, 1968–1999," October 25, 2005, http://ssrn.com/abstract=835204.

63. Frank Deford, "Racially Unbalanced," July 12, 2006, http://sportsillustrated.cnn.com.

64. Douglas Stark, "Paving the Way," *Basketball Digest,* February 2001, 74–78.

65. "Black Teams and White Coaches: Why African Americans Are Increasingly Being Shut Out of College Coaching Positions," *The Journal of Blacks in Higher Education* 33 (2001): 44–45; "African-American College Athletes: Debunking the Myth of the Dumb Jock," *The Journal of Blacks in Higher Education* 35 (2002): 36–40.

66. "March Madness Brings Ratings Uptick to CBS," March 21, 2005, http://tv.zap2it.com; John Consoli, "NBA Finals' Ratings Sink on ABC," June 14, 2005, http://www.mediaweek.com; Kurt Badenhausen, Michael K. Ozanian, and Christina Settimi, "The Business of Basketball," January 25, 2007, http://www.forbes.com.

67. The four women's leagues operating as of 2007 are the Women's Professional Football League, founded 1999 and offering 15 teams (http://www.womensprofoot

ball.com), the National Women's Football Association, founded 2000 and operating 40 teams (http://www.womensfootballassociation.com), the Independent Women's Football League, founded 2000 and offering 30 teams (http://www.iwflsports.com), and the Women's Football League, founded 2002, currently with four teams (http:// sportzon.com). The Lingerie Bowl was a pay-per-view game offered during Super Bowl halftime from 2004 to 2006; it is expected to return in 2008; Adam Hofstetter, "Trouble Averted: Lingerie Bowl Taking a Year Off," January 31, 2007, http://sport sillustrated.cnn.com.

68. Rick Horrow, "March Madness: The Business of the Women's Tournament," March 25, 2005, http://cbs.sportsline.com; Oscar Dixon, "WNBA Showcases Game as It Turns 10," *USA Today,* May 19, 2006, http://www.usatoday.com; Michael Hiestand, "Unlike WUSA, WNBA Has NBA," *USA Today,* September 16, 2003, http://www.usatoday.com.

69. "2006–2007 States of the Game," December 19, 2006, http://insidecollege hockey.com; "Old School Hockey Is Back," June 9, 2006, http://www.cbsnews.com; Michael K. Ozanian and Kurt Badenhausen, "The Business of Hockey," November 9, 2006, http://www.forbes.com.

70. Brian O'Keefe, "America's Fastest-Growing Sport," *Fortune,* September 5, 2005, http://money.cnn.com.

71. Emily Murphy, "NASCAR Not Just for the Boys Any More," *USA Today,* July 2, 2004, http://www.usatoday.com.

72. Tim Lemke, "Indy out of the Pits," *Washington Times,* May 24, 2006, C01.

73. Jeff Wolf, "Organizers Match Premier Rodeo Event with 'Old West' Locale, but Many Say Money Matters Most," *Las Vegas Review-Journal,* December 5, 2004, http://www.reviewjournal.com.

74. "Ali the Man," http://www.ali.com.

75. "Billie Jean King," http://www.wic.org.

76. National Sporting Goods Association, "2005 Youth Participation in Selected Sports with Comparisons to 1995," http://www.nsga.org.

77. Stephen Harris, "XX Olympic Games," *Boston Herald,* February 28, 2006, 60.

78. International Health, Racquet and Sportsclub Association, http://cms.ihrsa. org.

79. International Paralympic Committee, http://www.paralympic.org; Special Olympics, http://www.specialolympics.org.

80. National Park Service, http://www.nps.org.

81. Georgia State Parks and Historic Sites, "Indian Springs State Park," http:// gastateparks.org; State of Alaska, "Parks and Public Lands," http://www.dced.state. ak.us; Donald R. Leal and Holly Lipke Fretwell, "Parks in Transition: A Look at State Parks," RS-97-1, 1997, http://www.perc.org.

82. Disney, http://home.disney.go.com; Douglas Frantz and Catherine Collins, *Celebration, U.S.A.* (New York: Owl Books, 2000); Andrew Ross, *The Celebration Chronicles* (New York: Ballantine Books, 2000).

83. "Renaissance Faires by State," http://www.renfaire.com.

84. "How to Get Started in Civil War Reenacting," http://www.sutler.net.

85. Historical Miniatures Gaming Society, Eastern Chapter, "What Is Wargaming?," http://www.hmgs.org.

86. Alexa Stanard, "Make It a Game Night," *Detroit News,* December 23, 2006, D1.

87. "History of Monopoly," http://www.monopoly.com; "All About Scrabble," http://www.hasbro.com/scrabble.

88. David Parlett, "A History of Poker," March 3, 2005, http://www.pagat.com; World Series of Poker, http://www.worldseriesofpoker.com.

89. Jodi Lee Reifer, "Bars Cash in on Bingo's Popularity," *Times-Picayune,* February 21, 2007, 03.

90. Leonard Herman, Jer Horwitz, Steve Kent, and Skyler Miller, "The History of Videogames," http://www.gamespot.com; "The Essential 50 Archives," http://www.1up.com; "Pac-Man," http://en.wikipedia.org.

91. Rachel Conrad, "EBay Restricts Sale of Playstation 3," November 16, 2006, http://www.msnbc.msn.com.

92. Thor Thorsen, "Haitian-Americans Protest Vice City," November 25, 2003, http://www.gamespot.com; Thor Thorsen, "Grand Theft Auto Sparks Another Law Suit," February 16, 2005, http://www.gamespot.com. The *CSI: Miami* episode is "Urban Hellraisers" (http://www.cbs.com).

93. SimCity 4, http://simcity.ea.com; The Sims, http://sims.ea.com.

94. "Economic Statistics," http://secondlife.com; Rob Hof, "Second Life's First Millionaire," *Business Week Online,* November 26, 2006, http://www.businessweek.com.

95. Peter Fimrite, "A High-Flying Hobby," *San Francisco Chronicle,* March 6, 2007, http://www.sfgate.com.

96. Beth Burkstrand, "Homespun Scrapbooks Become Pricey Labor of Love for Some," *Wall Street Journal,* July 16, 1997; "Scrapbooking in America™ Survey Highlights," http://www.creatingkeepsakes.com.

97. Mark Aguiar and Erik Hurst, "Measuring Trends in Leisure" (working paper, Federal Reserve Bank of Boston, January 2006).

## BIBLIOGRAPHY

Berlage, Gail Ingham. *Women in Baseball: The Forgotten History.* Westport, CT: Greenwood Press, 1994.

Cantor, George. *Historic Festivals: A Traveler's Guide.* Detroit: Gale Research, 1996.

Chudacoff, Howard P. *The Age of the Bachelor.* Princeton, NJ: Princeton University Press, 1999.

Cohen, Hennig, and Tristam Potter Coffin. *America Celebrates!* Detroit: Visible Ink Press, 1991.

Djata, Sundiata. *Blacks at the Net: Black Achievement in the History of Tennis.* Vol. 1. Syracuse, NY: Syracuse University Press, 2006.

Draper, Joan E. "The Art and Science of Park Planning in the United States: Chicago's Small Parks, 1902 to 1905." In *Planning the Twentieth-Century American*

*City,* ed. Mary Corbin Sies and Christopher Silver, 98–119. Baltimore: The Johns Hopkins University Press, 1996.

Einhorn, Eddie. *How March Became Madness.* Chicago: Triumph Books, 2006.

Findlay, John M. *Magic Lands: Western Cityscapes and American Culture after 1940.* Berkeley: University of California Press, 1992.

Fisher, Jerry M. *The Pacesetter: The Untold Story of Carl G. Fisher.* Fort Bragg, CA: Lost Coast Press, 1998.

Gelber, Steven M. *Hobbies: Leisure and the Culture of Work in America.* New York: Columbia University Press, 1999.

Goodale, Thomas, and Geoffrey Godbey. *The Evolution of Leisure.* State College, PA: Venture Publishing, Inc., 1988.

Green, Ben. *Spinning the Globe: The Rise, Fall, and Return to Greatness of the Harlem Globetrotters.* New York: Amistad, 2005.

Groves, Melody. *Ropes, Reins, and Rawhide.* Albuquerque: University of New Mexico Press, 2006.

Hall, Lee. *Olmsted's America: An 'Unpractical' Man and His Vision of Civilization.* Boston: Little, Brown and Company, 1995.

Hauser, Thomas. *Muhammad Ali.* New York: Simon and Schuster, 1991.

Herman, Daniel Justin. *Hunting and the American Imagination.* Washington, DC: Smithsonian Institution Press, 2001.

Lavin, Maud, ed. *The Business of Holidays.* New York: The Monacelli Press, 2004.

Marling, Karal Ann. *Blue Ribbon: A Social and Pictorial History of the Minnesota State Fair.* St. Paul: Minnesota Historical Society Press, 1990.

McCarry, John. *County Fairs: Where America Meets.* Washington, DC: National Geographic Society, 1997.

Moss, Richard J. *Golf and the American Country Club.* Chicago: University of Illinois Press, 2001.

National Park Service. *The National Parks: Shaping the System,* 3rd ed. Washington, DC: U.S. Department of the Interior, 2005.

Nissenbaum, Stephen. *The Battle for Christmas.* New York: Vintage Books, 1997.

Perla, Peter P. *The Art of Wargaming.* Annapolis, MD: Naval Institute Press, 1990.

Pleck, Elizabeth H. *Celebrating the Family: Ethnicity, Consumer Culture, and Family Rituals.* Cambridge, MA: Harvard University Press, 2000.

Putnam, Robert. *Bowling Alone: The Collapse and Revival of American Community.* New York: Simon and Schuster, 2000.

Putney, Clifford. *Muscular Christianity: Manhood and Sports in Protestant America, 1880–1920.* Cambridge, MA: Harvard University Press, 2001.

Rader, Benjamin G. *American Sports: From the Age of Folk Games to the Age of Televised Sports.* Upper Saddle River, NJ: Prentice Hall, 1983, 2004.

Ratjar, Steve. *United States Holidays and Observances.* Jefferson, NC: McFarland and Co., 2003.

Rust, Edna, and Art Rust Jr. *Art Rust's Illustrated History of the Black Athlete.* Garden City, NY: Doubleday and Company, 1985.

Schor, Juliet B. *The Overworked American.* New York: Basic Books, 1992.

Sloane, David Charles. *The Last Great Necessity: Cemeteries in American History.* Baltimore: The Johns Hopkins University Press, 1991.

Smith, Lisam, Ed. *Nike Is a Goddess: The History of Women in Sports.* New York: Atlantic Monthly Press, 1998.

Smith, Ron. *The Ballpark Book.* St. Louis, MO: The Sporting News, 2000.

Wetzel, Dan, and Don Yaeger. *Sole Influence: Basketball, Corporate Greed, and the Corruption of America's Youth.* New York: Warner Books, 2000.

White, G. Edward. *Creating the National Pastime: Baseball Transforms Itself, 1903–1953.* Princeton, NJ: Princeton University Press, 1996.

Wright, Jim. *Fixin' to Git: One Fan's Love Affair with NASCAR's Winston Cup.* Durham, NC: Duke University Press, 2002.

Zimbalist, Andrew. *Unpaid Professionals: Commercialism and Conflict in Big-Time College Sports.* Princeton, NJ: Princeton University Press, 1999.